MW01616737

Timothy Verdon
Alessandro Coppellotti
Patrizia Fabbri

# Churches
# of Florence

arsenale 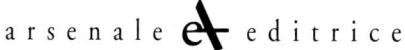 editrice

Timothy Verdon
Alessandro Coppellotti
Patrizia Fabbri
CHURCHES OF FLORENCE

*photographs*
Antonio Quattrone

*layout*
Stefano Grandi

*printing*
EBS Editoriale Bortolazzi-Stei
Verona

*first edition*
May 2000

Arsenale Editrice srl
via Querini 100
30172 Venice Mestre
Italy

*Arsenale Editrice © 2000*

ISBN  88-7743-217-9

# Contents

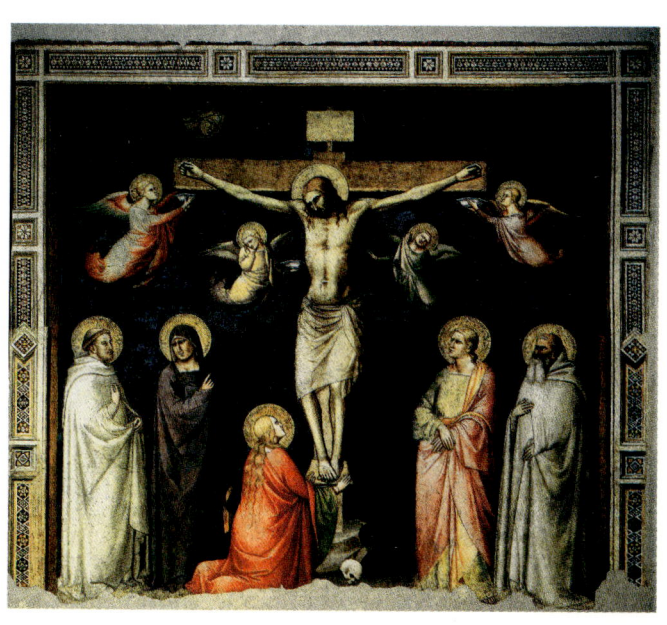

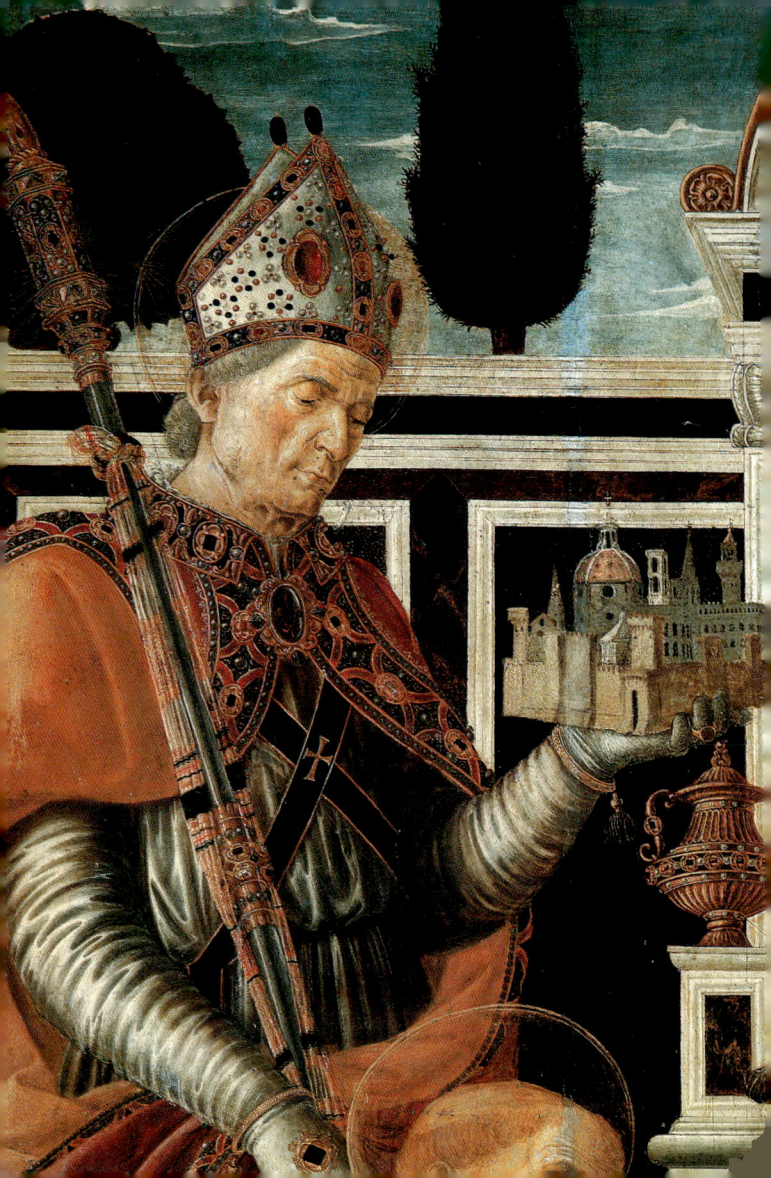

# The Church, the churches, the city

Perhaps more than other cities, Florence identifies with her churches, recognising the values of her life and history in the network of ecclesiastical buildings that, century after century, signal the city's development. The very 'image' of Florence – the visual and spiritual impression this city makes on citizens and visitors alike – takes shape around a church: the vast cathedral commissioned by the Commune in the late thirteenth century, paid for with public funds, and brought to completion in the fifteenth century by Filippo Brunelleschi, architect of the bold dome.

The relationship between this emblematic church and the city above which it looms is suggested in Ferdinando Leopoldo Del Migliore's seventeenth-century text, *Firenze città nobilissima illustrata*, where the cathedral's titanic size is explained in light of the planners' supposed conviction that "they should not undertake projects for the City unless the idea be to make them like a human heart, dilated because composed of the souls of many citizens united in a single will".[1] In Florence, that is, a great church was considered a 'project for the City': a civic as well as religious symbol, translating into architectural terms the moral process by which men overcome prejudices and transcend individual interests to join with others "in a single will". A church might thus be compared to the collective heart of those who use it, a heart made large by fraternal harmony experienced as political commitment.

THE CHURCH, THE CHURCHES, THE CITY
This ideal vision has ancient roots, going back to the beginning of Christian civilisation and beyond, to Judaism and the culture of the synagogues. The very term 'church' – *ekklesia* in New Testament Greek – indicates

Workshop of Andrea del Verrocchio, *Madonna and Saints* (detail), church of San Martino a Strada, Grassina

first of all the community of believers, and only secondarily the building in which they gather. "Brothers, *you* are God's building", the Apostle Paul told the Christians of Corinth in the mid-first century (1 Cor. 3,9); and another Pauline text extends this metaphor, arguing that those who make up the church community are "fellow citizens of the saints and members of God's family, built upon the foundation of the apostles and prophets, with Christ Jesus himself as the cornerstone. In Him", the text goes on, "every structure rises in an ordered way, as a holy temple in the Lord; in Him you too, along with others, are being built up to become God's dwelling place, by means of His Spirit" (Eph. 2,19-22).

A third New Testament text develops the specifically *civic* dimension of this ecclesial-architectural metaphor. "Clinging to Christ, the living stone (...), you also are being used as living stones in the construction of a spiritual edifice", the first Letter of Peter says. "You are a chosen race, a royal priesthood, a holy nation, the people that God has acquired for himself, that you might proclaim the wondrous deeds of Him who has called you out of darkness into his admirable light" (1 Pt. 2,4-9). And – since this 'holy nation', this 'people' already considered itself 'God's dwelling place' among men – it was natural to transfer the term used to identify the community to the architectural space in which it came together[2]: the 'Church' in fact lives and celebrates its passage from darkness to light in places called 'churches', which constitute architectural expressions of the way in which the 'holy nation' experiences its own identity. As a modern ecclesiastical text puts it, "Christian places of worship correspond to the awareness which the Church, the people of God, has of itself in history. Their concrete forms, from period to period, are partial images of this self-awareness".[3]

ANTIQUITY OF THE ECCLESIAL IDENTITY

In its character as historical *community*, the Church in Florence (whose foundation in fact goes back to the early Christian era) feels a special bond with the wellsprings of Christian life in the Church of Apostolic times. Del Migliore's characterisation of the Cathedral as a 'heart composed of the souls of many citizens united in a single will', for example – in the passage cited above – explicitly echoes the language of the Acts of the Apostles, where the first Christians at Jerusalem are described as having "one

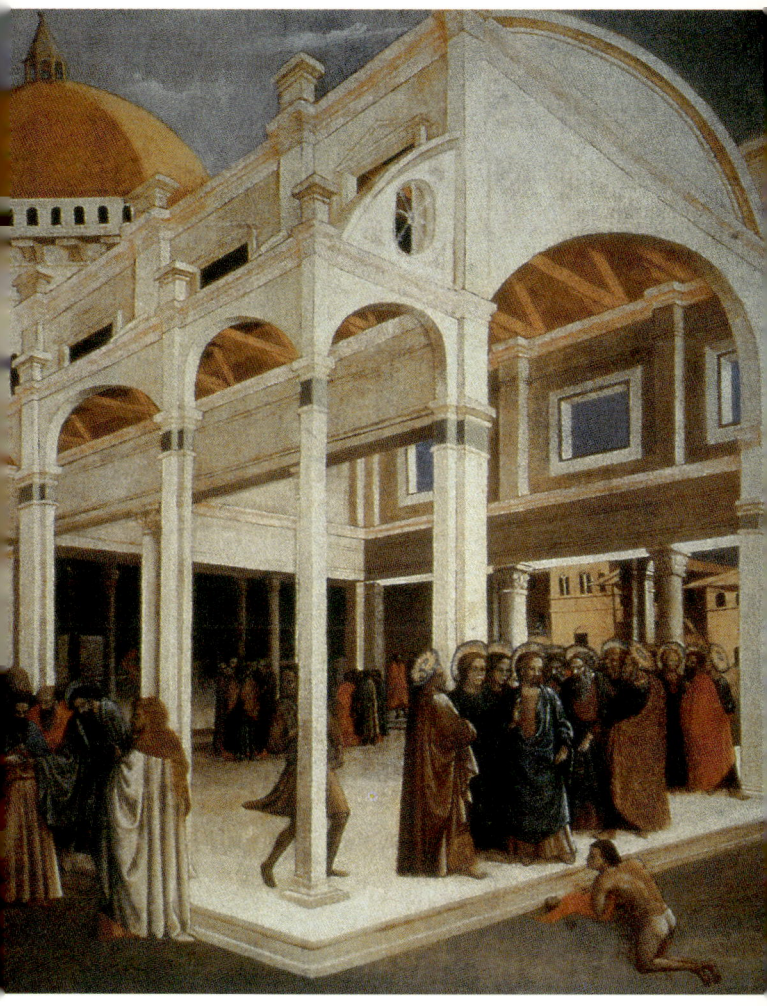

heart and one soul".[4] The use of this expression is meant to suggest ideal continuity: a spiritual thread linking the founders of Santa Maria del Fiore, in the thirteenth century, with the disciples who in the first century comprised the infant Church.

To the antiquity of its concept of Church, moreover, Florence adds a venerable idea of civic life also: a political self-consciousness derived from the city's never forgotten Roman origin. The religious identity of 'holy nation' is thus grafted onto a civic identity passed down from the late Empire, and the Judeo-Christian notion, 'people of God', overlays a Roman one, dating to the Republican era in which Florence was founded: the concept of *plebs* – an autonomous 'people' with rights and duties, able to defend itself and willing to make necessary sacrifices. This conceptual overlay, which deeply marks the development of the Church and its churches from the fifth through the ninth centuries, leads to the Mediaeval 'pleban' (rural parish) system and to the *pievi* – literally, 'places in which the *plebs* gathers: assembly halls for one or another 'people'. For the whole Middle Ages, in fact, parish membership was indicated with this term, 'people'. "We gave eight *soldi* to Mistress Dada, wife of Martin who lodges in Neri del Giudice's house", we read in a register of 1324 recording donations made at Orsanmichele; "very poor, she belongs to the *people* of San Michele Visdomini".[5]

Taking the place of the ancient *plebs*, the parochial 'people' became in effect the natural ambient of individual freedom, fraternal assistance and the defence of values.

A third aspect of the ecclesial and civic self-understanding of Florentines derives from the origin and social condition of the first Christians on the banks of the Arno, traditionally held to be Eastern immigrants working as artisans and traders. The conservatism of Florentines – their sense of preserving an ancient and precious heritage – comes in part from this consciousness of having received the faith straight from its source: from men and women who came from the same 'holy' lands where Christianity was born. Local tradition in fact stresses the Eastern origin of two archetypal figures of the early Florentine Church: Minias, 'King of the Armenians',

*Preceding page: The Duomo as an Open Structure*, school of Masaccio, Johnson Collection, Philadelphia
*Carta della Catena*, detail showing four churches

martyred in Florence in the year 250 in the persecution of Decius, and the great fifth-century bishop Zenobius, whose family was held to be Greco-Syrian in origin.

The modest social condition of the Eastern immigrants who evangelised Florence was also important for the ecclesial identity taking shape in these early centuries. Their 'poverty' likened them to the 'least brethren' and 'poor' to whom Jesus had directed his mission, and – in the spiritual economy of Christian faith – this fact constituted a warrant of authenticity. "Among you there are not many who are wise according to the world's lights", Saint Paul had written to believers in Corinth: "there are not many powerful people, not many of noble birth. But God has chosen that which in the world is weak to confound the strong, that which in the world is ignoble and despised and that which is nothing at all, so as to reduce to nothing the things that are, so that no one may boast before God" (1 Cor. 1,26-29).

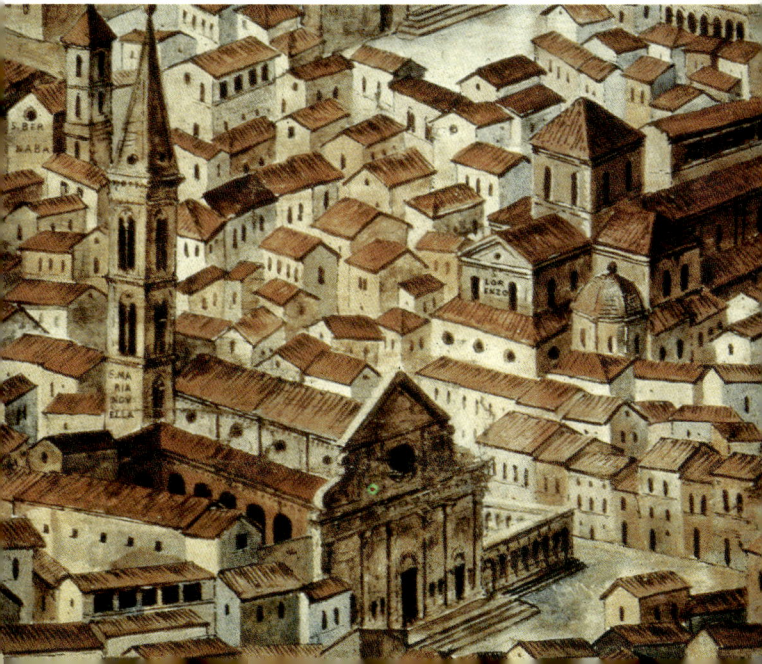

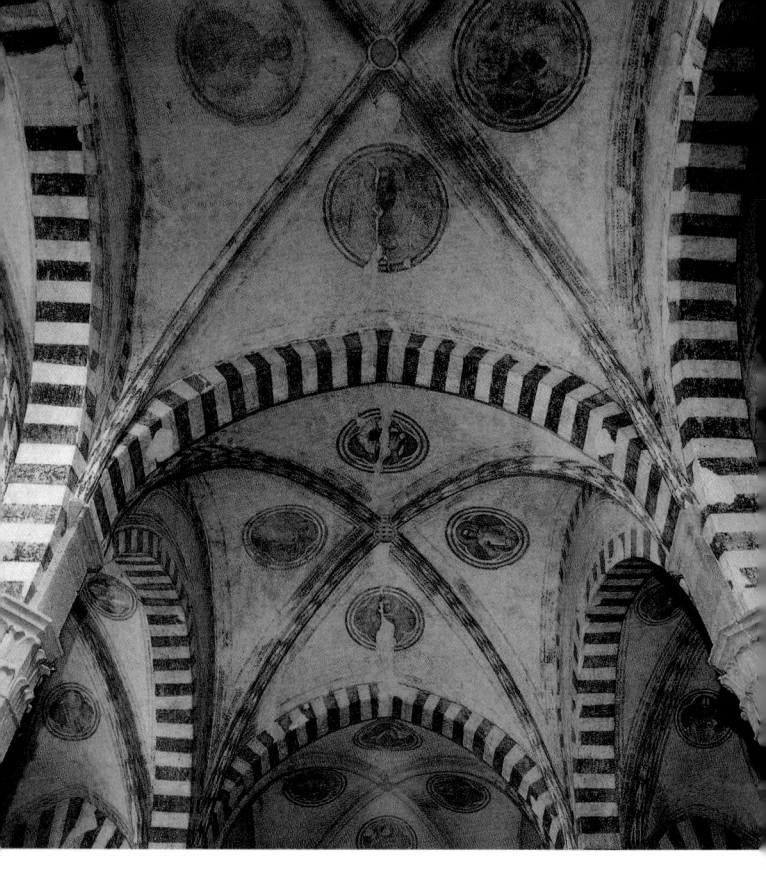

SPIRITUALITY AND STYLE

In time, these historical and moral features of the *Church* in Florence became constituent elements of an aesthetic that, despite changing styles, would endure in the city's *churches*: a taste that is also 'character', in the sense in which that term is used in moral theology, a deep orientation influencing people's aspirations and behaviour. 'Humility' in the choice of vernacular materials, the 'poverty' of sober decoration, 'simplicity' expressed through clear planning and structural legibility: these are the ethical and aesthetic components calculated to guarantee authenticity of ecclesial and civic experience. Seen from outside, the churches of Florence rise amid their surrounding houses like speakers at a public meeting, each determined to have his say. And they speak, with rough eloquence or fine, to the 'people' in whose midst they stand, inviting to brotherly unity men and women who live in houses fashioned of the same materials, members of the 'body' of which the neighbourhood church is the 'heart'.

And seen from within, these churches effectively convey the unity to which they invite: they are assembly halls for a 'nation' of priests and prophets, a 'chosen race' whose dignity consists in remaining united. From the clear, uncomplicated space of Sant'Ambrogio, defined in a single nave, to the basilican articulation of Santi Apostoli, which perfects in the city a plan developed in rural *pievi*; and from the Gothic spatial logic of Santa Trinita, Santa Maria Novella and San Remigio, complex yet clear as a Scholastic syllogism, to the radiant lucidity of Brunelleschi's interiors: notwithstanding different architectural languages, visitors grasp the ongoing search for a dynamic harmony able to mould shared life, in the Church and in the city. In such interiors, religious people will feel something like what Saint Augustine experienced on entering a church of his time: "what happened here, as this church took shape", he says, "is repeated whenever Christians come together. Through their faith, in fact, they become available as building material, as when trees and stones are cut from forests and mountainsides. When believers are catechised, baptised and 'shaped', it is as if they were being hewn, dressed and polished in the hands of craftsmen and builders. Yet they do not become the Church of God unless they are also bound together by charity. It is the same with the beams and stone blocks of this building: if they were not knit together in a certain ordered way – if they weren't connected to each other harmoniously and, in reaching out to one another, if they did not in some sense 'love' one another – no one would enter here. In fact, it is only when you see stone and wood well connected that you enter a building without fear of structural collapse. Since therefore Christ wanted to enter and to live in us, he said – almost as if constructing a building – : 'I give you a new commandment, that you love one another' ".[6]

CHARACTERISTICS OF DEVELOPMENT

In Florence as in other ancient urban agglomerations, the formation of a network of ecclesiastical buildings – a socio-religious *system* expressed in architecture – was closely related to the development of the city. The first Christian churches were outside populous urban centres, like Christianity itself, which was marginal to the life of the Roman Empire in which it was born and spread. At a somewhat later period, with the so-called 'Peace of the Church' or 'Peace of Constantine' (313 A.D.), and above all after the definitive closure of pagan temples by order of the Emperor Theodosius (391 A.D.), Christian communities established themselves within the walls, cutting spaces of their own from the close-knit fabric of late Antique cities. Such spaces still tended to be peripheral, with respect to the urban centre, except where they were mere substitutions, as in the case of Christian churches carved out of disused pagan temples. The consolidation of the new religion between the fifth and tenth centuries, and Christianity's assumption of the range of civic connotations noted above – the definition of the Christian 'people' as a political as well as spiritual reality – inverted the co-ordinates of this equation. In the lava-like spread of medieval cities, churches were often the only really public structures and, practically speaking, the only kind of building with a clearly defined socio-architectural character.[7] From 'spiritual appendages', as they had been in the early centuries, Christian places of worship became dynamic nuclei of social and political life, fostering the crafts and even a kind of industrial activity.

As time went on, the growth of cities and definition of urban plans unfolded in function of the position of the city's churches, particularly with the advent of the Mendicant Orders in the thirteenth and fourteenth centuries. And, even as new socio-architectural typologies took shape churches remained the chief symbolic spaces of city life, with a range of new public functions. They came to house State monuments and memorials, as well as the tombs and chapels of upper class families; they provided devotional and meeting space for special groups, such as confraternities and professional associations. From the fifteenth to the nineteenth century, an uninterrupted process saw old churches enlarged, modernised, embellished, and new ones built, in an ever-increasing centrifugal rhythm as, from already saturated urban centres, cities expanded toward new outer boundaries. Right up to the 1960s, the construction of parish churches in working class and middle income neighbourhoods created by the post-World War II economic boom retained something of the symbolic significance, at once civil and religious, that it had in the Middle Ages.

## THE FIRST BASILICAS

This developmental pattern, more or less standard in those areas of Europe formerly part of the Roman Empire, emerges with particular clarity in Florence. The earliest church for which there is archaeological and epigraphic evidence in fact was outside the walls of Roman 'Florentia', to the South of the city, near an intersection of busy roads: the new Via Cassia, the Pisa Road and that leading to Volterra. Of seventy-five funerary inscriptions found on the site of this building, moreover, twenty are in Greek and offer proof that a Christian community of Eastern origin had settled just out-

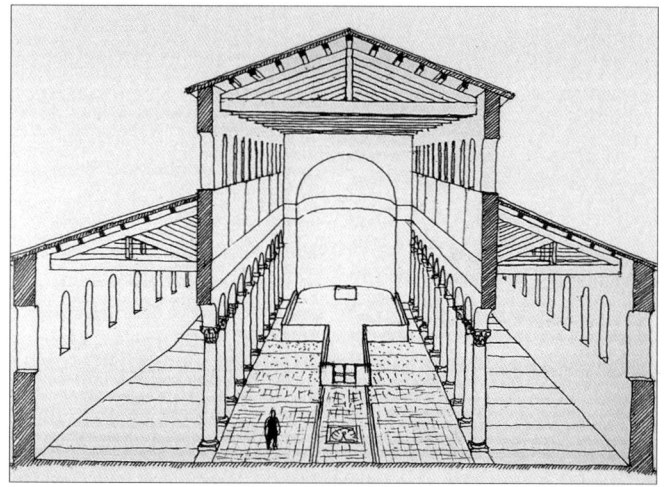

Suggestions for a reconstruction of Santa Reparata in the 5th-6th centuries.
*Preceding pages*: Gothic arches of San Remigio

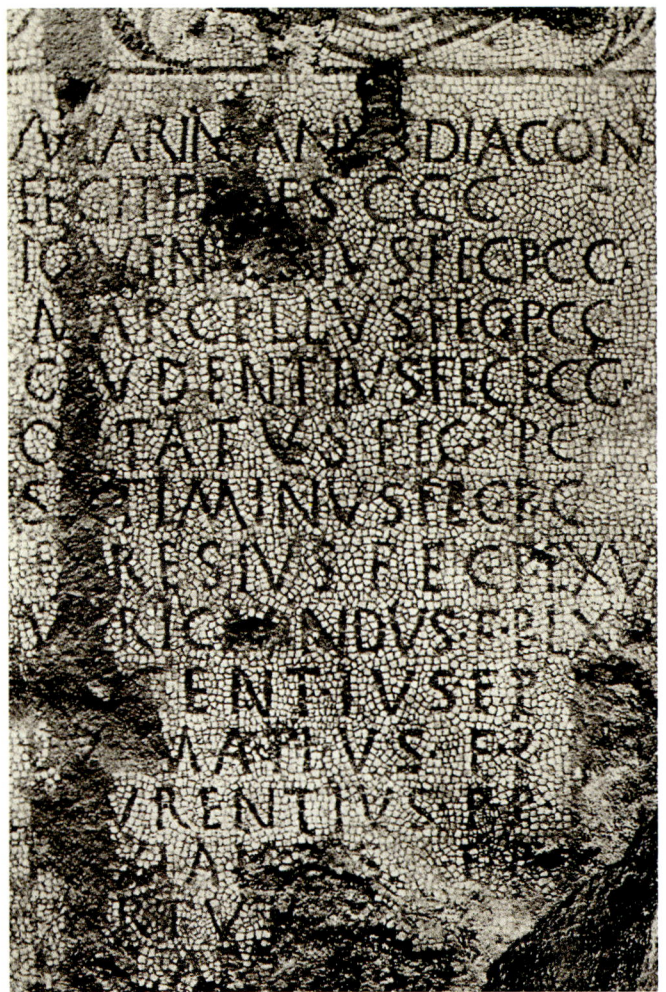

side the city gates: probably Greek-speaking Syrian dyers and merchants come up from Rome.[8] The historian Mario Lopes Pegna drew the evident conclusion, that "those who brought the Gospel to Florence were almost certainly Greek-speaking Syrians", and noted the existence, on the Hadrianic 'new' Via Cassia, not far from the crossroads where the first place of Christian worship in Florence stood, of an inn called "Ad Graecos".[9]

The church in question was Santa Felicita, which today we see in the elegant eighteenth-century form given it by the architect Federico Ruggieri. Excavations done in 1948 showed that the original church was a basilica with central nave and side aisles, separated by colonnades, all on a monumental scale: 26 metres wide and 40 long![10] This structure, dating from the late fourth or early fifth century, had been built in an already existing Christian cemetery, probably taking the place of a still older *domus ecclesiae* – a 'domestic church', that is, adapted from the main room of a private residence.

The period of foundation of the *domus ecclesiae* of Santa Felicita, thought to correspond to the beginning of the Church in Florence, is not certain. Local tradition claims that, as early as the first century Florence had a Christian community with its own bishop, a certain Frontinus who died for the faith around 56 A.D., under Nero.[11] Yet there is no documentary evidence of organised Christian life in Florence at so early a period; the first sure references to a stable Church community appear only in the fourth century, when the presence of Bishop Felix "*a Florentia Tuscorum*" ("from Florence in Tuscany") is mentioned in a list of prelates summoned to Rome in 313 A.D. for the Synod that dealt with the Donatist question.[12] Even so, there must have been a group of Christians active in Florence before that date, if around 250 A.D. Saint Minias and other believers gave their lives for Christ and were buried on the hill later 'christened' with the proto-martyr's name. This second Christian cemetery, on Mount San Miniato, was south east of the Roman city walls. Its position above Santa Felicita, together with the insistence of older writers on Saint Minias' Eastern origin, thus reinforce the hypothesis of a Church of Florence whose first growth was in the Greco-

Mosaic floor with names of members of the Florentine Christian community in the 5th-6th centuries. Santa Reparata excavations.

Syrian suburb along the Via Cassia Nova. In the newly tolerant climate of the fourth and early fifth century, it would have been natural to enlarge the early Christian meeting place (the *domus ecclesiae*) in monumental terms, erecting the Basilica of Santa Felicita the remains of which were discovered some fifty years ago.

The second of Florence's churches, in chronological order, was also founded *extra moenia* and near an important access road: San Lorenzo, built in the late fourth century North of the walls, near the intersection of the ancient Faenza road with the original Via Cassia. Consecrated in 393 A.D. by Saint Ambrose, Bishop of Milan, the new basilica was made possible through the generosity of a wealthy widow, Giuliana, who on the day of consecration publicly vowed her only son to the Church's service. Disregarding the legendary tone in which they are recounted, these facts suggest the increased importance of a Church community able to draw a personage of Ambrose's stature, and which availed itself of its own means and considered its institutional future sure.[13]

The third of the early Christian basilicas in Florence confirms this impression of a prosperous, well-organised Church. Built not outside but *inside* the Roman city walls, larger than Santa Felicita (and perhaps than the old San Lorenzo, of which no trace remains) and embellished with splendid mosaic pavements visible today thanks to the excavations directed by Guido Morozzi between 1965 and 1973, this structure with a main nave and side aisles allows us to speak at last of a 'network' of churches: a series of places of worship extending from one end of the urban area to the other and which, at least in an inchoative way, gave the impression of a 'Christianised' city. Dedicated to Saint Reparata, the third-century Palestinian martyr on whose feast-day a victory had been won over the barbarians in 405 A.D. (as tradition maintains), the new church had a civic as well as religious character. In time it would be considered the 'city *pieve*' – the main urban church, that is – and claim the status of cathedral, replacing San Lorenzo, where Bishop Zenobius had established his episcopal headquarters in the fifth century.

Santa Reparata floor mosaic, detail.

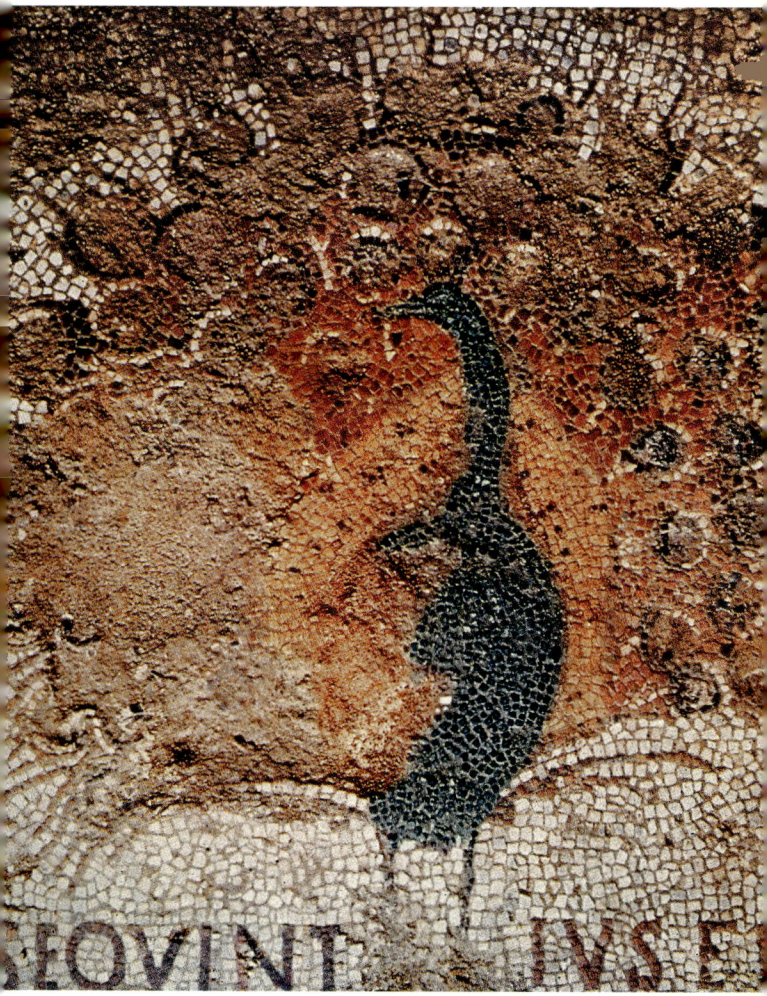

## FORMATION OF THE RELIGIOUS CENTRE

Together with the urban basilica of Santa Reparata, other buildings of note-worthy importance to the Christian community arose. New studies on the religious centre of Florence between late Antiquity and the Renaissance claim that the construction of a baptistery in front of Santa Reparata should be considered contemporary with the basilica: part of a unified plan that also included the bishop's palace.[14] According to this theory, the dimensions and shape of the new Christian ecclesiastical complex so constituted, in the city's north eastern corner, were similar to those of the old pagan enclave at the centre of the urban grid, in the forum dominated by the temple of Capitoline Jove: a Christian 'sacred enclosure' replacing that of the old faith, in token of the cultural renewal which the new system of belief promoted.[15] The main difficulty with this, as with other theories regarding the primitive growth of this area, is the lack of undisputed co-ordinates for dating Santa Reparata and the baptistery, both in the absolute and relative sense. While for Santa Felicita and San Lorenzo we have epigraphic and documentary evidence, for the 'new religious centre' there is only archaeological data allowing different interpretations. Today no one accepts the late mediae-val myth of the baptistery built in the Classical period as a temple of Mars, but it not clear whether the present structure is late Antique or rather Romanesque: a discrepancy of six hundred years! (Unless, indeed, with Lopes Pegna, we consider the baptistery and Santa Reparata as belong-ing to the Byzantine or Lombard period).[16]

What can be claimed with certainty is that the relationship between bap-tistery and cathedral which we see today goes back to very remote times. Whether we accept the traditional dating, which holds Santa Reparata was built in the early fifth century and the baptistery even earlier, or choose a different chronology, the axis connecting the place of *initiation* to that of *full communion* – font to altar, baptistery to cathedral – appears to be original. And even if until the eleventh century there was a baptistery of modest dimensions its shape, like that of the present baptistery (which there-fore would be a medieval enlargement) was octagonal. Thus the volumet-ric and spatial relationship we see today – between a centrally planned

The baptistery in the *Codice del Biadolo* (14th century)

building and another one, basilican in layout – is probably ancient, conceived in function of the numerological symbolism and liturgical rhythm of the baptismal rite in the first centuries.[17] The relationship between the baptistery and Santa Reparata was also meant to recall the configuration of the most famous church complex of the early Christian world, Constantine's Holy Sepulchre at Jerusalem, comprised of a basilican church aligned with another one, centrally planned. The proud Florentine conservatism mentioned earlier should be read in light of this singular continuity in the evolution of the city's most important religious complex, the authentic 'centre' of Florentine Christianity, formed by cathedral, baptistery and – perhaps even in those early days – bishop's palace.[18]

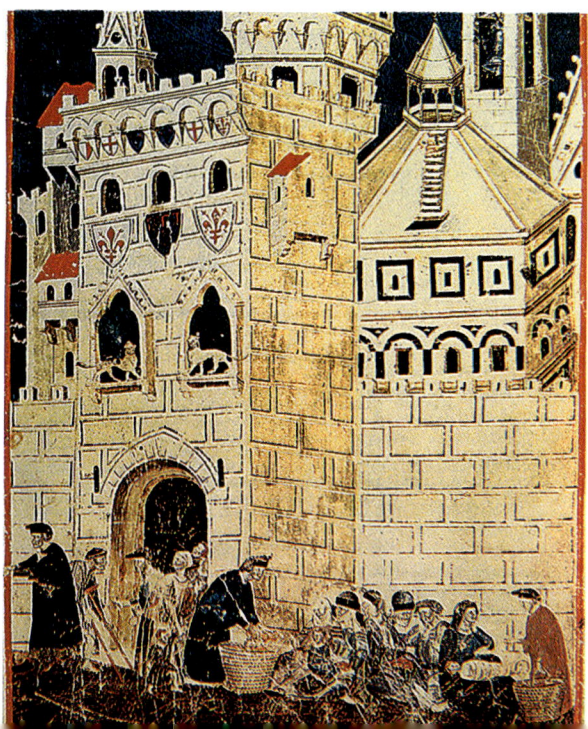

THE END OF ANTIQUITY, THE BEGINNING OF THE MIDDLE AGES

Accepting the traditional dates, what becomes clear is that the basilica of Santa Reparata and its baptistery were built in the last decades of peace the Western Roman Empire was to know. The victory over the Goths of King Radagaisus, on Reparata's feast day in 405 A.D., had not been final. With the taking of Rome by the Vandals in 455 and the deposition of the last Latin emperor, Romulus Augustulus, in 476, even the semblance of a central power disappeared, and, with it, all hope of systematic development for the Church and other institutions. The budding network of Florentine churches, with Santa Reparata and the baptistery at its centre (accepting, again, the traditional dates), not only could not be extended, but was partially dismantled: Santa Reparata, destroyed by the barbarians, remained outside the defensive rampart hastily erected further south by the Byzantine garrison come to 'defend' Florentia from Gothic forays.

The years of the Byzantine occupation (552-568) saw few new churches built, and small ones at that, of which none have survived to our time. The structure that might serve to symbolise the conditions of the city and ecclesial community in the sixth century is Santa Maria Odigidria, called 'in the Capitol' because built within the colonnade of the old temple of Capitoline Jove, in the central forum. Suppressed in the eighteenth century and turned into a hotel, this structure disappeared entirely under the arcades of Piazza della Repubblica at the end of the nineteenth century; but its small size, and situation inside the portico of a pagan building, eloquently express the state of Florence and its Church during the Byzantine era: a population of perhaps fewer than a thousand people, who – behind defensive walls reduced to a bare minimum – did not construct, but occupied and adapted the spaces of a vanished empire.[19]

This inertia did not last long. By the end of the sixth century Tuscany was part of the Lombard kingdom, and the conversion from Arianism to the Catholic faith of Queen Theodolinda brought renewed prestige to Church and the resumption of ecclesiastical building projects, even in secondary centres like Florence. In the seventh and eighth centuries, a series of churches – of which some were built north of the forum, in the area that had been left outside the re-dimensioned Byzantine defences – reintegrated and extended the system of ecclesiastical structures begun three centuries before, laying the foundations for a jurisdictional subdivision into what later would be called 'parishes'. A nation of warriors, the Lombard invaders took Saint Michael the Archangel, captain of the heavenly host, as their patron, and at least four churches bearing his name go back to that period: San Michele Bertelde, San Michele Visdomini (in the original location, corresponding with the present-day choir of the cathedral), San Michele 'ad Hortum' (Orsanmichele) and San Michele alle Trombe (later Santa Elisabetta, suppressed in 1785) – of which the first two were built beyond the Byzantine walls.[20]

### THE ROLE OF MONASTICISM

The Lombard kings, like the Carolingian emperors who followed them, used monasticism and monks in the religious and civil organisation of the emerging feudal system on which their power rested. Among the churches founded in Florence between the seventh and eighth centuries, several in fact were served by monastic communities: San Michele in Orto, for example, and San Michele Bertelde, both under the authority of the Abbey of Nonantola, at Modena, in the heart of Lombard territory. Another of the Lombard churches, San Piero Celoro (meaning 'in ciel d'oro', *'in a golden heaven'*: now the Archive of the Chapter of Santa Maria del Fiore), was under the authority of the abbey of the same name in Pavia, founded by King Luitprand.[21] The local ecclesiastical 'network' was thus linked to the international system of major monasteries, in an infrastructure destined to play a determining role in the history of the universal Church in the following centuries. Charlemagne's conquest of the Lombard kingdom, ensured by the capture of Pavia in 773-774, would confirm the monastic development of the ecclesiastic network in Florence and throughout the 'empire' entrusted by Pope Leo III to the king of the Franks in the year 800. Leaving aside the question of whether Charlemagne personally founded churches such as Santo Stefano al Ponte and Santi Apostoli, it remains true that the administrative re-organisation of the Holy Roman Empire spurred the expansion, in Florence, of important ecclesiastic institutions.

In 854, the emperor Lothair united Fiesole to Florence in a single imperial county, and Florence became one of the most important centres in Tuscany, with a *contado* (rural subject territory) stretching from the summit of the Apennines to Siena, from Pistoia to Arezzo. Lothair then opened

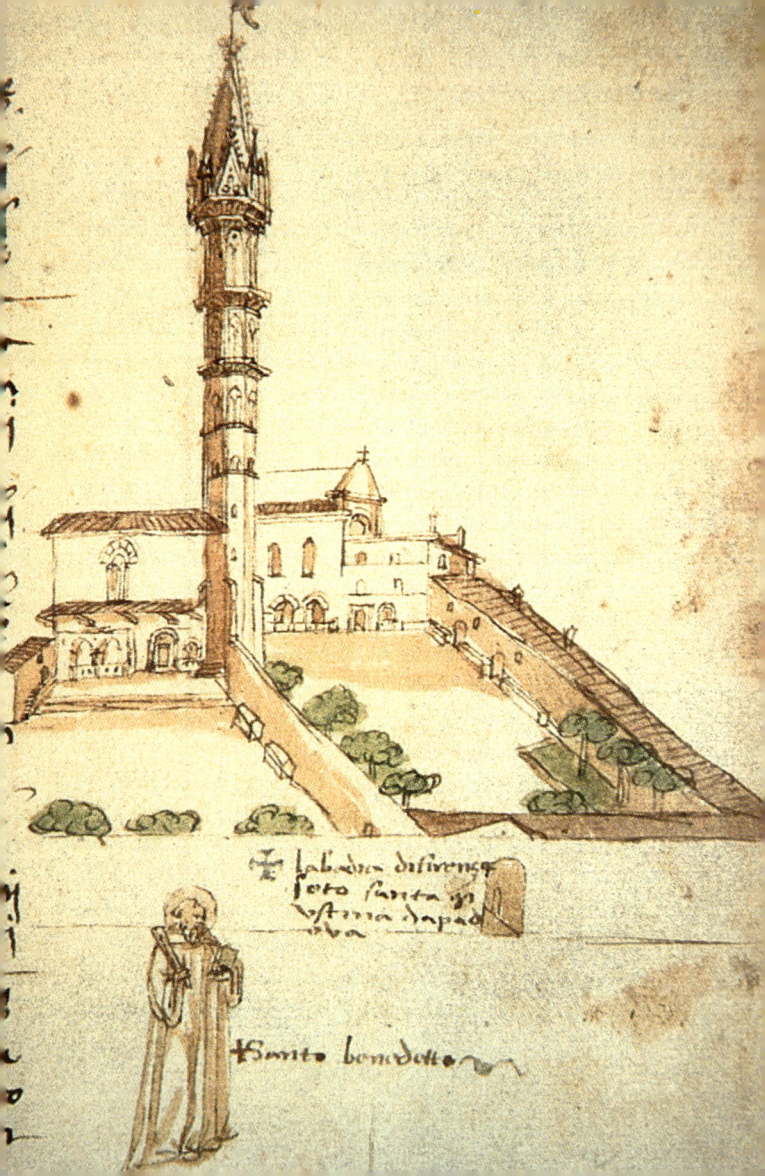

labadia difirenge
foto fanta in
ftina dapad
oua

Santo benedetto

an public church school in Florence, giving rise to an imperial bureaucracy formed in part of priests and monks.[22] A document of March 897 gives an idea of the 'image' of the Church in the Carolingian era: it says that the palatine count Amadeo, envoy of Emperor Lambert, sat in judgement "under the portico in front of the basilica of San Giovanni Battista, with the Margrave Adalbert, to render justice and pass sentence on one and all. With them sat Elwing, Bishop of Parma; Lupo, Bishop of Siena; Adalbert, Bishop of Luni; and Grasulf, Bishop of Florence".[23] In fact the bishop's palace and the imperial margrave's residence were in the same group of buildings behind the baptistery, where the Arcivescovado stands today: an overlay of Church and State inspired by the Holy Roman Empire, which derived its legitimacy from ecclesiastical authority.

The imperial administration was often run by monks, and it is no surprise that the most important ecclesiastical foundations in Florence between the tenth and eleventh centuries were monastic. The first deserving mention is the Badia Fiorentina or 'Florence Abbey', "within the ancient walls", as Dante specifies (Par. XV, 97-98), founded in 987 by Willa, widow of the Margrave Hubert, with patrimonial holdings that assured its prestige.[24] Willa's son, Count Hugo, would found at least seven abbeys in Tuscany, and the friendship of the Emperor Henry II with the Bishop Hildebrand of Florence led in 1018 to reconstruction of the Benedictine abbey of San Miniato al Monte, which belonged to the extensive monastic federation with its centre at Cluny, in Burgundy. Another abbey, San Salvatore a Settimo (Badia a Settimo), in 1004 was given by Count Lothair of Cadolo to the Cluniac Benedictines, and in 1024 Hildebrand placed the old church of Santa Felicita in the care of the monks of San Miniato. In 1059, Santa Felicita became the residence of a community of Benedictine nuns under the direction of the abbess Teitberga.[25]

The abuses unavoidable in this complicity between the Church and the State would, in the eleventh century, provoke a series of reforms which included the renewal of Benedictine monasticism by Saint John Gualbert (985-1073), from his Abbey of Vallombrosa, forty kilometres south of Florence. In 1048, construction of the Abbey of San Salvi was begun for the 'Vallombrosans'

Badia Fiorentina with St Benedict in the *Codice Rustici* (15th century)

not far from the walls of Florence, and twenty years later the abbey complex at Settimo was entrusted to John Gualbert's followers. In the same period, the Vallombrosans were granted the city monastery of Santa Trinita, on the south-west corner of the Roman walls, just beyond the moat.[26]

The spirit of reform would later spread from the monastic sphere to the official hierarchy of the Church. In Florence, in 1055, Pope Victor II presided over a council that brought together a hundred and twenty Italian and foreign bishops, and in 1068 the simoniacal bishop of Florence Pietro Mezzabarba was discredited by a Vallombrosan monk, Pietro Igneo, in the famous ordeal by fire that took place at Badia a Settimo. To rid the Church (and with it the local civil administrations) of imperial interference, the countess Matilda of Tuscany would become an ally of the reformer pope Gregory VII.[27] One of the most significant events for the Florentine Church and for its churches in that period was the election in 1058 of Godfrey of Burgundy, Bishop of Florence, as pope, with the name Nicholas II. The new pope spent more time in Florence than in Rome, and consolidated the prestige of the city by refounding one of the oldest churches inside the walls, the baptistery of San Giovanni. An old source claims that in 1059 Nicholas II 'consecrated' the baptistery: in the most widely-accepted interpretation, that means he began the process of amplification and embellishment which, between the eleventh and thirteenth centuries, replaced the late-antique baptismal hall with the vast structure we now see, conceived on a monumental scale that clearly had Imperial Rome as its model. Nicholas II also began the enlargement of Santa Reparata and the reconstruction of Santa Felicita (1056) and San Lorenzo (1060), in what – if we add San Miniato al Monte, rebuilt starting in 1018 – seems to have been a Romanesque 'rebirth' of the entire original network, with all the early components renewed and enlarged.

THE CHURCHES OF THE COMMUNE

This eleventh-century renascence took place in a context of political and economic change which saw the Church assume a leading role in asserting the city's identity. The resistance to imperial power organised by the 'great countess' Matilda in support of Gregory VII laid the foundations of Florentine Guelphism, and at Matilda's death (1115) the Commune was

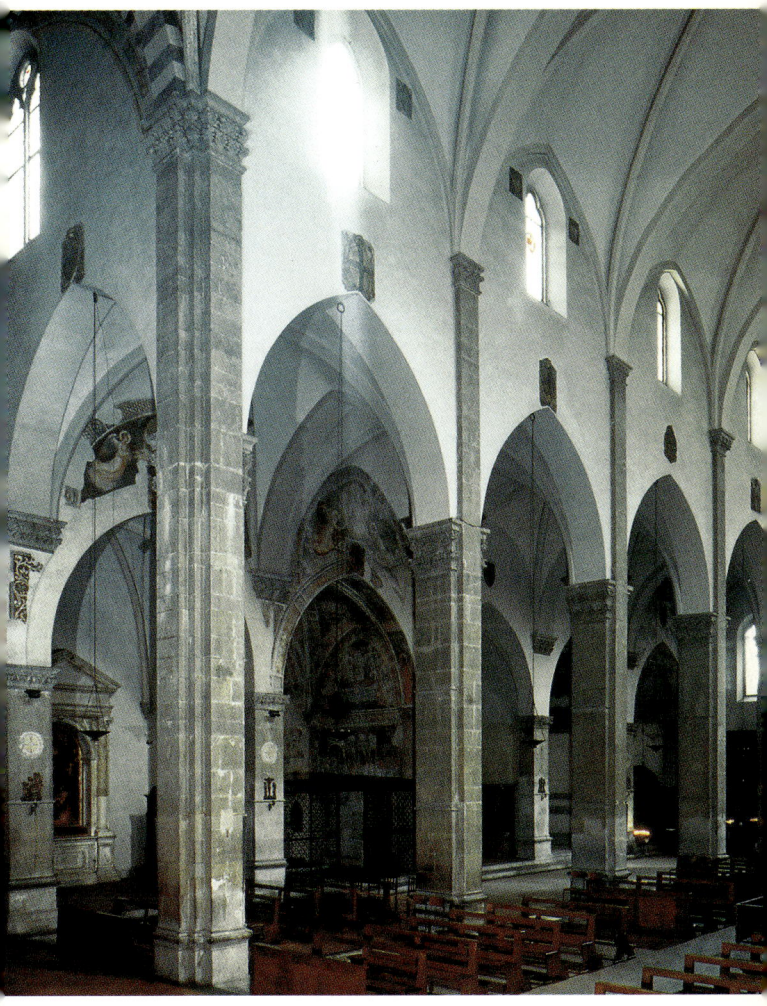

already virtually established. The Florentine Republic was born, owing its *libertas* to the pope, ideal guarantor of legitimacy in the face of the Emperor's pretensions and those of Imperial vassals in the Tuscan marquisate.

With the destruction in 1125 of a hated foe in a hilltop fortress – Fiesole – and the submission of her bishop, a feudal lord with vast possessions, thereafter obliged to reside in Florence, the power of Guelph *Fiorenza* was significantly strengthened. As early as the mid-eleventh century, the population had grown to over twenty thousand, and the services made necessary by such rapid development were a-forming. The nucleus of the remarkable hospital system for which Florence would become famous goes back to this period: in the small space between the baptistery and Santa Reparata stood the Spedale di San Giovanni Evangelista, and a document of 1117 speaks of a hospital alongside San Lorenzo.[28]

These buildings, which had several functions – they were hospices for travellers and the poor, nursing homes for the sick, orphanages – also developed in light of the monastic presence, as a natural extension of the community ideal of Benedictine life and of the insistence, in the *Regula Benedicti*, on fraternal assistance. Sources in fact mention hospitals at the Badia Fiorentina (1031), at the suburban monastery of San Pier Maggiore (1065), and another one (1068), under the authority of the Abbey of San Miniato but located at the foot of the hill, near Santa Felicita.[29] Henceforth the Church would play a significant part in the city's economic life. Before the year 1000, sources already speak of a *laboratorium* for wool making connected to the monastery of San Michele in Orto, and another in the now extinct monastery of Sant'Andrea 'in Foro Vetere': an association of functions that foreshadowed the role the Mendicant orders would play in the industrial development of Florence in the thirteenth and fourteenth centuries. And since San Michele in Orto was dependent on the Abbey of Nonantola – which, aside from providing precious wool from Modena, also provided the labour – that kind of ecclesiastic commitment led to a primitive system of commercial and artisan exchange. In an analogous development, when, at the end of the thirteenth century the Commune had to demolish part of the old walls rendered superfluous by urban expansion, the Abbot of the Badia Fiorentina bought the section contiguous with the monastery property, had the walls torn down, filled in the moat and built a series of

shops which the monastic community then leased at low rents.[30] In this fashion the ecclesiastic bodies had, and were perceived as having, a central
role in the economic and urbanistic development of the Commune. The
monastic ideal of brotherly charity found expression in a series of hospices supported by the intelligence and hard work of the monks themselves,
and labour serving the common good thus became an ideal of Florentine
civil life, encouraging the early organisation of artisan corporations, the
guilds. The very shape of the city – the growth of the fabric of streets and
piazzas – was in part shaped by the intervention of ecclesiastical organ-
isms : churches that owned urban and suburban property (often through
legacies) sold it at reasonable rates, on condition that houses and shops
be built – as in a document of 1057 regarding a piece of land near Santa
Felicita.[31] By this point, it is fair to say, the past and above all the future
of Florence were inseparably linked with the life of the city's churches.

THE MENDICANT ORDERS AND THE MONUMENTAL BASILICAS

These were the dynamics, civic and ecclesiastical, that gave Florence and
its network of religious buildings definitive form in the thirteenth and fourteenth centuries. A true demographic explosion, bringing the population
to over one hundred thousand before the cataclysmic epidemic of 1348, had
created an urgent need for services that neither Commune nor Church could
satisfy in the eleventh and twelfth centuries. The new town walls of 1173-
1175 soon proved inadequate, and thousands of immigrants drawn by jobs
in the wool factories settled outside the walls, which between 1284 and 1333
would have to be enlarged again to absorb these new residential areas.
With the immigrants came small religious communities serving the 'new
poor' created by this medieval industrial revolution. After the 1220s, representatives of the new 'Mendicant' orders appear (religious orders supported by people's contributions, that is, rather than by their own capital,
as the older monastic orders were). The Commune, dominated by the Guilds,
grasped the role these 'friars' might play in the socio-economic as well as
religious development of the city, and made available vast tracts of property to the Franciscans, Dominicans, Servites, Augustinians and Carmelites
– to mention but the most important groups – : land where the friars
established convents around which populous districts developed that in the

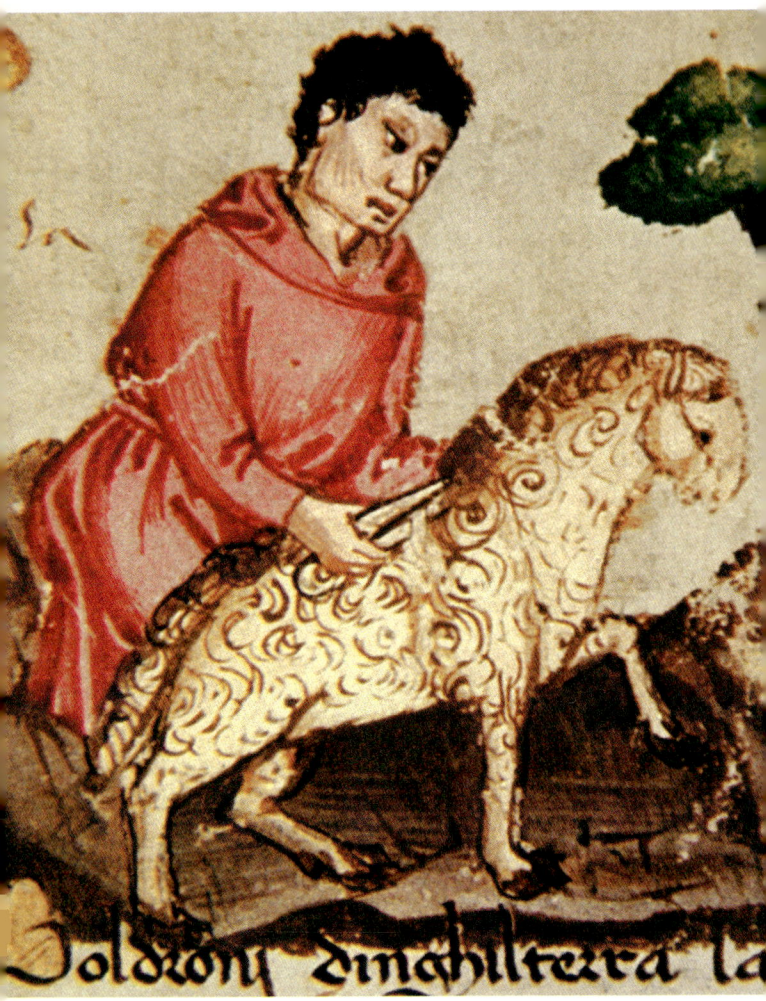

space of two generations were woven into the urban fabric, thanks to construction of the above mentioned new fortifications in 1284-1333. Simultaneously, the small outlying churches occupied or built by the friars when they first came were enlarged, creating around the old Roman centre a constellation of large modern basilicas which even today define our perception of Florence as a city: Santa Maria Novella (Dominicans), Santa Croce (Franciscans), Santissima Annunziata (Servites), Santo Spirito (Augustinians) and Santa Maria del Carmine (Carmelites).[32]

In addition to the major orders, other communities settled in the same fashion: the Umiliati at Ognissanti, the Silvestrines at San Marco. And the churches of the old monastic orders were enlarged as well: Santa Trinita, Santa Maria Maggiore, the Badia Fiorentina and Badia a Settimo, entrusted in 1236 to the Cistercians of San Galgano. The ties with the city's economic and public life born in the monastic context were strengthened, eventually involving the new Mendicant orders as well. The Cistercians of Badia a Settimo supervised river navigation, essential for trade; the Umiliati were experts in wool processing; the Camaldolese and the Franciscans were arbiters and guarantors in the affairs of city administration. Santa Maria Novella, the first of the Mendicant churches to be enlarged on a monumental scale (and for many years the only large public building in the city), was the seat of a citizen parliament in 1301, and a 'papal apartment' was created, supported and run by the Commune: an official facility for prominent guests, popes or princes. In front of the friars' churches large squares were laid out, an innovation at once costly and striking since medieval cities were constricted within defensive walls. These spaces were for preaching, a religious activity in which the Mendicant orders were highly skilled, but served also for the civil assemblies of the 'Second People' which, between 1282-1283, forged an alliance between the greater guilds (the banker and merchant bourgeoisie) and the class of artisans and trained workers living in the districts served by the new basilicas. The new monumental churches, with their piazzas, were public structures, built *"ad utilitatem animarum et decorum civitatis"*.[33] They represented in concrete terms the citizens' will to live together in peace: the enlargement of Santa Maria Novella

Miniature from Antonio Ventura's *Libro delle gabelle* (14th century)

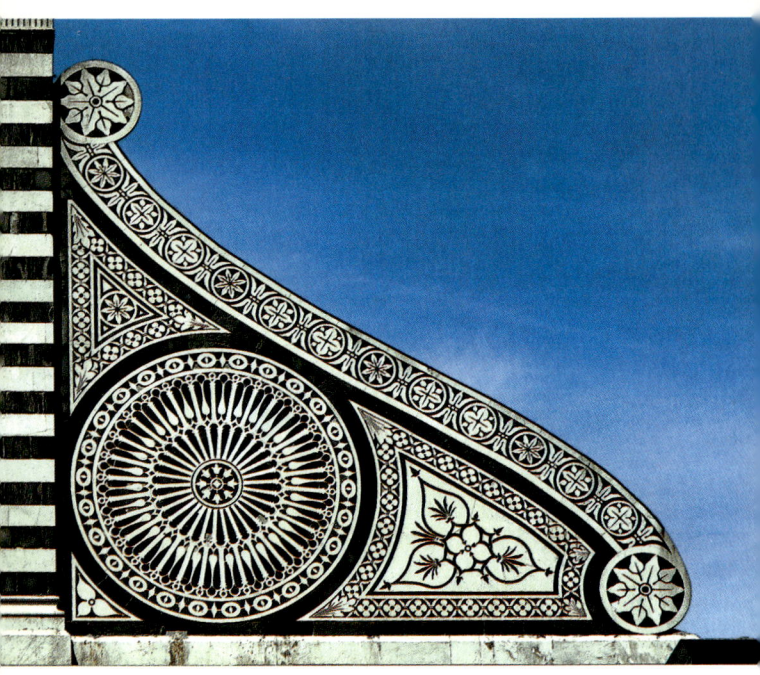

towards the south – the addition of the majestic main nave – was begun
when the 'Cardinal Peace-Maker' Latino Malabranca, a Dominican, was
sent by Pope Nicholas III on a mission to the warring Florentine factions
in 1279. It is significant moreover that, as soon as the nave was completed, the façade was decorated (the lower part, at least) with green and
white marble like that of the then 'new' facing of the baptistery. That is, the
first of the large suburban churches was given a 'Florentine' appearance
similar to that of the old centre's most revered place of worship, in token

Leon Battista Alberti, façade of Santa Maria Novella, detail
*Following pages:* Andrea di Bonaiuto, fresco in the chapter house, Santa Maria
Novella

of full participation in the history and life of the city.[34] The architectural style in which the new churches were conceived, a soberly functional Gothic borrowed from the Cistercians, must have given an impression of modernity, and the vast wall surfaces inside the basilicas – naves and chapels which in the space of two generations would be covered with frescoes – offered rich patron families the opportunity to contribute to the city's decorum, while the poor might be proud to belong to so well-organised a society (both sentiments becoming part of the Christian faith illustrated in the murals). In this way the new thirteenth- and fourteenth-century churches became the religious sign of a civic destiny, a 'vocation' to moral as well as economic and cultural greatness.

THE NEW CATHEDRAL

In the dynamic context thus outlined – with the construction of the basilicas of the Mendicant orders and the enlarging of existing monastic churches like Santa Trinita – the old cathedral facing the baptistery began to seem inadequate to the self-image Florence was in the process of defining. As Giovanni Villani wrote in the early fourteenth century, Santa Reparata "was small and very crude in form compared to such a city".[35] Seen in relation to the monumental new baptistery, and especially to the cathedrals of other Tuscan and Italian cities – Pisa, Siena, Orvieto – the old cathedral of Florence was indeed modest in size and decoration, and could not but embarrass the Florentines. Thus was born the project of a new cathedral church, the 'emblematic' structure mentioned in the first page of this essay. Together with the city hall begun a few years later, the new cathedral was meant to confirm in architectural terms the strength and the stability of the Florentine Republic and its Guelph government, defeated at Montaperti in 1260 but once again victorious at Campaldino in 1289.

Even more than the basilicas of the Mendicant orders, the new cathedral was a public work, undertaken *"ad honorem et laudem Dei et beatae Virginis Mariae"* (according to a document going back to the planning phase in 1294), *"et ad honorem comunis et populi florentini, et ad decorem iam dicte civitatis Florentiae"*.[36] The work was entrusted to the architect who was already working on the construction of the new city walls and the basilica of Santa Croce, and who two years later would be called to build Palazzo

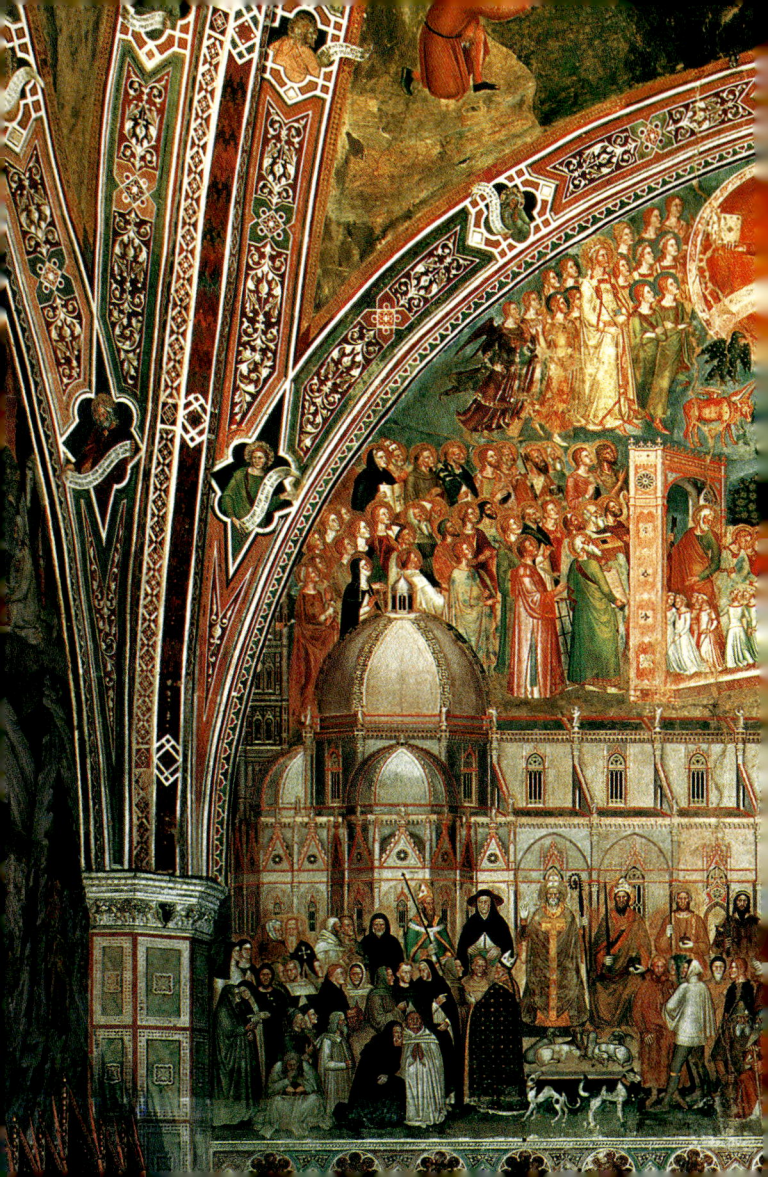

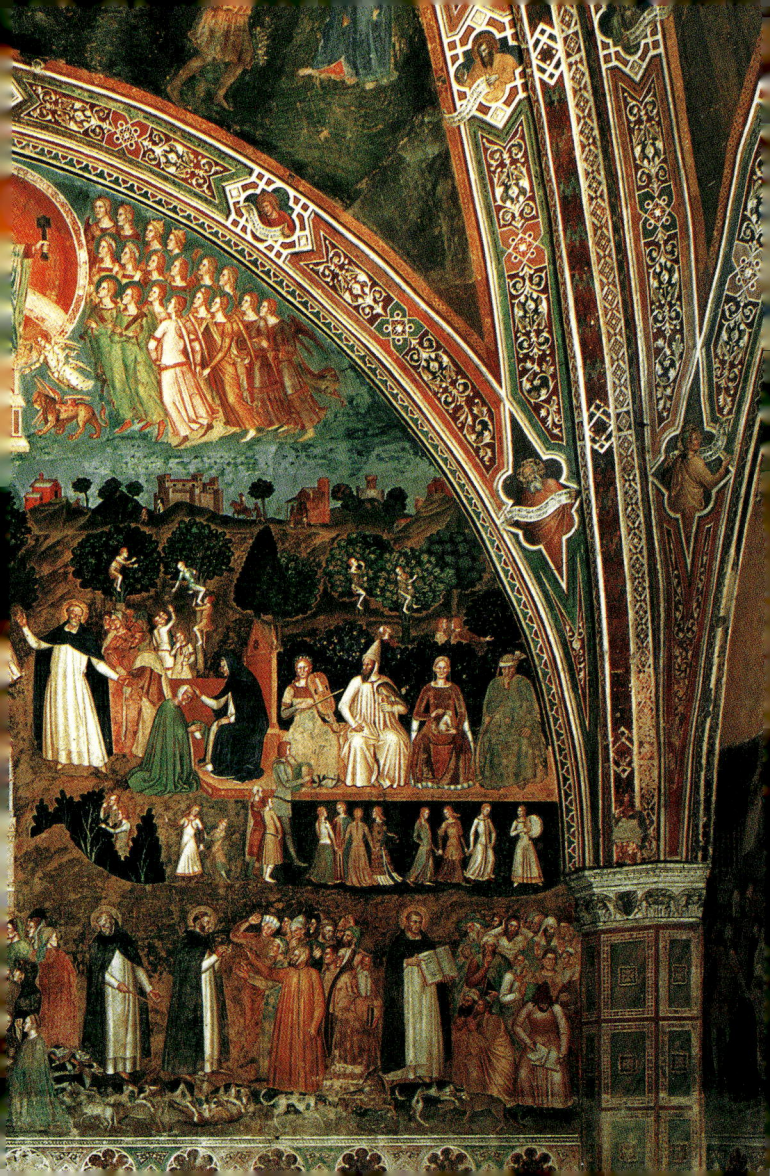

della Signoria: Arnolfo di Cambio, whom we should consider the 'official' architect of the Commune in that period. The new dedication of the cathedral – no longer to Saint Reparata but to the Virgin Mary, with the title 'Santa Maria del Fiore' (a reference both to *Fiorenza* and to the *flower* seeded in Mary's womb, Christ)[37] – makes clear that the rising cathedral was seen both as 'state church' and as the main symbol of Florentine faith.

The economic machinery devised to realise this project suggests the interaction of social and religious messages which the new cathedral embodied. After an initial series of contributions from the clergy, funding became the responsibility of the State. Taxes and special levies assured the necessary sums, which were entrusted to a body created to supervise the construction and embellishment of the cathedral, called the 'opera' (from *opus*, 'work': 'office of works' that is, or 'cathedral foundation'). In 1331 the commune assigned direction of the Opera to the most important of the Florentine artisan corporations, the powerful Wool Guild, which re-organised the administrative structure of the body along the lines of its own statutes. In the fourteenth and fifteenth centuries, skilled craftsmen employed by the Opera on the 'cathedral project' would be lent to other city projects, among which the Loggia della Signoria, next to the town hall, and the new 'palace' of the Guilds, Orsanmichele.[38]

Thus cathedral and city merged, the one an integral part of the other, born of a single will: the cathedral planned and paid for by the Commune, but Communal monuments then built by the cathedral Opera, and all of it guided by the same political-economic interests. In the perception of the people of the time, Santa Maria del Fiore became virtually a 'sacrament' of the city's growth: an *efficient sign* begetting other signs. And when the great commercial loggia, Orsanmichele, was turned into a church and embellished by the Guilds, the merging of roles was complete: every dimension of Florentine public life seemed to emanate from its ecclesial life, which in turn was conditioned by the political and economic life of the city. The socio-sacramental implications of the new cathedral are suggested in a fresco of 1365, in the Chapter House of Santa Maria Novella. A work by Andrea di Bonaiuto, the fresco aligns the major representatives of the ecclesiastic and the power structures, the pope, the emperor, a king, a cardinal, a bishop, and so on, in front of Santa Maria del Fiore: as if to subsume the social structure of the Middle Ages in a single symbolic module, the Church, symbolised by the still-unfinished temple already heralded as the greatest church – in size – of the Christian world (an honour that Santa Maria del Fiore could claim until the completion of Milan cathedral and the Vatican Basilica designed by Bramante in the sixteenth century).

BRUNELLESCHI'S DOME

The most characteristic architectural and symbolic element of the new cathedral, the dome, was already part of the overall project in the fourteenth century, as is evident in Andrea di Bonaiuto's fresco. It was built at the beginning of the fifteenth century, in barely fourteen years between 1420 and 1434. "A structure so grand (...) vast enough to cover all Tuscans with its shadow..."[39], as Brunelleschi's friend, Leon Battista Alberti, described it, this 'greater dome' of the new cathedral did indeed 'cover' an entire area of early medieval Florence: in the late fourteenth century, in order to lay its foundations, houses and palaces had been torn down (among which that of the Bischeri family, notorious for having foolishly opposed the project). Also demolished was the old parish church of San Michele Visdomini, whose name was transferred to a new construction located 150 meters to the north. With the dome of Santa Maria del Fiore, architecture – and specifically religious architecture – made an irreversible step forward on the related planes of symbolism, urban planning and technology. The breath-taking curve of the exterior ribs, and the stupendous effect of the eight huge roof segments, communicate – through form and titanic volume – the 'boundless capacity to inspire awe' that Giorgio Vasari would later attribute to Filippo Brunelleschi, considering it an inner quality. As pure sublime 'form', the dome gathers and unifies the other forms over which it looms: it is not only big, but *monumental*, imposing itself as the dominant central element of its world. Practically speaking, it is so monumental, compared to everything near it, that it becomes a visual symbol of the entire city. With its mass it covers and ennobles palaces and houses, offering a concrete image of the 'mother Church' who spreads her tent to extend God's grace to all his children. It defines the central Christian temple of Florence as an irresistible unifying force, absolute pivot of the city's topography.[40]

A cause of particular astonishment to fifteenth century viewers was the tech-

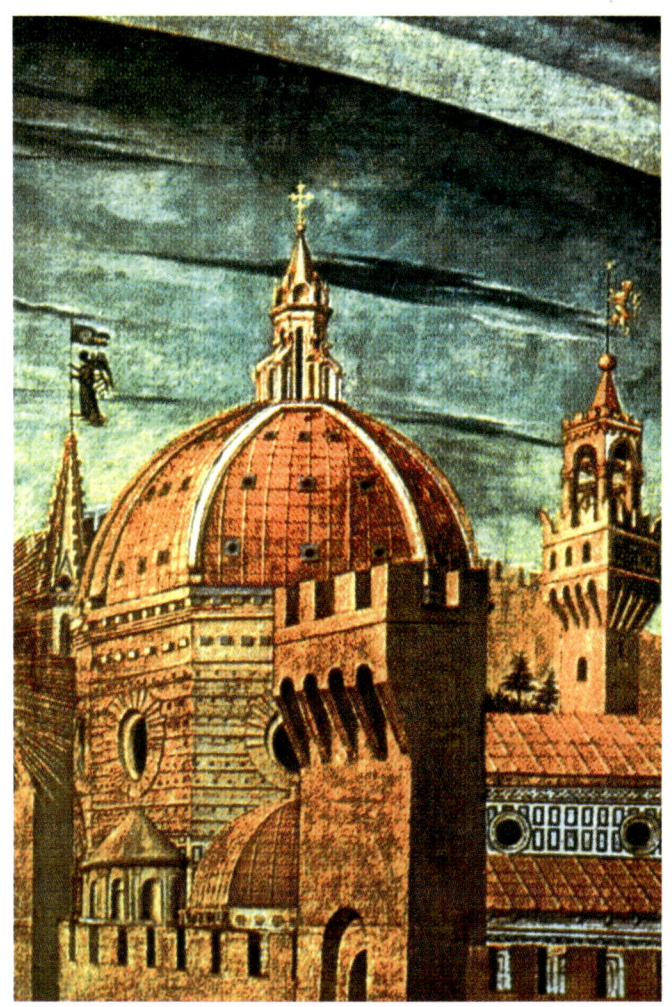

nological triumph the dome represents. Built 'without visible support' outside or in, it confirmed modern man's capability, on a par with that of ancient builders, to comprehend and replicate the order of the universe, creating a microcosm fashioned according to laws of divine origin. It is no coincidence that a Florentine philosopher, Pico della Mirandola – in his *Orazione sulla dignità dell'uomo* – would later present God as "the Architect [who] fashioned the world as a dwelling for divine beings, an august temple designed according to the arcane laws of His wisdom". From Pico's neo-platonic point of view, the human vocation is in fact to understand and admire the masterpiece of the Architect-God: "having completed his work, the divine Artificer wanted there to be someone able to grasp its logic, love its beauty, admire its greatness". Pico concludes by calling man *universi contemplator*, "contemplator of the universe".[41]

If we interpret, from this 'contemplative' point of view, the religious architecture Brunelleschi created while he was directing the titanic undertaking of the dome – the Spedale degli Innocenti, San Lorenzo, Santo Spirito, Santa Maria degli Angeli, the Pazzi Chapel at Santa Croce – perhaps we can pierce the veil that seems to separate Renaissance Humanism from the experience of faith. In the luminous structural logic of Brunelleschi's churches, the believer discovers that he truly is 'made in the image' of God: capable of understanding the laws 'structuring' the universe, the unchanging mathematical relationships in which the Creator's perfection is manifest; capable of analysing these laws and living them, reshaping his own existence in light of this Christian Humanism expressed in architecture.

### TAM ANTIQUA ET TAM NOVA

The fifteenth-century Renaissance renewed, in forms recalling its remote late-antique origins, the original 'system' of Florentine ecclesiastical buildings. Along with San Lorenzo and Santa Reparata (henceforth 'Santa Maria del Fiore'), Santa Felicita and San Miniato also underwent transformations – not full reconstruction but enrichment with exquisite chapels in the new style. The first *aggiornamento* of the network of Florentine churches, which had taken place four centuries earlier, in the days of Hildebrand and Nicholas

Domenico di Michelino, *Dante with His Poem*, detail, 1465, Duomo

II, was thus repeated, as if in token of perennial youth. If then we substitute Santo Spirito for Santa Felicita as the 'modern church' beyond the Arno, we can say that the primitive ecclesiastical network, comprised of three structures spanning the city from north to south, had been reconstituted: an explicit reference to the antiquity of the Florentine Church, which perceived itself as *"pulchritudo tam antiqua et tam nova"* (in Saint Augustine's phrase), a "beauty ever ancient, ever new".[42]

Other churches were brought into line with this vision of a city that renews itself through return to its ancient origins: the façade of Santa Maria Novella, left incomplete in the fourteenth century, was given a magnificent upper story, designed by Leon Battista Alberti. At the Santissima Annunziata, radical redesign of the thirteenth-century structure was begun, with the addition of a new choir rotunda, planned by Michelozzo and modified and completed by Leon Battista Alberti. And at the Carmine, San Marco, Santa Trinita and Santa Maria Novella important programmes of frescoes served to update church and convent, in a more or less systematic process that extended to the whole city. In Santa Maria del Fiore, a great number of medieval artworks transferred from Santa Reparata to the new cathedral, or commissioned for it in the fourteenth century, were sold, and – once the dome was finished – an astounding creative effort was made, with the aim of giving the cathedral a modern appearance. The new works included: the *cantorie* by Luca della Robbia and Donatello; the stained-glass windows of the drum; Luca della Robbia's reliefs for the sacristies and his bronze doors; the superb marquetry of the Sagrestia delle Messe; the frescoes depicting military leaders; the clock; the commemorative reliefs and busts. Apart from these commissions for Santa Maria del Fiore, which came from the Opera del Duomo, the other renovation projects were all financed by private patrons: the Medici, Brancacci, Barbadori, Rucellai, Pazzi, Sassetti, Tornabuoni and Strozzi families – patricians who, for the most part, were also and simultaneously building magnificent palaces in town and villas in the country. Even foreign princes were involved: the royal family of Portugal, at San Miniato al Monte, and the marquess of Mantua at San-

Domenico Ghirlandaio, *Young Woman of the Tornabuoni Family*, detail of the fresco in the Tornabuoni chapel, Santa Maria Novella

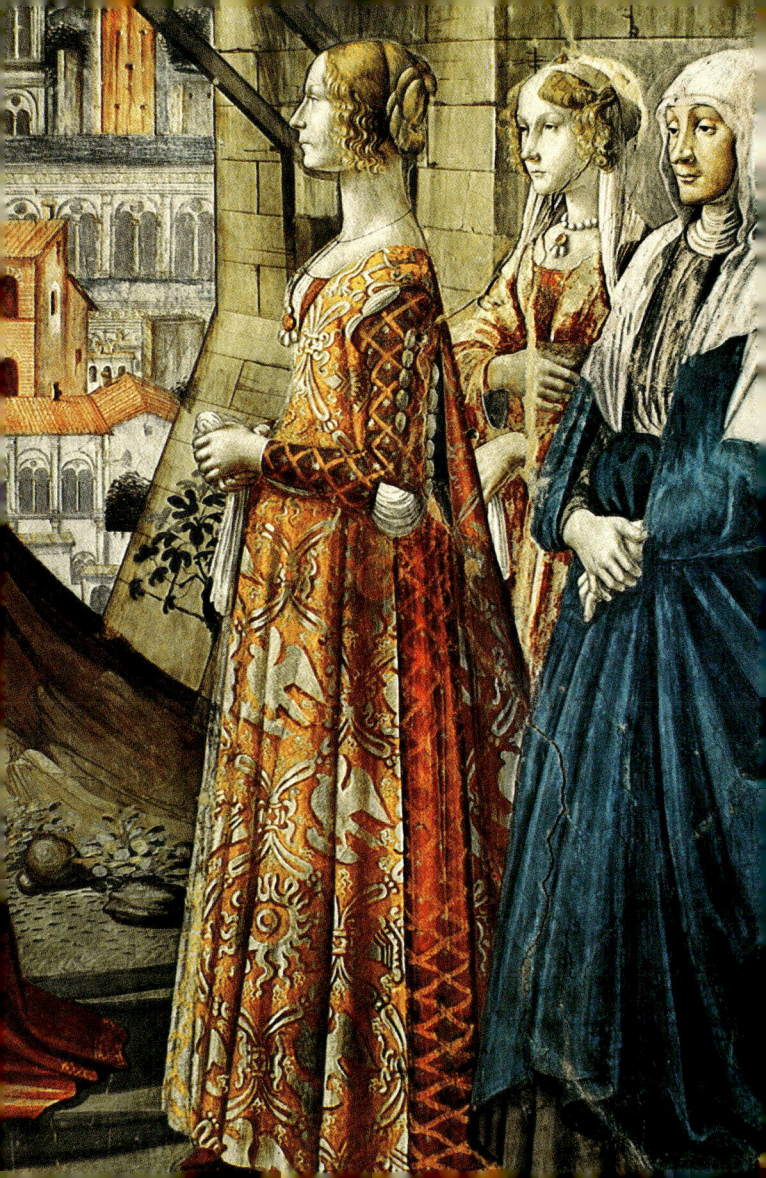

tissima Annunziata. The new splendour of the old network of Florentine churches cannot, therefore, be interpreted in the same communal, civic terms that had marked it prior to the year 1000: no longer was it the diocese, the parish, the monastery and the convent, nor even the Commune, but the great families who renovated the churches of Florence, which in many cases must have seemed to be external chapels serving the palaces that rose beside them. The coats of arms and the portraits of the patrons could be seen everywhere: the Medici at San Lorenzo, San Miniato, San Marco, at the Santissima Annunziata and in the Novitiate Chapel of Santa Croce; the Rucellai at Santa Maria Novella and San Pancrazio; the Pazzi at the Chapter House of Santa Croce; the Sassetti at Santa Trinita; the Tornabuoni at Santa Maria Novella.

## GRAND DUCHY AND COUNTER-REFORMATION

The process of aristocratic renovation begun in the fifteenth century was intensified over the next three centuries, in the radically changed atmosphere of the Medici principate. The churches in which Savonarola had preached at the end of the fifteenth century were transformed with splendid furnishings in line with the taste and sense of 'decorum' of the late Renaissance. At the behest of Duke (later Grand Duke) Cosimo I, beneath Brunelleschi's dome Baccio Bandinelli's heavy choir enclosure took shape (partially dismantled in 1842): a structure that, in the original version of 1547-1572, had seventy pillars in polychrome Serravezza marble, more than eighty marble reliefs (of the three hundred planned) and titanic statues on the high altar.[43] While Bandinelli was elaborating the choir, Bartomoleo Ammannati enriched the cathedral nave, and especially the octagonal space around the choir, with twelve aedicules or monumental niches for statues of the apostles, thereby conferring solemn splendour on the liturgical area of the cathedral. And as soon as Bandinelli's choir was finished, attention shifted to the inner decoration of the huge dome: three thousand six hundred square metres of fresco painting, executed between 1572 and 1579 by Giorgio Vasari and Federico Zuccari. Similar Grand Ducal programmes in Santa Croce and Santa Maria Novella removed the old lateral altars, which were replaced by a uniform series of monumental sixteenth-century *aedicula*; the impression, in the 'functional' area of these churches where the liturgy was celebrated and where the perceptions of the faithful took shape, was of an old building 'ennobled' through solemn reference to Classical culture: a kind of architectural metaphor for the Roman reform movement then making its influence felt.

The Catholic Counter-Reformation found fertile terrain in Florence, owing both to the conservative religious and cultural disposition of the Florentines and to the close ties the Medici had with the Papacy and with Spain. The iconographic programme of the Bandinelli choir and the dome frescoes, for instance, fully reflects the controversial spirit of the times, emphasising doctrinal aspects of traditional Catholicism challenged by the Protestants.[44] The same was true of the series of monumental paintings executed for the new altars of Santa Croce and Santa Maria Novella, which programmatically develop themes stressed by the Council of Trent. In these two basilicas, as in other churches – in compliance with the Council – the fourteenth-century rood screens (architectural dividers that, in the Middle Ages, separated the friars' choir from the nave of the church) were demolished.[45]

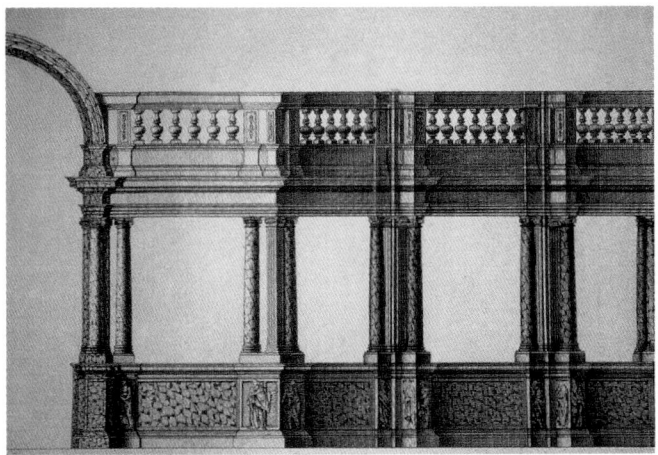

Baccio Bandinelli, view of part of the choir in an 18th century engraving

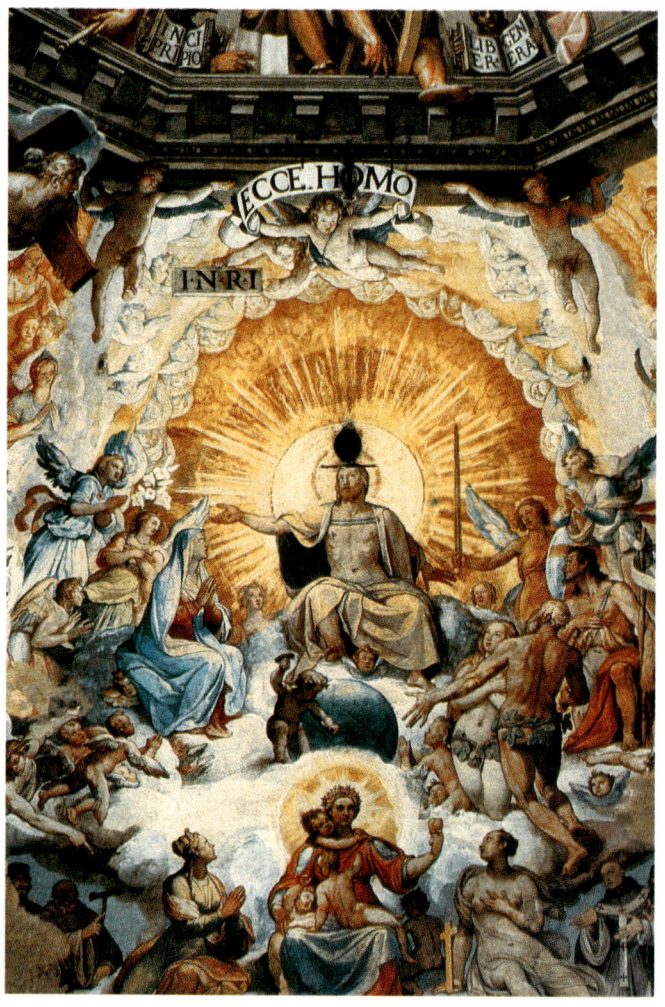

Aside from its more or less radical transformation of existing structures, the Counter-Reformation also built new churches from the ground up: San Giovannino next to the palazzo Medici Riccardi, begun by Ammannati in 1579; San Gaetano (by Nigetti, 1601, and the Silvani family, 1648), on the site of the Lombard church of San Michele Berthelde, of which it would keep the name coupled with the new dedication; San Filippo Neri, called San Firenze, built by Gherardo Silvani (1633-1648), with its superb façade added in the eighteenth century.

These three churches, erected for the most important of the religious orders created in the Catholic Reformation – the Jesuits (San Giovannino), the Theatines (San Gaetano), and the Oratorians or 'Filippini' (San Filippo Neri) – perfectly fulfill the liturgical and iconographic ideals of Tridentine Catholicism. They are unified halls without side aisles, affording an unbroken view of the high altar and with gorgeous furnishings that express the prestige of the Church as institution and the doctrinal and devotional contents required by religious orthodoxy.

A number of old churches 'went baroque': the Badia Fiorentina was subjected to a radical intervention begun in 1627 (in forms consistent however with the 'Tuscan' manner of the previous century rather than with contemporary Roman models). In 1644 the baroque modernisation of the Santissima Annunziata began, destined to drag on for the next two centuries; Santa Felicita was entirely redone by Federico Ruggieri, in 1736, and even Santa Maria del Fiore and the baptistery of San Giovanni would be retouched in the modern spirit: a painted façade for the cathedral was executed in 1689 by Ercole Graziani, who drew his inspiration from San Gaetano, and a baroque altar appeared in the baptistery San Giovanni, with a dramatic figure of the Baptist borne heavenwards in glory, a work by Girolamo Ticciati, removed in the early twentieth century.[46] Nineteenth-century efforts at 'restitution' and 'restoration' of the supposed original decoration of religious buildings, often carried out with surprising brutality, make it difficult to have a clear vision of the former appearance of Florentine churches. Gone are Vasari's niches in Santa Maria Novella and the imposing eucharistic tabernacle once on the altar of Santa Croce; gone too are the

Federico Zuccari, detail of fresco in Santa Maria del Fiore

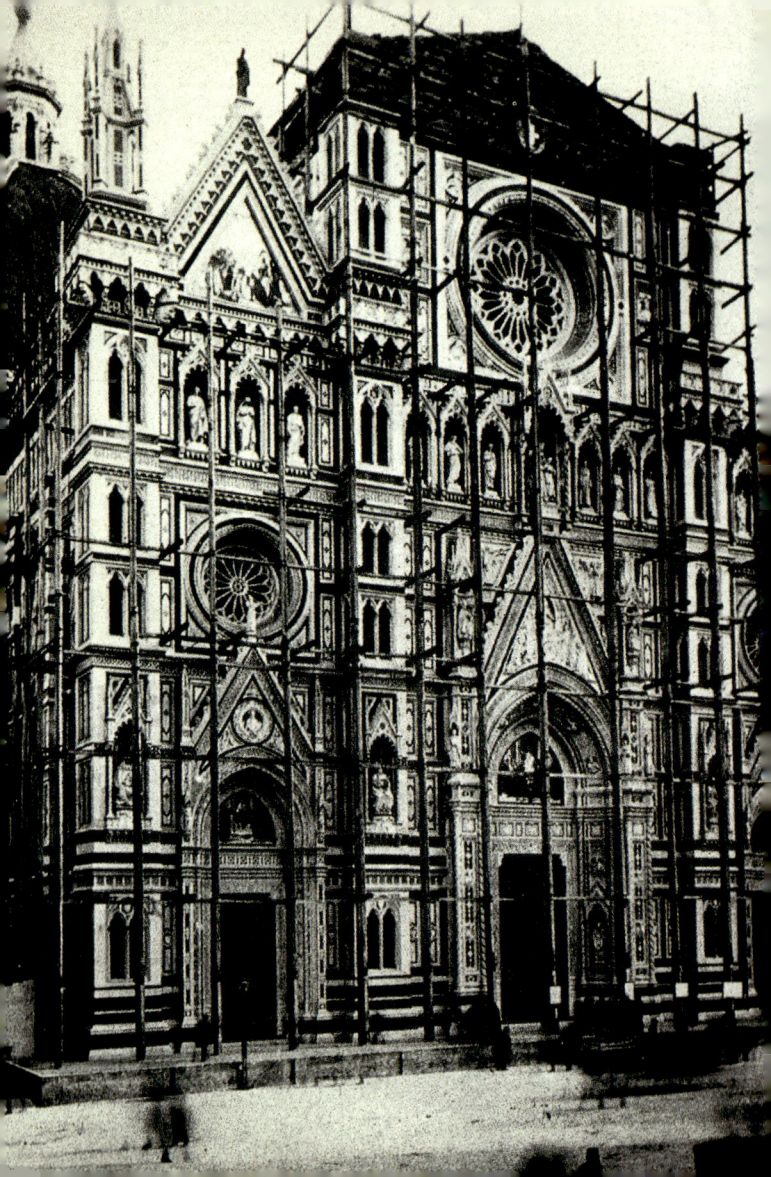

frescoes on the façade of the Misericordia, illustrating the works of Charity, and those by Graziani on the front of the cathedral, with their titanic allegorical figures and historical-ecclesiastical scenes. The strong colours, dramatic forms, concentrated meanings and ecstatic atmosphere in which iconography and style were conceived must have given Florence, like other cities of the time, a festive, celebratory look, 'theatrical' but not artificial, like the elegant backdrop for an erudite drama of the period.

THE MODERN AGE

The nineteenth century rejected the effervescent staginess of baroque decor, striving after 'historical authenticity'. In 1884, a text eulogising the neo-Gothic façade of the cathedral would claim that "the Middle Ages were not fond of abstruse symbols or allegorical abstractions, preferring those truths which then reigned in every mind, being graven in every heart [...] these great churches [...] were to our fathers a kind of synthesis of Christian society, and of the union of man's city with the city of God".[47]

The style that seemed to favour this 'synthesis' was the Gothic. In Italy as elsewhere in Europe, the re-invention of architectural and decorative modules recalling the thirteenth and fourteenth centuries became part of the search for meaning imposed by an age of violent social and political upheaval, offering the appearance of ideal continuity with the end of the Middle Ages. In Florence, reference to the cultural values of the fourteenth century – the time of Dante and Petrarch, Arnolfo and Giotto – was a kind of 'return to the future': simultaneously memory and prolepsis, celebration of the past and augury for the future. The principal works were those made for the main churches: the bell tower and façade of Santa Croce, the neo-gothic altars of Santa Maria Novella, the new organ lofts in Santa Maria del Fiore and the simplification of Bandinelli's choir enclosure (which lost its entire superstructure of pillars, along with the altar statues). The most challenging project was the façade of the cathedral, executed by Emilio de Fabris and his collaborators between 1871 and 1884 in a 'railroad gothic' style that sought to reproduce the fourteenth-century Florentine decorative taste seen in the campanile and side doors of the cathedral. In a similar way, non-Catholic and non-Christian late nineteenth and early twentieth-century places of worship sought to reproduce characteristic features of their respective religious and architectural traditions. The twentieth century would build many churches, in the new districts created at the end of the last century and considerably extended in the post World War II period. A series of late neo-Gothic experiments (among which the church of the Santi Sette Fondatori, consecrated in 1910) give an idea of the difficulty – in Florence as everywhere in the Catholic world – of finding an architectural language suited to modernity. Among post-war churches that are functional and also possess architectural interest, two works by the architect Lando Bartoli deserve mention: Saints Gervasio e Protasio, consecrated in 1957, and Sacro Cuore in via Capodimondo, built between 1956 and 1962. Both structures replaced small earlier churches, and illustrate – with very different solutions – the attempt to meet the needs of believers with a contemporary architectural idiom, elevating this to the dignity of sacred architecture.

The most successful contemporary Florentine church is the one called "the freeway church", located at the north toll-booth of the Autostrada del Sole. Dedicated to San Giovanni Battista, this inspiring structure is a masterpiece of Giovanni Michelucci's mature period. It freely echoes the language developed by such twentieth-century masters as Le Corbusier, presenting an image of temporariness – inspired by the traveller's tent, a provisional halting-place during man's journey – while in its materials and massed volumes it recalls the permanency of ancient Etruscan architecture. It is significant that this last 'great' church of Florence is located alongside a road – just like the early Christian basilicas that between the fourth and fifth centuries rose near the consular roads. Judeo-Christian faith does not recognise a permanent city in this world, in fact, but – as we read in the Letter to the Hebrews – keeps its eyes on "the city with sound foundations, whose architect and builder is God Himself" (11,10). A 'tent' on the freeway is a fitting symbol for the pilgrim Church on earth, in movement towards its heavenly homeland, a travelling companion for modern man as he seeks meaning in history and in individual existence. At the gates of Florence, city of monuments and mass tourism, Michelucci's building speaks of a church community that is, to be sure, ancient, but at the same time – like Saint John the Baptist – free to live "in desert regions" until the day of its manifestation to Israel (Luke 1, 80).

NOTES

[1] F.L. Del Migliore, *Firenze città nobilissima illustrata*, Florence, 1684, p. 6. The passage is quoted by Del Migliore from a communal document dated 1294, no longer available. G. Richa, *Notizie istoriche delle chiese fiorentine*, Florence 1757, vol. 6, p. 14, quotes Del Migliore, reproducing the entire passage.

[2] C. Mohrman, *Les dénominations de l'église en tant qu'édifice en grec et en latin au cours des premiers siècles chrétiens*, in «Revue des sciences religieuses», XXXVI, (1962), pp. 155-177.

[3] *La progettazione di nuove chiese*, document of the Episcopal Commission for Liturgy (CEI), Bologna 1993, p. 7.

[4] Acts of the Apostles 4, 32.

[5] See J. Henderson, *Piety and Charity in Late Medieval Florence*, Oxford 1994, p. 255, n. 49.

[6] Discorso 336: 1-6. *Patrologia latina* (Migne) 38, 1471-1472. 1475.

[7] G. Fanelli, *Firenze*, Bari 1981, p. 11.

[8] M. Lopes Pegna, *Le più antiche chiese*, Florence 1972, p. 47. Id., *Firenze dalle origini al medioevo*, Florence 1962, p. 370.

[9] M. Lopes Pegna, *Itinera Etruriae*, 1, in «Studi etruschi», XXI, (1951), p. 434.

[10] Lopes Pegna, *Le più antiche chiese*, cit., p. 47.

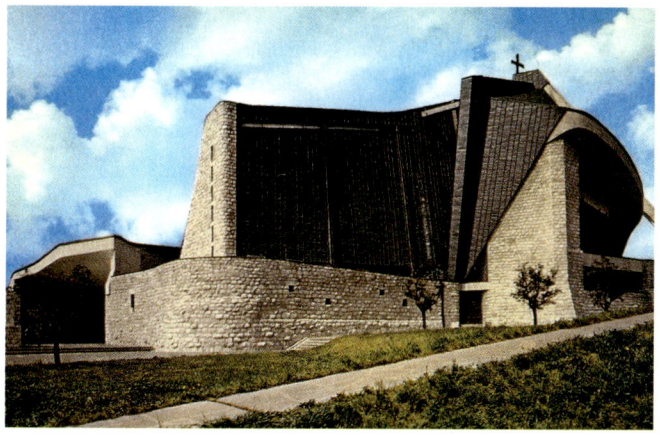

*Preceding pages*: Neogothic façade of the Duomo (still under construction) with two possible solutions for side area – cusped on the left, and "basilical" on the right

Giovanni Michelucci, San Giovanni Battista on the freeway

[11] *Ibid.*, p. 27.

[12] Optatus Milevitanus, *De schismate Donatistarum*, 1, 23 in G.D. Mansi, *Sacrorum conciliorum nova collectio*, Florence 1759, II, 436. See F. Lanzoni, *Le diocesi d'Italia dalle origini al principio del secolo VII*, Faenza 1927, pp. 570 and following, and *Annuario della Chiesa Fiorentina*, edited by G. Villani and V. Cirri, Florence 1993, pp. 21-28.

[13] Lopes Pegna, *Le più antiche chiese*, cit., p. 50; R. Davidsohn, *Storia di Firenze, 1. Le origini*, Florence 1956, pp. 56 and following; D. Vinvenzo Borghini, *Discorsi*, II, Florence 1755, p. 366; G.B. Ristori, *Della venuta e del soggiorno di Sant'Ambrogio a Firenze*, «Archivio Storico italiano», 36, (1905), pp. 267-268.

[14] G. Morozzi, *Santa Reparata, l'antica Cattedrale fiorentina*, Florence 1987; and by the same, the chapter devoted to Santa Reparata in the book edited by D.Cardini (see next note), with an updated bibliography. See also F. Toker, *Excavations Below the Cathedral of Florence, 1965-1974* in «Gesta», XIV, (1975), pp. 17-37.

[15] D. Cardini (edited by), *Il Bel San Giovanni e Santa Maria del Fiore. Il centro religioso di Firenze dal Tardo Antico al Rinascimento*, Florence 1966, pp. 35-38.

[16] Lopes Pegna, *Le più antiche chiese*, cit., p. 53-57, 74-81. Also see Cardini (edited by), *Il Bel San Giovanni*, cit.; P. Degli Innocenti, *Le origini del Bel San Giovanni: Da Tempio di Marte a Battistero di Firenze*, Florence 1994; G. Rocchi, *Santa Maria del Fiore. Rilievi, documenti, indagini strumenti, interpretazioni*. II. *Piazza, Battistero, Campanile*, Florence 1996, pp. 27-66; A. Paolucci (edited by), *Il Battistero di San Giovanni a Firenze*, Modena 1994, II, essays by T. Verdon, pp. 9-32 and G. Morolli, pp. 33-132.

[17] L. Crociani, "La liturgia battesimale" in Cardini (edited by), *Il Bel San Giovanni*, cit., pp. 49-63; T. Verdon, "Da Santa Reparata a Santa Maria del Fiore: il mistero della fede", in *La cattedrale di Santa Maria del Fiore (Alla riscoperta di piazza del Duomo in Firenze)*, II, Florence 1993, pp. 19-40.

[18] T. Verdon, "'Forma ecclesiae homo': per un'antropologia teologica dell'architettura ecclesiastica" in *Spazio e rito: aspetti costitutivi dei luoghi della celebrazione cristiana* (Minutes of the XXIII week of studies of the Associazione dei Professori di Liturgia, Torreglia 1994), Rome 1996, pp. 113-135.

[19] Lopes Pegna, *Le più antiche chiese*, cit., p. 72.

[20] *Ibid.*, p. 84; see also B. Quilici, *La chiesa di Firenze nell'alto medioevo*, Florence 1938, pp. 23 and following.

[21] Lopes Pegna, *Le più antiche chiese*, cit., p. 84.

[22] Fanelli, *Firenze*, cit., p. 8; R. Davidsohn, *Storia di Firenze, 1. Le origini*, Florence 1956, pp. 124-125; 129-130.

[23] Lopes Pegna, *Le più antiche chiese*, cit., p. 75; see A. Bertini, G. Barsuchini, *Memorie e documenti per servire alla storia del Ducato di Lucca*, Lucca 1818-1856, Appendix I, p. 70, doc. LV.

[24] Fanelli, *Firenze*, cit., p. 9; R. Davidsohn, *Storia di Firenze, 1. Le origini*, Florence 1956, pp. 172 and following.

[25] Fanelli, *Firenze*, cit., p. 9.

[26] R. Nicola Vasaturo, *Vallombrosa. L'Abbazia e la congregazione*, Vallombrosa 1994, pp. 3-79 (with a rich bibliography).

[27] Davidsohn, *Storia di Firenze*, cit., pp. 331-351.

[28] Fanelli, *Firenze*, cit., p. 9. On the medieval baptistery see Paolucci (edited by), *Il Battistero*, cit., essays by T. Verdon and G. Morolli; also see C. Pietramellara, *Il Battistero di San Giovanni a Firenze, rilievo e studio critico*, Florence 1973, pp. 33-34. For the lost document relative to the 'consecration' on behalf of Nicholas II in 1059,

see A. Busignani, R. Bencini, *Le Chiese di Firenze. Il Battistero di San Giovanni*, Florence 1988, p. 26.

[29] R. Stopani, "Ospedali e xenodochi a Firenze e lungo le vie maestre del suburbio fiorentino nei secoli XIII e XIV" in *Storia della solidarietà a Firenze*, Florence 1985, pp. 5-22.

[30] Lopes Pegna, *Le più antiche chiese*, cit., p. 92; Fanelli, *Firenze*, cit., p. 16.

[31] Fanelli, *Firenze*, cit., p. 20.

[32] *Ibid.*, pp. 23-38. See also B. Quilici, *La Chiesa di Firenze nei primi decenni del secolo XIII*, Florence 1965; A. Benvenuti Papi, "Una città e un vescovo: La Firenze di Ardingo (1230-1247)", in *L'Ordine dei Servi di Maria nel primo secolo di vita*, Florence 1986.

[33] Fanelli, *Firenze*, cit., p. 25.

[34] J. Wood Brown, *The Dominican Church of Santa Maria Novella at Florence*, Edimburgh 1902.

[35] G. Villani, *Cronica*, VIII, 9, edited by F.G.Dragomanni, Florence 1885 [first edition?]

[36] C. Guasti, *Santa Maria del Fiore: la costruzione della Chiesa e del Campanile secondo i documenti*, Florence 1887, n. 3.

[37] *Ibid.*, p. CXIII (document of March 29, 1412). See also T. Verdon, "Costruire una casa per il Signore", in *Dal Battistero al Duomo (Alla riscoperta di Piazza del Duomo in Firenze)*, edited by T. Verdon, Florence, 1992, pp. 93-115 (particularly p. 106).

[38] *Opera. Carattere e ruolo delle fabbriche cittadine fino all'inizio dell'Età Moderna*, edited by M. Haines, L.Riccetti, Florence 1996, essay by M. Haines, "L'Arte della Lana e l'Opera del Duomo di Firenze, con accenno a Ghiberti tra due istituzioni", pp. 267-294.

[39] L.B. Alberti, *Opere volgari*, edited by C. Grayson, Bari 1973, vol. III, pp. 7-8 ("Della pittura").

[40] T. Verdon, "Struttura sì grande, erta sopra e' cieli: la cupola e la città nel 1400", in *La cupola di Santa Maria del Fiore (Alla riscoperta di piazza del Duomo in Firenze, IV)*, edited by T. Verdon, Florence 1995, pp. 9-32.

[41] G. Pico della Mirandola, *De hominis dignitate*, edited by B. Cicognani, Florence 1942, pp. 4-6. See T. Verdon, "Urbs beata: riflessioni sulla città ideale rinascimentale", in *Ostliches Westliches. Studien zur vergleichenden Geistes -und Religionsgeschichte*, edited by M. Sladek, Heidelberg 1995, pp. 321-336.

[42] *Confessioni*, 10.27.

[43] D. Heikamp, *Baccio Bandinelli nel Duomo di Firenze*, in «Paragone», 15, (1964), pp. 32-42; T. Verdon, "*Ecce homo*. Contesto e senso degli affreschi della cupola", in *Il Giudizio ritrovato. Il restauro degli affreschi di Santa Maria del Fiore*, Florence 1995, pp. 27-32; F. Vossilla, "Dal coro alla cupola. Linee di mecenatismo di Cosimo I a Santa Maria del Fiore nell'epoca del Concilio di Trento", in *L'Uomo in cielo. Il programma pittorico della cupola di Santa Maria del Fiore: teologia ed iconografia a confronto (Vivens Homo 7/1)*, edited by T. Verdon, Bologna 1996, pp. 41-56.

[44] M. Hall, *Renovation and Counter-Reformation. Vasari and Duke Cosimo in Santa Maria Novella and Santa Croce, 1565-1577*, Oxford 1979.

[45] *Ibid.*

[46] T. Verdon, "La facciata e le facciate. L'arredo esterno di Santa Maria del Fiore nella sua piazza", in *La facciata di Santa Maria del Fiore (Alla riscoperta di piazza del Duomo in Firenze, V)*, edited by T. Verdon, Florence 1996, pp. 103-130.

[47] "G.R.", *L'Arte cristiana. Augusto Conti e la facciata del Duomo di Firenze*, Prato 1884, p. 3.

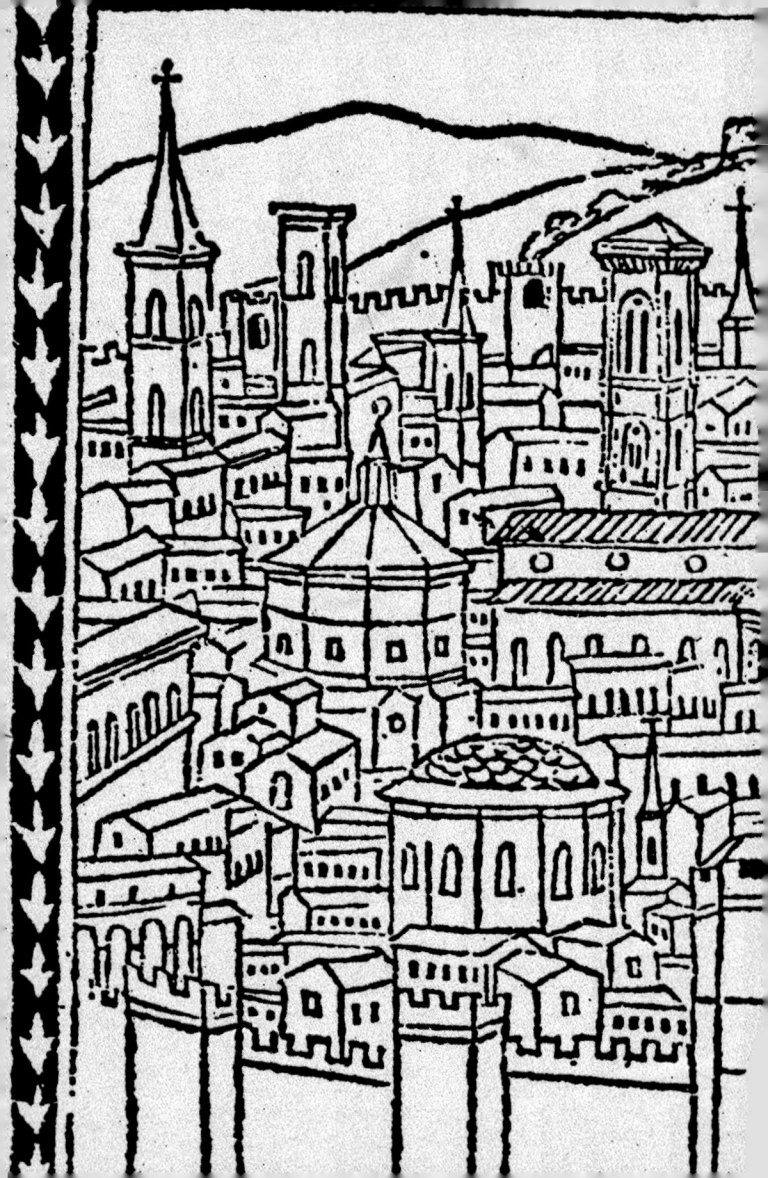

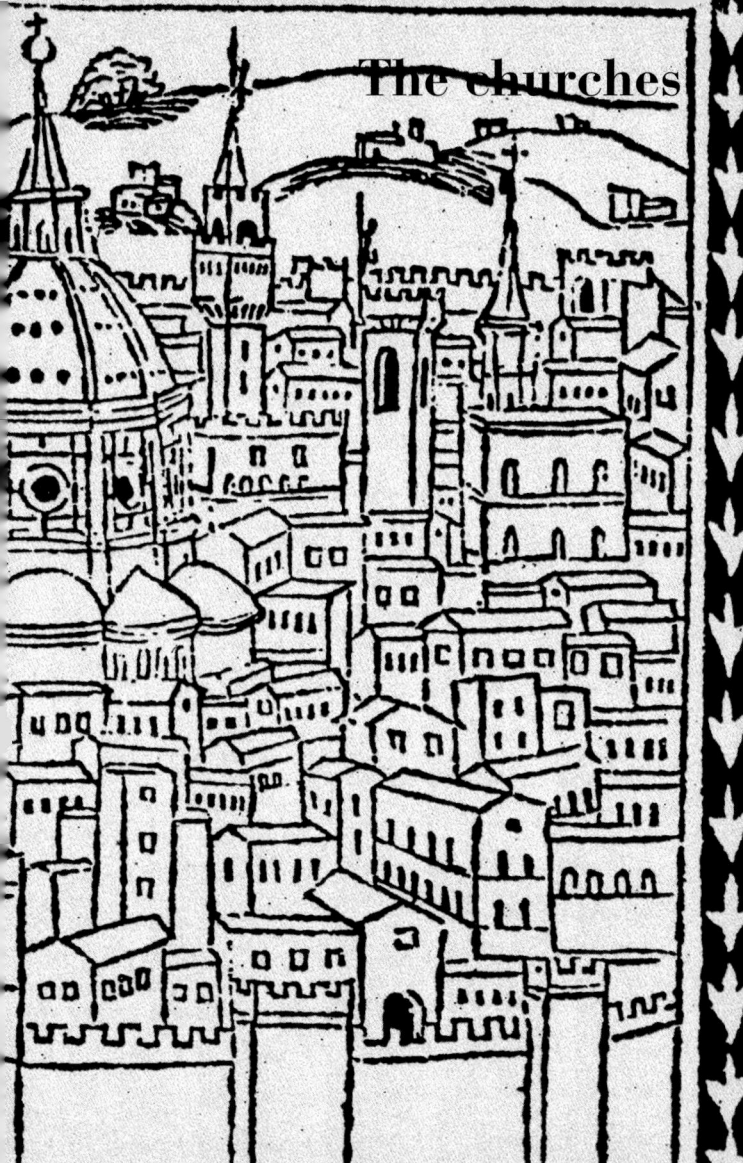

# Santa Felicita
*piazza Santa Felicita*

In the late IVth or early Vth century on the left bank of the Arno, near Ponte Vecchio, stood a church with a nave and two side aisles in the midst of a large cemetery spreading towards the hillside behind. This was the burial place of a great many Greeks and Syrians, often teachers or tradesmen, populating late-antique Florence. In 1024 the church's founder Hildebrand assigned it to the monastery of San Miniato al Monte. In 1059 the complex was occupied by a convent of benedictine sisters administered by Teitberga, for whom Nicholas II dedicated the church, putting it under his own protection. Throughout the XIIth century other popes would also show it the same good will. In 1209 Santa Felicita became a parish church. This meant giving Florentine bishops a series of rights – sanctioned by Innocent III – on the abbatial church, above all the capacity of naming its abbess. And indeed during the fourteenth century the abbesses belonging to the local patrician families would embellish and enrich the inside of the church, with works by outstanding artists like Niccolò di Piero and Spinello Aretino. It was actually a common practice, up to recently, for the abbesses to come from the city's most influential and wealthy households, and in particular from those from the vicinity. In the fourteenth century abbess Costanza de' Rossi undertook a thorough renovation of the church, this being the first substantial structural intervention concerning Santa Felicita, to which it probably owes its gothic appearance. On the other hand, over the following centuries, there would be a great number of artistic commissions and alterations involving single chapels, like the Barbadoris' – designed by Filippo Brunelleschi (1420) – with Pontormo's *Deposizione* as altarpiece. With the building of Vasari's Passage – which directly connected, on the upper level, palazzo Pitti with palazzo della Signoria, running along the façade of the old church, one side giving onto it – Santa Felicita became a privileged place for court sacred functions, and to attend them Grand Duke Ferdinand had several galleries built. In 1736, just when the Medici dynasty was dying out, Ferdinando and Giuseppe Ruggieri thoroughly altered the church giving the edifice a stylistic unity rhythmed by colossal order pilasters. After centuries the monastic role of the ensemble ended

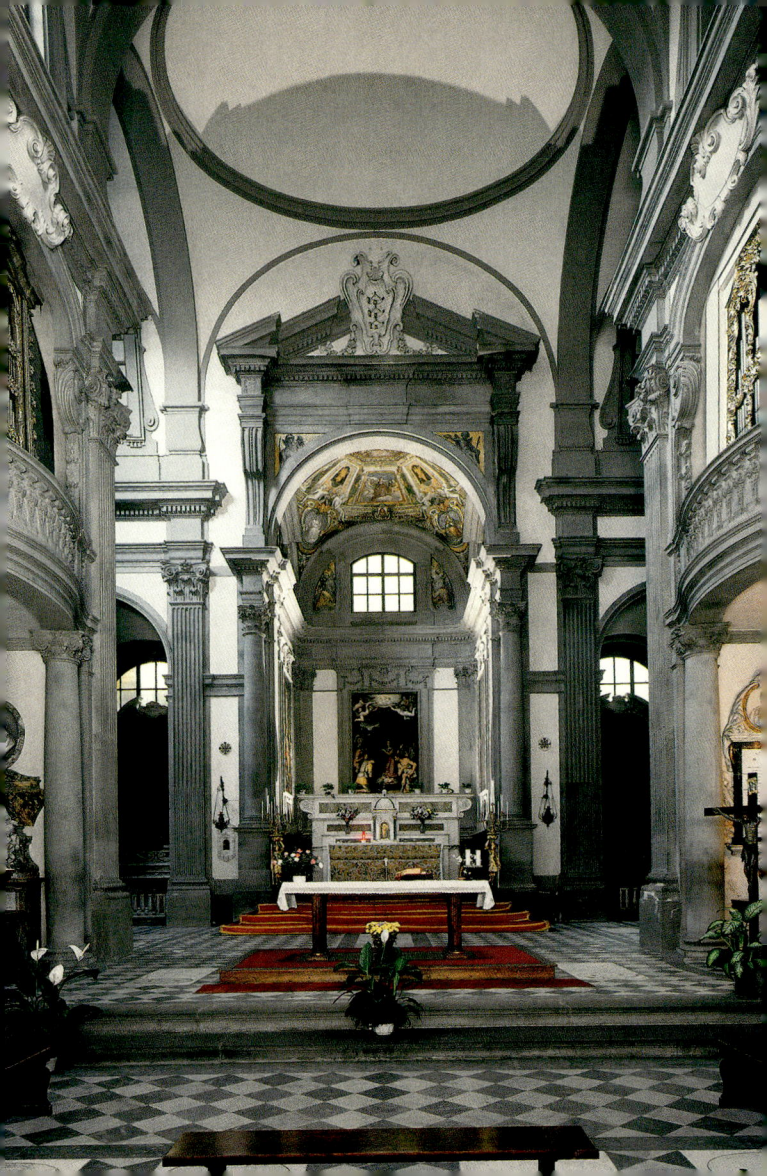

with its suppression by Napoleon in 1808, the church keeping its role as priory and parish church.

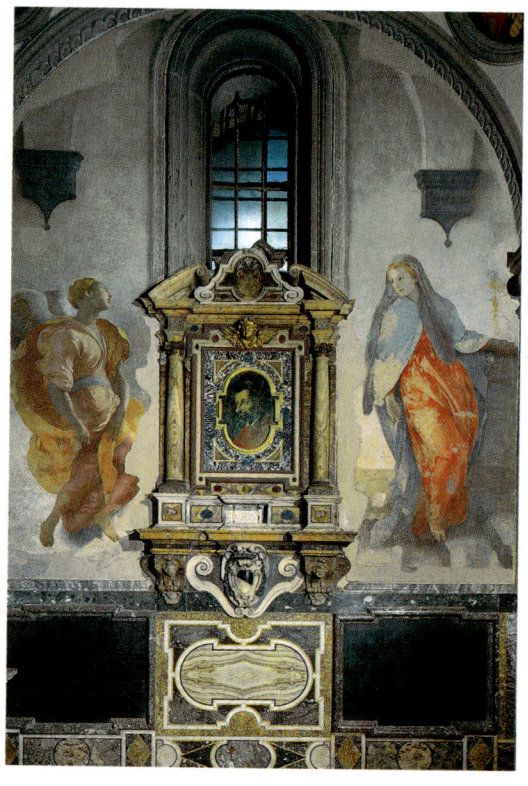

The Barbadori Chapel
Pontormo, *The Deposition*

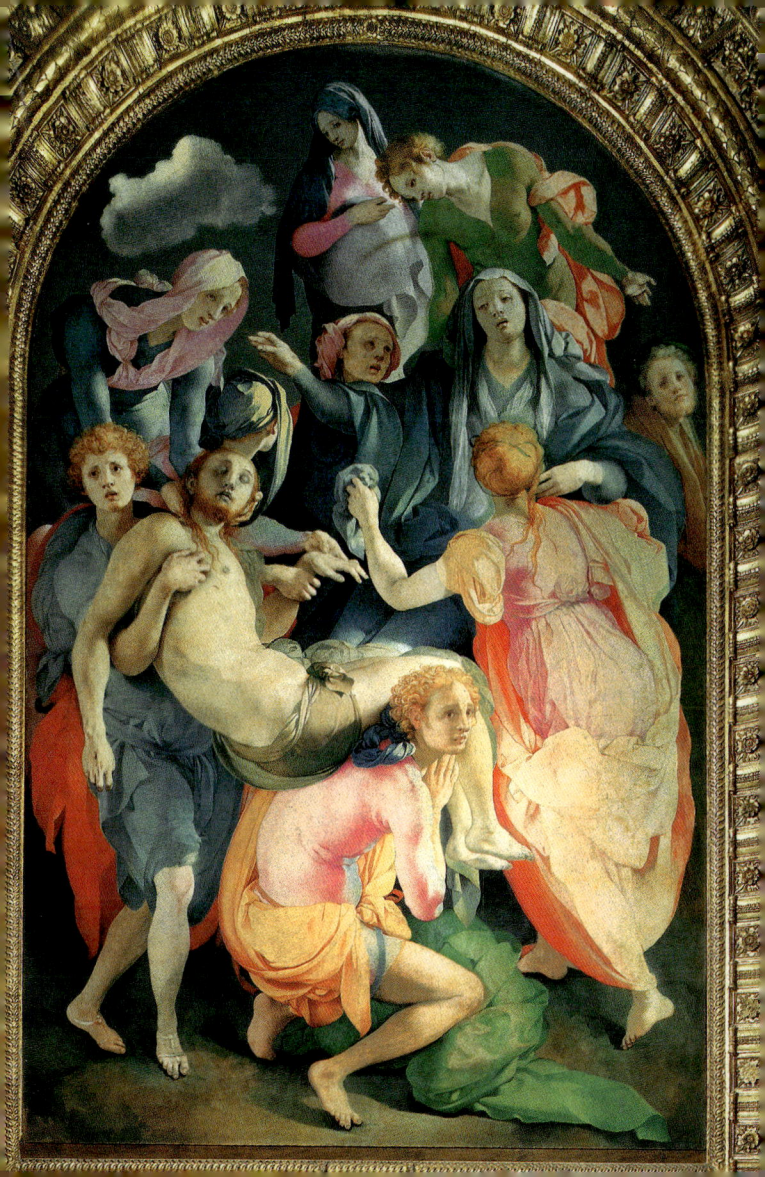

# San Lorenzo

*piazza san Lorenzo*

This is one of the oldest Florentine churches, standing beyond the Roman city walls, near the *Porta contra Aquilonem*, and consecrated during the Easter celebrations of 393 by saint Ambrose, bishop of Milan. On that occasion he deposed in the altar the relics of the martyrs Vitale and Agricola, brought from Bologna, and pronounced a homily, titled *Exhortation to virginity*, praising also that Giuliana – a rich widow perhaps of Eastern ori-

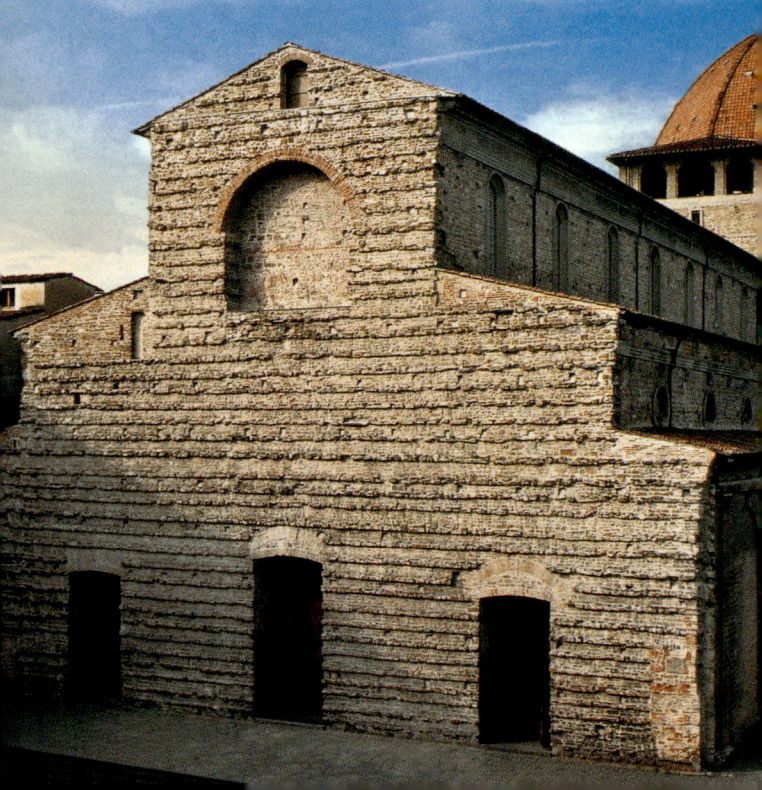

gins – who had generously backed with her own donations the new Florentine yard. Thus the church was given the title of *Ambrosian basilica*, also preserving for some time that type of liturgy. A while later, as pontifical bulls attest, it was even given the title of Florentine mother church, although it would never actually be recognised as the city cathedral. Rebuilt in romanesque style, it was consecrated anew in 1060 by Nicholas II (who before becoming pope, while still cardinal Gerald of Burgundy, had funded the work), just before it was absorbed in the new, larger walls, in which a gate, then named Porta del borgo di San Lorenzo, was opened. The church

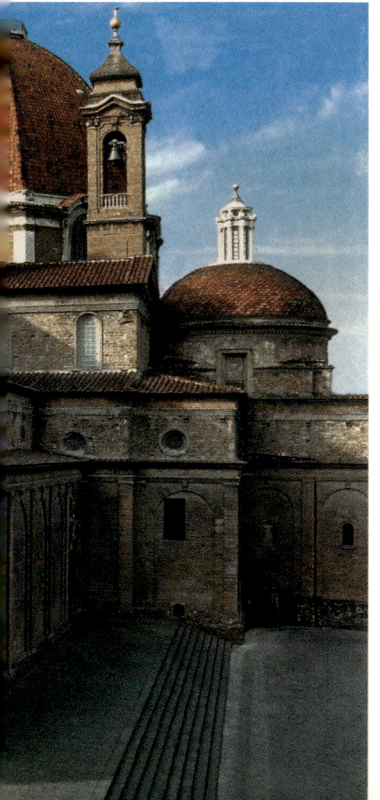

was continuously used as a neighbourhood parish church. A hospital was connected to San Lorenzo as well, run by a layman supervised by a rector. In 1423 Giovanni di Bicci de' Medici, belonging to the family that owned houses in the area and was about to rule the city, commissioned Filippo Brunelleschi to undertake a radical restructuring of the church. The work lasted at length; in 1446, when Brunelleschi died, Cosimo de' Medici took over the expenses, and first Antonio Manetti the Elder and then in 1460 his son Antonio the Younger the artistic supervision. Meanwhile, the Medicis' role continued to grow: the family not only handled the commissions, but even distributed chaplaincies and rectories. And the identification of the basilica with the Medicis became even clearer at the time of their restoration – after the first republican parenthesis – , when

59

Leo X commissioned Michelangelo for the outer and inner walls of the façade (even if only the second was executed), and then for the new sacristy and the library. Aside from the Medicis', the great church received the tombs of other important families connected to the ruling dynasty and for the most part local residents, like the Rondinellis, the Della Stufas, the Ginoris, the Neronis and the Martellis. After mid-seventeenth century, the Medicis' tombs were given large separate premises, completed in early XVIIIth century: the chapel of the Principi, an extension of the apse section of the basilica, whose purpose was to embody the Medici family's wealth by the scope of the decoration, and whose plan was carried out with the advice of the Grand Prince Ferdinand himself. On that occasion the church was thoroughly altered, and on October 23, 1712 Pope Pius VI declared it *basilica insigne in perpetuo*. On the other hand, the bell tower was built in 1740 by Ferdinando Ruggieri. Later, the ruling dynasty that would replace the Medicis, Asburgo Lorena, would display a like predilection for the Medicean church *par excellence*, choosing its crypt for their own tomb. In our century the work to build the stairway, in 1912-1913, and then – about forty years later – the archeological digs that explored the crypt, brought to light scarce traces of the primitive building, but also an interesting Roman urban fabric, with close-set houses and shops.

Filippo Brunelleschi, the old sacristy. In the centre, tomb of Giovanni di Bicci de' Medici and his wife Piccarda Bueri. Sculptures by Donatello on walls

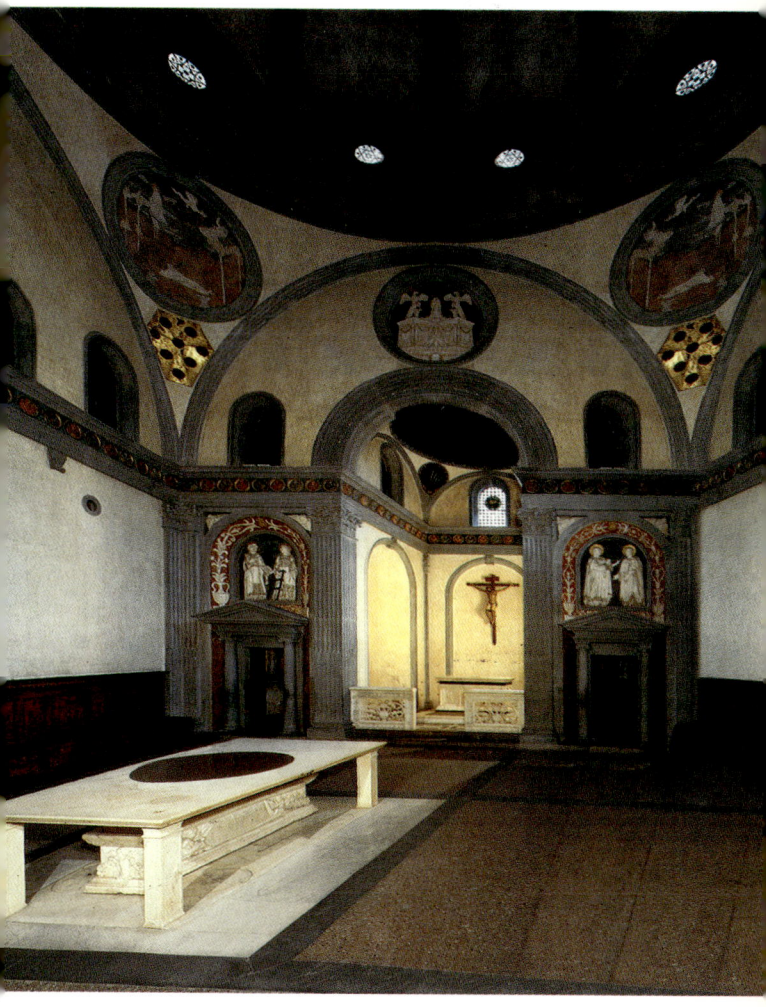

# Baptistry, cathedral and bell tower

*piazza San Giovanni, piazza del Duomo*

Where the cathedral now stands, the church of Santa Reparata used to rise, far more modest in size and decoration, yet fully deserving to be considered one of the most important paleo-Christian complexes in Tuscany. Tradition has it built in thanksgiving for the victory of Stilicone's Christian armies over Radagaisus, leader of the Goths, in 405. Instead, fourteenth-century chronicler Giovanni Villani claims it goes back to before that date, and was originally dedicated to Santo Salvatore, but without further significant confirmation, there being no ancient documents mentioning it (the first being relatively late, in 987). However, it is certain that the church has always been the city cathedral, even if at one time, up to the beginning of the second millenium, it lay outside the city walls. Demographic growth, Florence's accrued prestige and prosperity were later to prove it inadequate, and even in a way detrimental to the city's image. However, on June 11, 1293, a first deliberation of the Florentine communal authorities regarding it seemed to tend to a large-scale restoration of the old cathedral. But what finally won out was the idea of building an entirely new church, far more majestic and rich, and which because of its size should have been placed farther from the baptistry. Nonetheless, old Santa Reparata would keep its previous role until the actual completion of the new cathedral, which was to rise around it, and only then would have been torn down. In 1296 Arnolfo di Cambio was charged with the works, but only partly finished a first version of the carved decoration of the façade. After a time of transition, he was succeeded by Andrea Pisani, and in 1343 by Francesco Talenti, after an interruption of a few years during which Giotto was master builder. The presence of such famous names, the constant attention chronicles paid to the events concerning the new cathedral, the contribution of economically influential groups, such as the city guilds' confraternities, prove the yard's great importance for the entire city, not just from the religious point of view. This value of the image is confirmed by the substantial urban interventions in the area, aiming systematically at providing more space around the new building to make it more handsome and more visible, even at the expense of old and socially useful func-

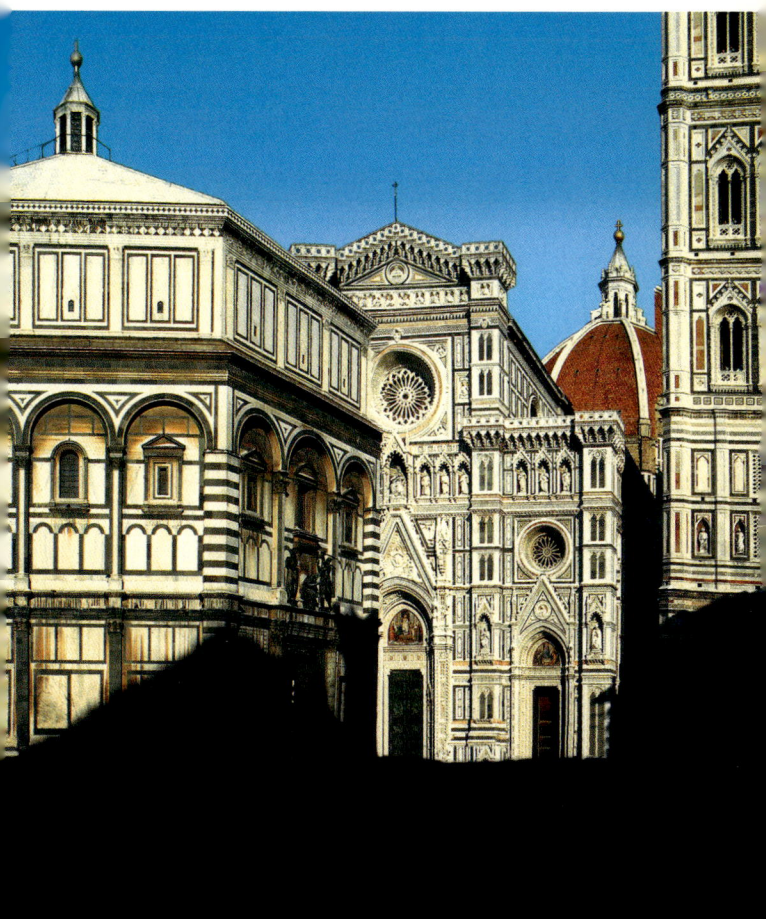

tions like hospitals, churches and fraternities. A like significance was attributed to the construction, designed by Giotto, of the monumental bell tower, which he himself began to build in July 1334. His death, in 1337, limited his work to the first order. Building continued under Andrea Pisani, and then, after the interruption owing to the dramatic plague of 1348 and the critical times ensuing, was completed by Francesco Talenti. The decoration, finished in the next century, forms a kind of synthesis of Florentine culture and society between Middle Ages and Renaissance, with the representation, in the carved reliefs, of the various human activities and the virtues presiding them under the aegis of the Christian faith.

The plan for the new cathedral with the bell tower had to deal right away with the issues of the surrounding space and the presence of other important buildings which, along with Santa Reparata, had formed the religious heart of the city for centuries. In front of the façade of the old church, in fact, and close by, the baptistry of San Giovanni had stood for ages, probably built at the end of the VIth century – according to tradition on the site of a pre-existing pagan temple dedicated to Mars – , by the Florentine bishop Zenobius. Octagonal and probably smaller than the present build-

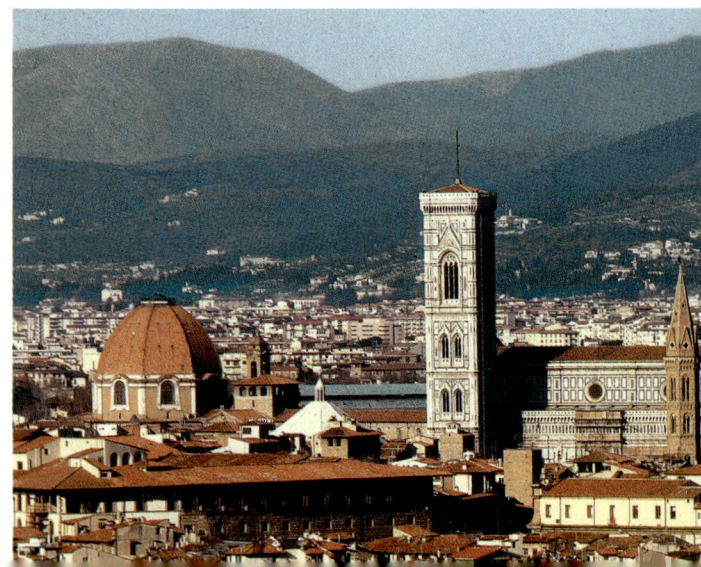

ing, the early baptistry, a sort of walled enclosure – perhaps without a roof – around an immersion baptismal font, from the start must have been connected with Santa Reparata facing it, since indeed its only entrance opened towards the cathedral and on the same axis, implying a direct, straight course between baptismal font and cathedral high altar. Every year on Easter morning, the flight of the symbolic metal "dove" follows this axis: starting from the high altar, it reaches the parvis, thus opening the ceremony for the explosion of the cart, a spectacular rite wherein in the old days the Florentines read auspices regarding crops and the coming year's fortunes. With the growth of the city and its political and administrative importance, the need was also urgently felt to adapt the old baptismal complex to new needs. Thus the new baptistry was built, probably taller than the previous one and embellished by a first white and green marble inner and outer facing. The new holy building was consecrated in 1059, in presence of pope Nicholas II. In the XIIth century the octogon was reinforced at the angles and endowed with thicker outer walls permitting the construction of a masonry vault resting on arches. In 1174 the lantern was completed, and in the early XIIIth century the old curved apse was replaced

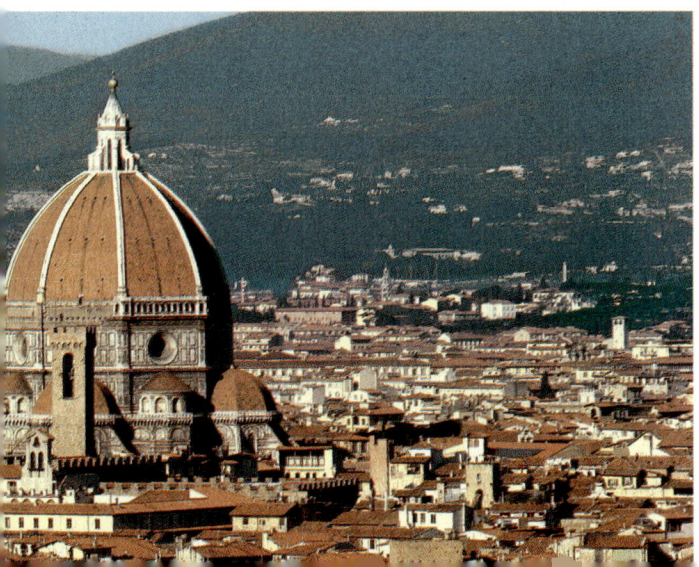

by the present-day rectangular chevet. The rich gold-background mosaics are also XIIth and XIIIth-century, replacing, with relevant decorative value, the old wooden covering. Subdivided in narrative strips answering to didactic principles, they illustrate meaningful episodes of the lives of Saint John the Baptist and Jesus, as well as numerous Bible scenes, culminating with the huge image of Christ in the *Universal Judgement*, by Coppo di Marcovaldo, representing the climax not only of the symbolic and didactic level underlying the mosaics, but also of every Christian's earthly course. In 1330 Andrea Pisano made over in bronze the baptistry door, composed of plaquettes devoted to the life of Saint John, in composition and technique drawing on the one that Bonanno had executed in 1180 for the cathedral in Pisa. To the original door two others were then added, cutting orthogonally the main axis. In 1401 the Calimala Guild launched the famous contest for the execution of bas-reliefs for a new main door, in which artists like Lorenzo Ghiberti and Filippo Brunelleschi competed. So between 1402 and 1424 Ghiberti executed, on a plan not unlike that of the existing door, an authentic *Door of Our Saviour*, where the plaquettes narrate New Testament stories from the Annunciation to the Pentecost. Placed on the main axis, they were the theological introduction to the mosaic representation of the *Universal Judgement* inside the baptistry. In its new configuration, Andrea Pisano's door was transferred to the south entrance, whereas Ghiberti's was placed to the north to allow this same artist to create, between 1425 and 1452, another door which, by its absolute aesthetic perfection, won the privileged position on the axis facing the cathedral, and soon the explicit name of Door of Paradise.

Meanwhile the cathedral had nearly achieved its present form, after the outer walls of old Santa Reparata were definitively torn down in February 1375. In 1412 the church was given the name of Santa Maria del Fiore and in 1436, on the occasion of the Council of Florence, it was consecrated by pope Eugene IV, while Brunelleschi's great dome was still under way. Under the dome there was a first octogonal wooden choir, also by Brunelleschi, then replaced by one in marble, commissioned in 1547 of Bandio Bandinelli and completed in 1572 by his pupil Giovanni Bandini, with a series of carvings iconographically based on the value of redemption from original sin through Christ. This programme was to be completed

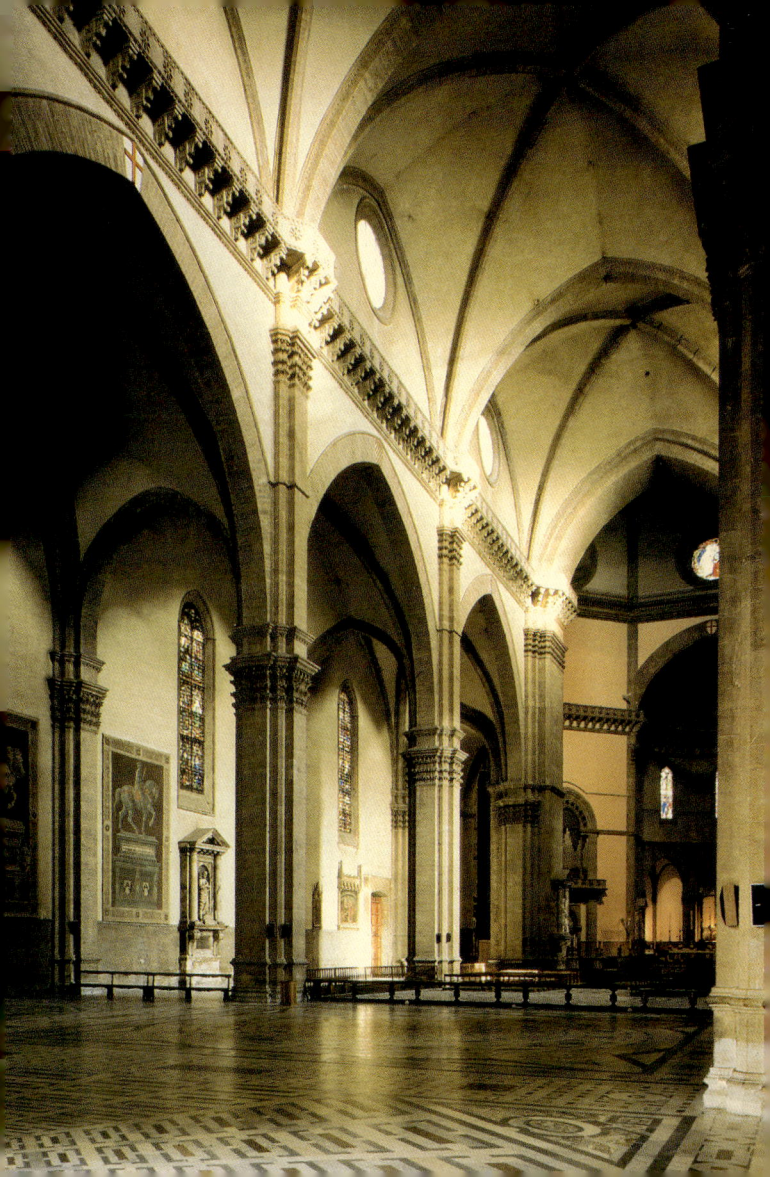

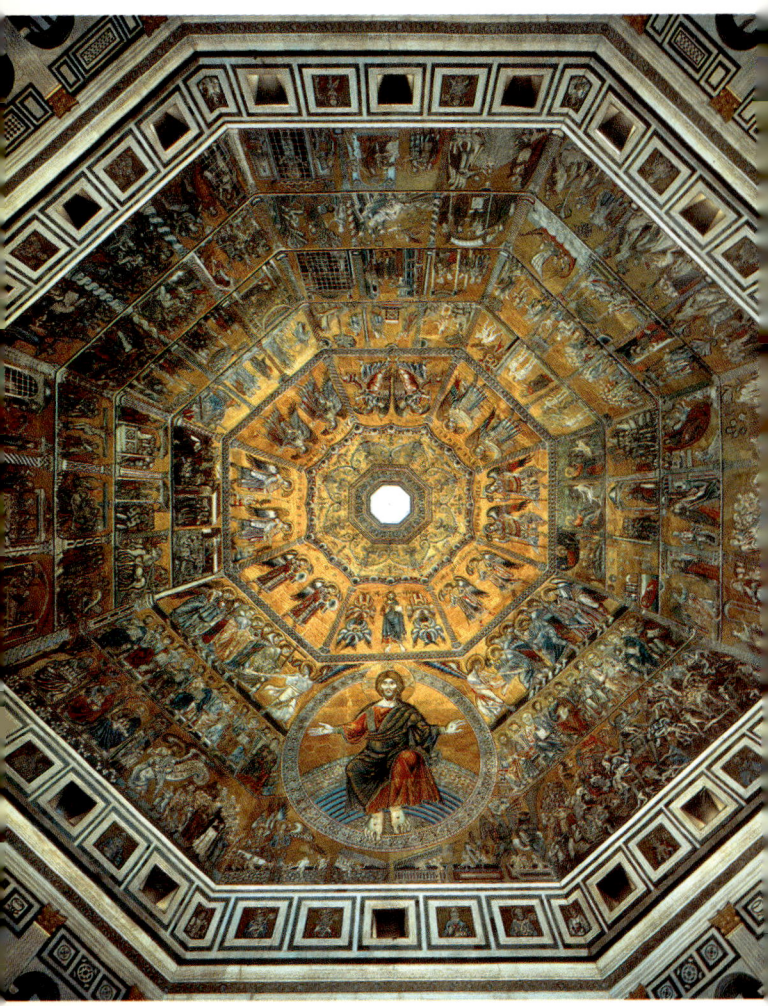

by the huge fresco on the dome intrados, focused on the *Universal Judgement* and executed by Giorgio Vasari and Federico Zuccari between 1571 and the end of the decade. Despite these vast transformations, the cathedral still retained the fragmentary incrustation of Arnolfo's façade. It was not until 1587 that grand duke Francesco I had it torn down, and then, after a series of temporary decorations for weddings and celebrations, a century later it was plastered and painted by a Bolognese corporation on a design by Ercole Graziani for Grand Prince Ferdinand's ill-starred marriage to Violante of Baveria. During the first half of the XIXth century the interior of the cathedral was "cleaned up" according to a purist design seeking to recreate its fourteenth-century forms. At mid-nineteenth century, in the very years when Florence was capital of the new kingdom of Italy, a series of contests were launched to finally provide Santa Maria del Fiore with a proper, definitive façade. Of the many imaginative designs presented, Emilio de Fabris' was chosen; in 1870 he was named official architect of the façade of Santa Maria del Fiore, and in June of the following year he began his artistic project, which would be inaugurated after his death, in 1887, with a gorgeous ceremony in which Florentine patricians and notables took part, dressed in the costumes of their fourteenth-century ancestors.

Mosaic decorations on baptistery ceiling

# San Michele Visdomini

*piazza san Michele Visdomini*

The history of San Michele Visdomini – familiarly called San Michelino – begins in another location, near Matilda's wall, later occupied by the apsidal area of the new cathedral. In fact the old church was torn down in 1364 to make room for it. But the same year, on February 29, Andrea Corsini, bishop of Fiesole, in stead of his relative Pietro, archbishop of Florence from 1361 to 1369 and apostolic legate to emperor Charles IV of Prague, laid the foundation stone of the edifice replacing it, just beyond the old walls, henceforth absorbed in the larger fourteenth-century ones. The name Visdomini was kept in memory of the family that used to boast patronage of the church; although in time other families joined them, the Visdominis kept the privilege for centuries until, with their consent, Cosimo I transferred patronage from the wealthy Francesco Grifoni – owner of the palazzo designed by Ammannati in piazza Santissima Annunziata – to the celestine monks, who moved there from the church they had previously occupied, San Pietro in via San Gallo. The fourteenth-century church whose entrance was on the present via Bufalini, in the course of its two hundred-years existence was embellished by works of art, such as the frescoes recently found under later white-washing, mainly owed to aristocratic patronages, but also to local craftsmen's families' donations. A thorough renovation was begun in 1552 by the Celestines, who stayed on until 1782, moved the entrance to via dei Servi and gave the church the appearance of a mannerist hall with side altars, enriched by works by great artists of the times, among whom Pontormo, Empoli, Passignano, Poppi and Agostino Ciampelli. In 1813 San Michele was confirmed as parish church.

Pontormo, *The Sacred Conversation.* The standing figure on the right is traditionally thought to be a self-portrait of the artist

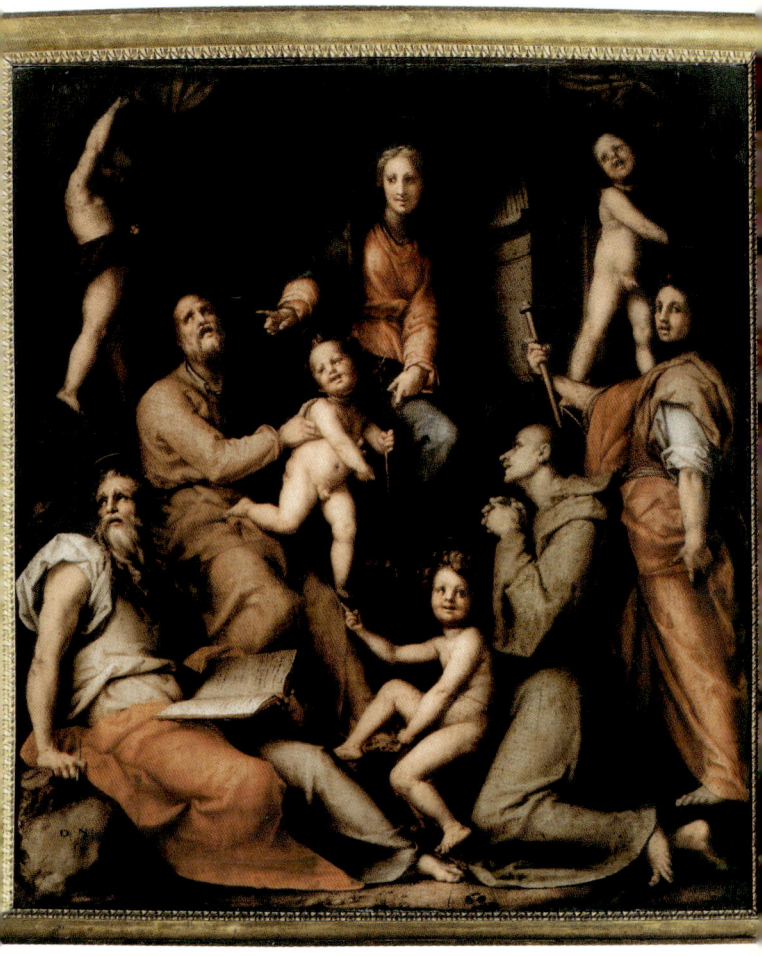

## Orsanmichele
*via de' Calzaiuoli*

The dedication to San Michele in Orto, reflected in the church's odd popular name, probably goes back to the small oratory that rose in the VII-IIth century in an open space which later became, perhaps after that religious building was torn down, the corn market. In 1290 Arnolfo built there a two-storey loggia, with storage spaces for corn supplies for times of scarcity. The images of Saint Michael Archangel and the Virgin were placed on two pilasters of the loggia, the latter soon becoming the object of popular veneration. The evening gatherings of the faithful who met here to pray and sing praises led to the birth of the Compagnia dei Laudesi. In 1304 a devastating fire destroyed, aside from a good part of the city, the log-

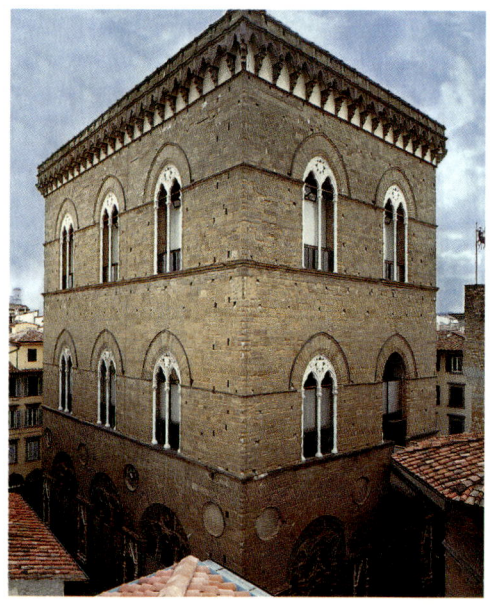

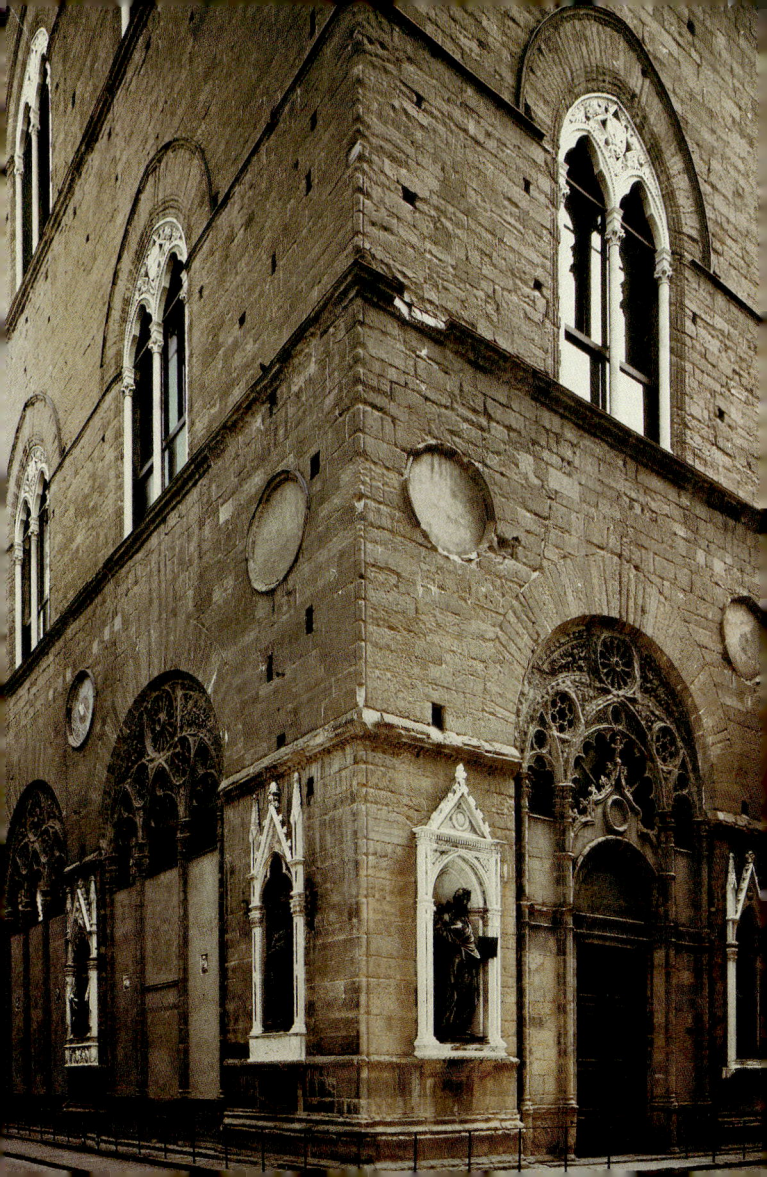

gia as well as the painting held to be miraculous. Its fame furthered the particular heed paid to the reconstruction, the replacement of the lost image with a panel by Bernardo Daddi and the building of a sounder edifice combining the practical role of corn-magazine and a religious and civic representative value. Actually, it was not until 1337 that the construction of the new, larger loggia began under three architects who were then also working on the great new cathedral yard: Francesco Talenti, Neri di Fioravante and Benci di Cione. After the 1348 plague many bequeaths can be noted – addressed to the Compagnia di Orsanmichele out of devotion to the holy image of the Madonna – which permitted to commission, in 1355, Andrea Orcagna for a shrine to set it off handsomely, completed four years later. In 1357, owing to the predominantly religious role of the loggia, Simone Talenti closed the large arcades and raised the building by two tall storeys, open also with large gothic windows, once again planned as storage for food supplies. Work can be considered completed by 1404. In 1415 the Florentine republic obtained its elevation to collegiate church, and on that occasion ten priests and two clerics under the authority of a provost were assigned to Orsanmichele. At the end of the century the market was moved elsewhere, the archives of the signoria were housed in the upper floors, and the loggia definitively turned into the church, both representative and meeting-place of the city corporations. To emphasise this role, the signoria had the Guilds adorn a series of shrines, more or less all the same size, open towards the outside of the pilasters of the ex-loggia, holding the images of the protector saints of their specific crafts. Nearly all the shrines were executed in the first three decades of the xvth century, with works by the greatest sculptors and artists of the times, ranging from Ghiberti to Nanni di Banco, Donatello to Niccolò Lamberti, Michelozzo to Filippo Brunelleschi. Some of these works were later replaced by statues by other great artists, such as Verrocchio, Baccio da Montelupo and Giambologna. With the suppression of the priory of San Romolo, February 10, 1796, Orsanmichele was elevated to parish church.

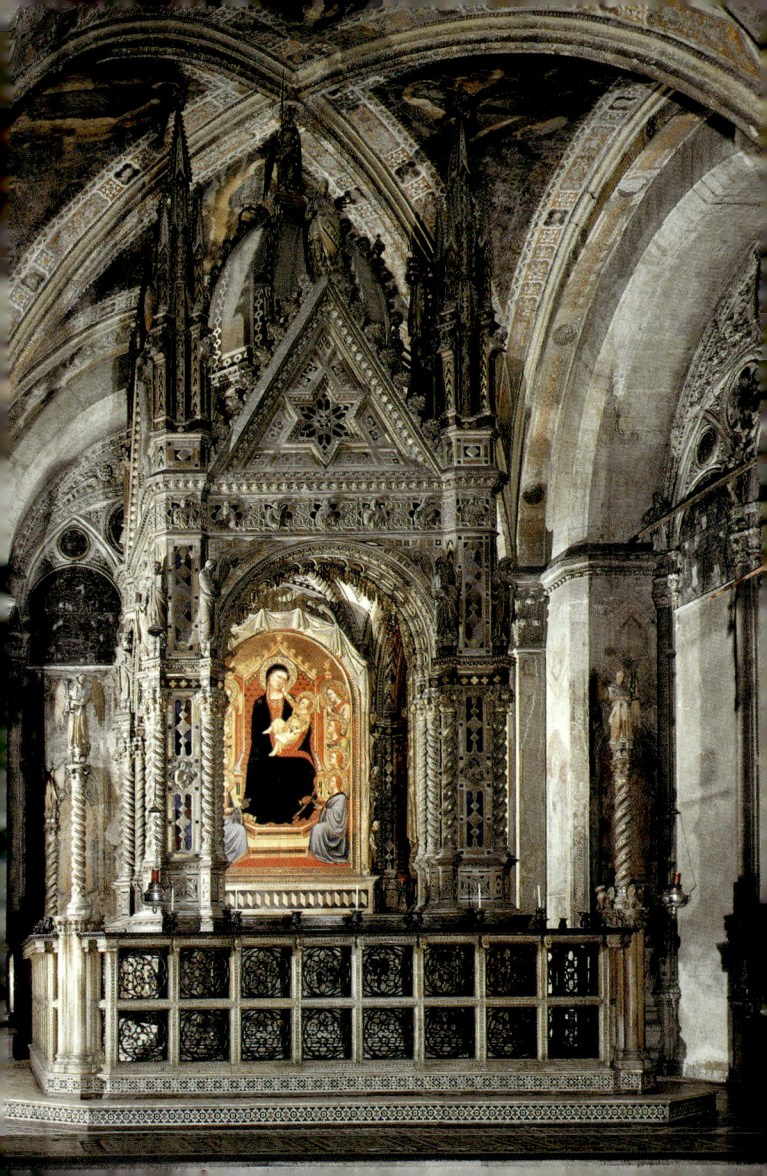

# Sant'Ambrogio
*via Pietrapiana*

The first dated document explicitly mentioning the church goes back to July 1001, while another document dated 1046 evidences a certain Raimberto's acquisition of the patronage. In 1141 pope Innocent II's bull grants the Sant'Ambrogio Benedictines several privileges, acknowledges their ownership of what they controlled up to then and the right to use bequeaths and profits to acquire new property. In 1163 a diploma signed by Algisius bishop of Milan bears witness of his predecessors' gift to the monastery of some property the Milanese diocese owned in various places of the florentine bishopric. In 1145 pope Eugene III confirmed and extended Innocent II's grants. In 1230, the abbess being sister Tada, a miraculous event occurred in the church that would determine its religious and artistic future. On December 30 of that year, in fact, after a priest named Uguccione had celebrated mass, and had not entirely dried the chalice, he discovered therein the remains of the eucharist transformed in coagulated blood. The event drew the faithful and, among them, Ardingo bishop of the city also who, for reasons of safety, wanted the miraculous chalice be moved to the bishopric. There a further transformation of the blood into flesh took place, a fact that accrued its miraculous nature. The chalice was returned to Sant'Ambrogio and soon later that same Ardingo, after a vision in a dream in which Christ complained of having been put back there "naked", endowed it with a precious ivory case. Another dream, this time with the Virgin appearing to a young girl named Aldobrandesca, led to creating a shrine, an event that triggered a gradual enrichment of the chapel where the precious relic is conserved. At the end of the thirteenth century the church underwent a large-scale renovation, evidenced by pope Clement IV's bull in 1266, in which indulgences were given to whoever gave alms to support the work. In 1280 cardinal Latino of Ostia and Velletri, sent to Florence as the papal legate for the peace between Guelphs and Ghibellines, granted perpetual indulgence to whoever visited the church on Sant'Ambrogio's feast day. That indulgence was further extended to the celebrative days of *Corpus Domini* and the Assumption. In 1320 Turino di Baldese paid for the renovation of the main chapel. Around 1486 the church

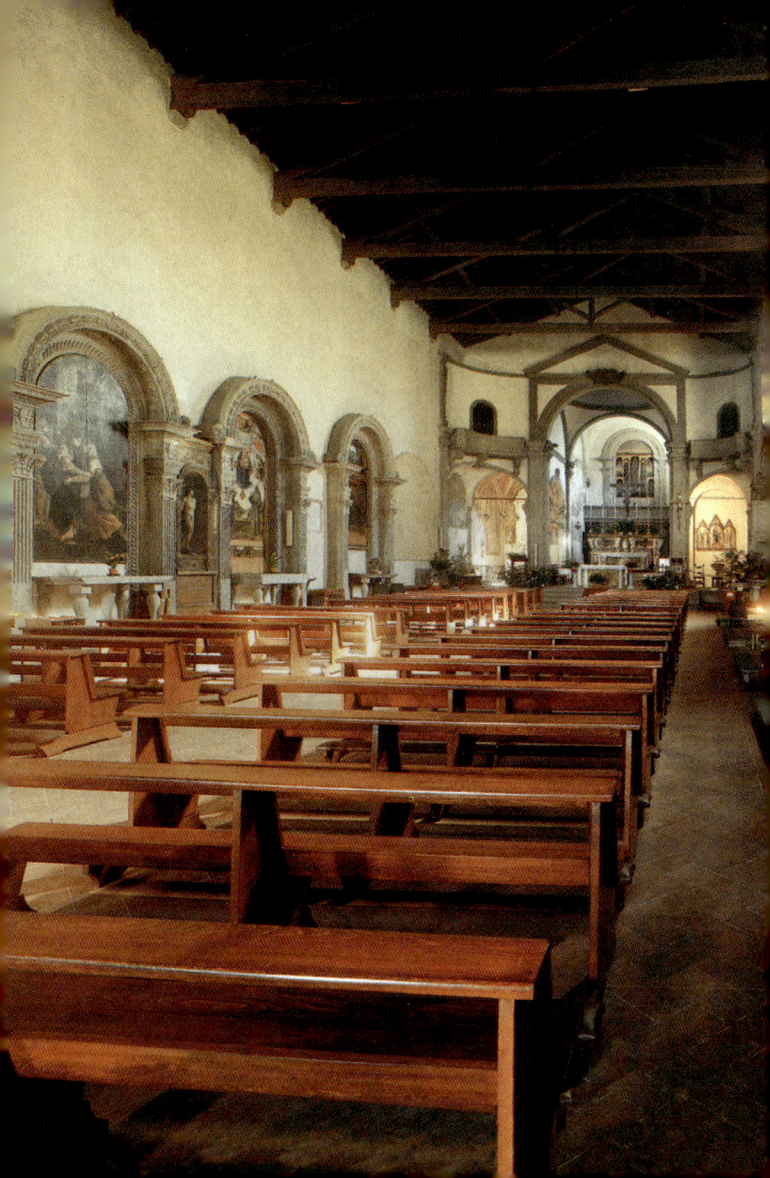

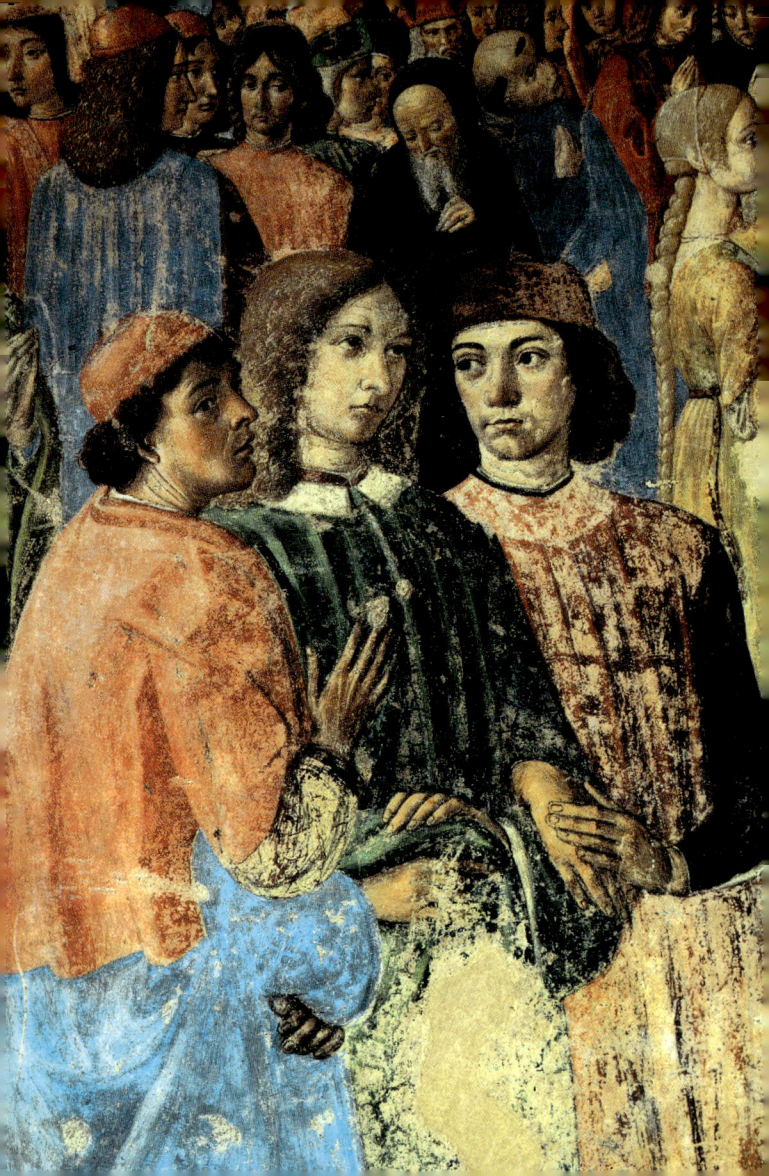

was again modernised, with the creation of arched side altars and the addition of Mino da Fiesole's marble shrine and Cosimo Rosselli's fresco in the chapel del Miracolo. In 1514 the Compagnia delle donne del miracolo di Sant'Ambrogio (*Society of the women of the miracle of Saint Ambrose)* was founded. In the XVth and XVIth centuries the tombs of a number of florentine artists were placed in the church, that same Mino da Fiesole (+ 1484) and Andrea del Verrocchio, who died in Venice in 1486 and was brought here. Another somewhat miraculous event was recorded in 1595 when on Good Friday the Sepulchre ornament (where the Holy Sacrament is kept for Holy Friday communion) caught fire and was practically destroyed despite attempts to put out the fire with water. The particles conserved in the shrine blended, perhaps owing to the water, forming a sort of small loaf which was then conserved as a sort of relic. A broader transformation was undertaken in the early XVIIIth century, to be precise in 1716, when the apsidal part was altered on a design by Giovan Battista Foggini and decorated by frescoes by Benedetto Fortini, the same one who painted the great trellised ceiling of the nave. The outside of the church mostly kept its Gothic style until the nineteenth century: in 1888 the present façade, still Gothic but slightly more elaborate, replaced the original one. Recent restorations have removed the false ceiling, bringing to light the trusses and fragments of fourteenth and fifteenth-century frescoes. Several of the alterpieces are now in the Uffizi galleries, such as the work known as *S. Anna Metterza* by Masaccio and Masolino, Filippo Lippi's *Incoronazione della Vergine* and the Botticelli work called *Pala delle Convertite*. The works still in the church are of great interest however, like the *Madonna in trono e Santi* attributed to Matteo di Pacino, second half of the fourteenth century, the *Sant'Onofrio*, an unusual drawing on the wall attributed to the Maestro di Figline, a triptych attributed either to Bicci di Lorenzo or Lorenzo di Bicci, the *San Sebastiano* in wood by Bernardo del Tasso and the three-part panel by Raffaellino del Garbo.

Cosimo Rosselli, detail of the fresco in the Cappella del Miracolo. The figure in the foreground on the right is a self-portrait of the artist

# Santi Michele e Gaetano Bertelde

*piazza Antinori*

Originally singly dedicated to Saint Michael, this church probably added the name Bertelde to recall an old family owning a house in the area. The founding of the old church goes back to 859 as a women's monastery supervised by the benedictine abbey of Nonantola, even if a secular priest were in charge of the offices, his nomination depending on the prior of San Felice in Piazza, another and more important Florentine abbey subordinate. The patronage of Nonantola probably ended around the thirteen-forties, when the church passed under the direct jurisdiction of the Florentine bishop Ardingo Trotti. During that period San Michele undoubtedly played a major role, the prior Buonaccorso being named procurator of the apostolic legates in Tuscany. The old building stood slightly outside the city

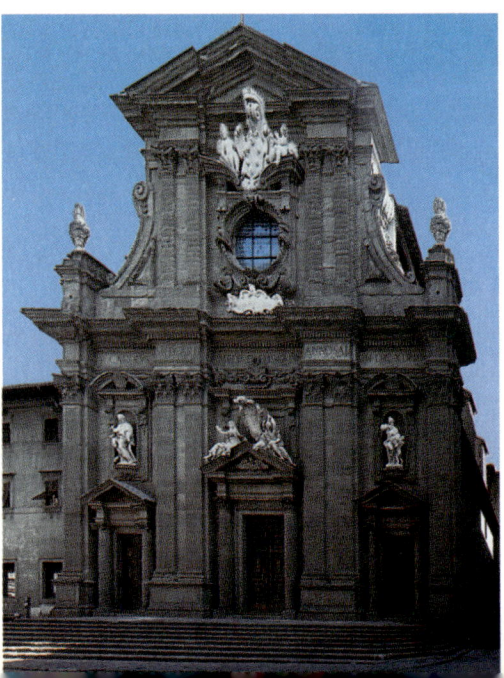

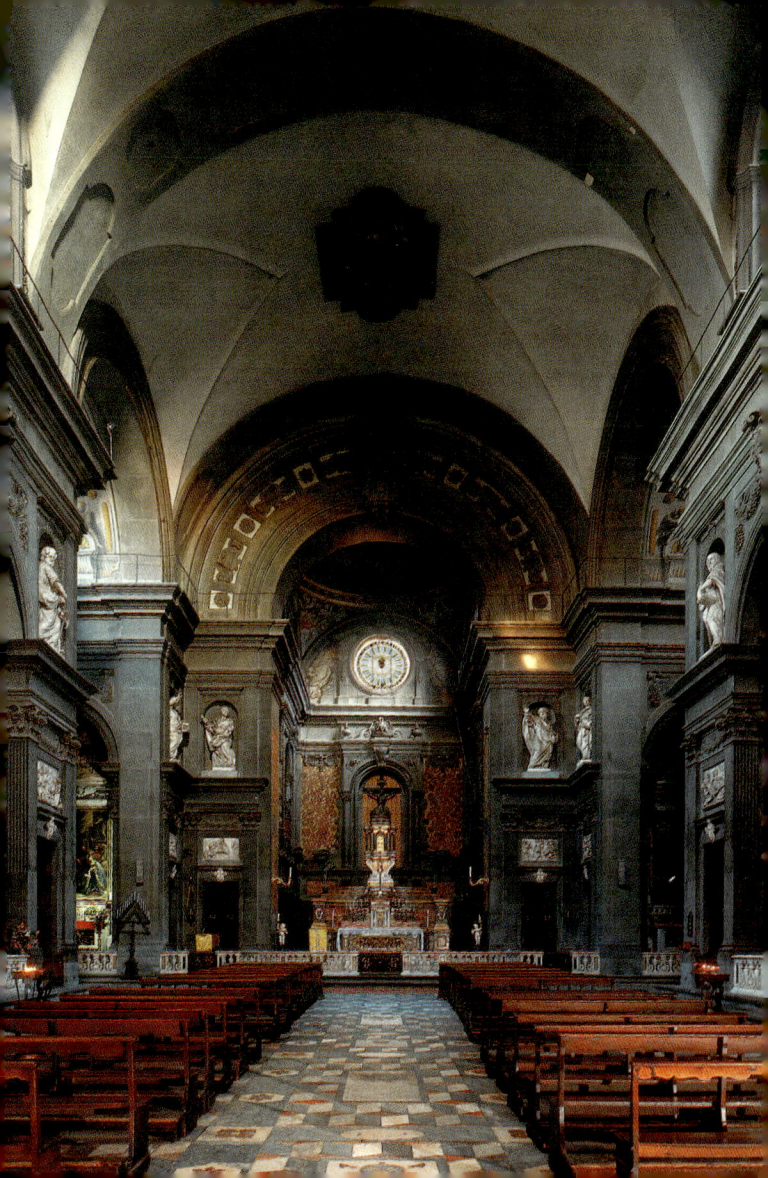

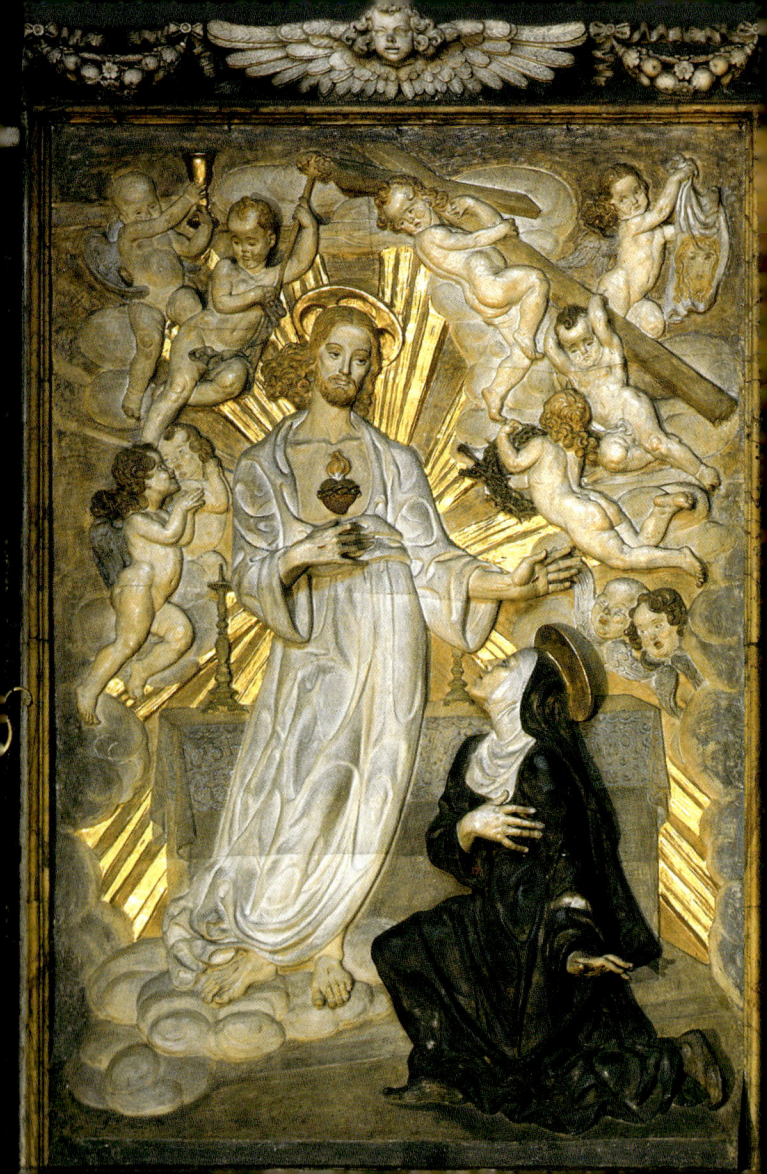

centre, in a rather ill-reputed district, due to the presence of public baths that drew persons of doubtful morality. However, in 1506 an image of the Virgin placed in front of the entrance of the place was seen to miraculously move, the prodigy attracting countless faithful and bystanders. In 1553 the olivetan monks were put in charge of the church but, by 1592, on a decision of cardinal Alessandro de' Medici – future pope Leo XI – it was handed over to the Chieti order, founded by Gaetano di Thiene in the spirit of the Counter-Reformation. The new friars purchased several buildings next to the original edifice and undertook a radical renovation, along with the moral rehabilitation of the district. Work began in 1604 with the Alessandro Marzi Medici's blessing (then bishop of Fiesole and later of Florence): the old church was gradually absorbed in the new one, and definitively torn down when the latter was completed, according to a common practice which had already been adopted for the cathedral in the fourteenth century. The authors of the building were, in chronological order, the architect Matteo Nigetti together with the Chieti order monk Anselmo Cagiano, then Gherardo Silvani – first coadjutor later replaced by his son Pier Francesco – who executed the façade. A number of Florentine baroque artists took part in the decoration, contributing to the rich iconography, mainly featuring sculptures by Balthasar Permoser and Carlo Marcellini. In August 1649, when the last works were nearly completed, the church was consecrated by the bishop of Arezzo Tommaso Salviati. On that occasion, the old dedication to Saint Michael was combined with that of Saint Gaetan, the founder of the order, a saint figuring in a handsome statue by Permoser on the façade. In 1783 the church assumed once again the title of priory and in 1795, after the Chieti order was dissolved, became a secular parish church by annexing several rectories suppressed in the neighbourhood. The church, recently restored, is also the spiritual meeting place of the German community in Florence.

# San Giorgio alla Costa e dello Spirito Santo
*via della Costa San Giorgio*

Alongside the Costa San Giorgio that climbs the homonymous hill south of the Arno until it meets the city walls at the gate also named after the warrior saint, stands a small church, founded before the year 1000 and originally dedicated to Saint George. Later on saint Mamiliano was added to this first dedication, when a nearby oratory named for that saint was attached to the parish church. This double name lasted a long time, and was also subject to a popular deformation often leading to confuse Mamiliano with the blessèd Florentine Umiliana dei Cerchi.

Subjected to frequent raids by armies descending upon the city (out of the bounds of which it remained until the last wall was built), and ruled by the powerful surrounding parishes, the church soon began a slow decline, until it was absorbed by the priorate of Sant'Andrea a Mosciano and transferred to the "Scopetinis", canon regulars from Santa Maria a Scopeti, near San Casciano, who settled in the rectory used as a convent. They stayed there until 1435, when pope Eugene IV – then residing in Florence – gave the Fiesole Dominicans, who wanted premises in the city, the church of San Giorgio. And since the adjacent monastery soon proved too small for them, they also took over the nearby houses of the abbot of Moscheta, which up to then had been used as a hospice and catered for pilgrims.

Soon, at Cosimo the Elder himself's request, the pope decided to move the Dominicans to the convent of San Marco, replacing the Silvestrinis, henceforth but a few and known for being deplorable administrators. They, in turn, replaced the Dominicans at San Giorgio, taking with them from San Marco all they could carry. In this new location they also succeeded in dissipating a huge patrimony, until pope Nicholas V, petitioned by the town authorities, definitively removed them from San Giorgio too, where some vallombrosian nuns from the monastery of Santa Verdiana settled under donna Alessandra da Vernio's guidance. They called themselves "nuns of the Holy Ghost", and thus the church assumed the new name, which is still its official denomination. The nuns also ran the parish, subject to the election of a priest responsible for the cure of souls, and a number of chaplains. The convent soon blossomed anew, supported also

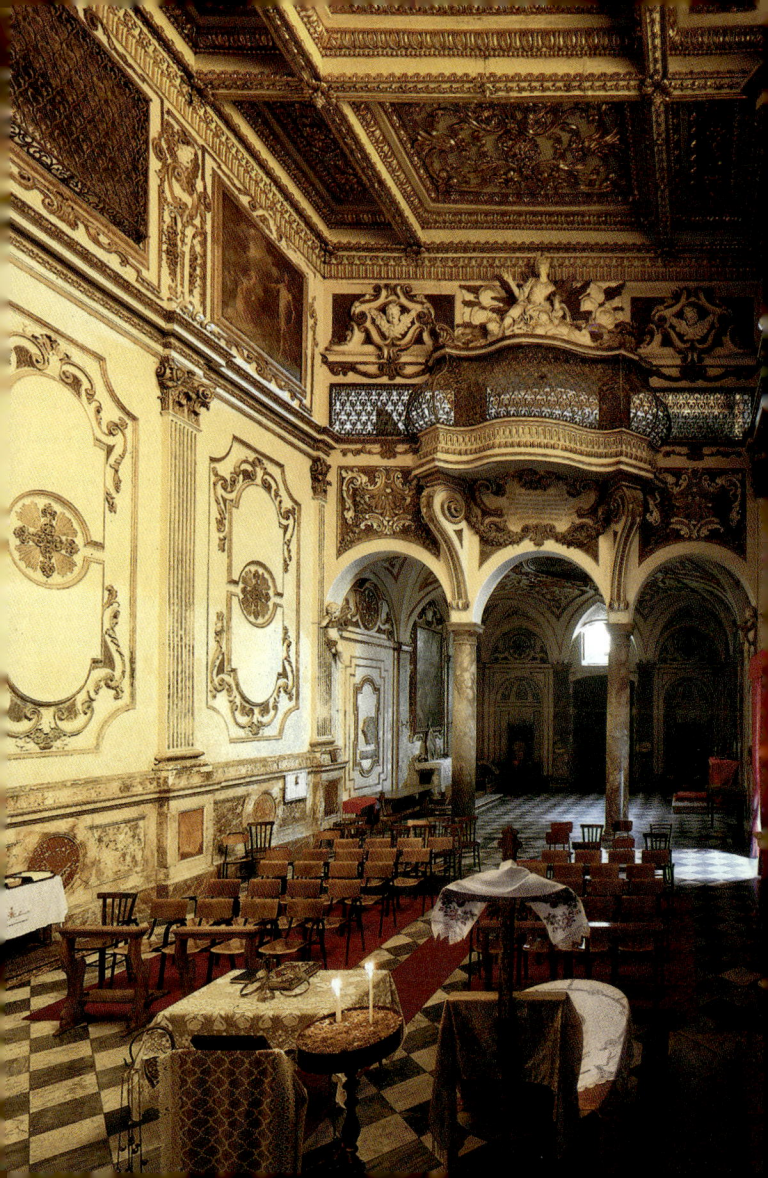

by the Medici family's favour, who in 1705-1708, massively contributed to the church's complete restoration, entirely supervised by Giovan Battista Foggini. The inside was richly stuccoed in white and gold in a gorgeous baroque style featuring a compositional and chromatic lightness, apparently heralding a rococo slightly unsuited to the sparse, unfinished exterior; the entrance area was lowered to hold with an elaborate balcony the nuns' overhanging choir; the panel of the *Madonna della Costa* – held to be a youthful work of Giotto and venerated for centuries in the church – was placed on a monumental high altar (whence it has been removed today for security reasons); a number of famous artists, including Tommaso Redi, Jacopo Vignali and Alessandro Gherardini, were called upon to execute works for the new church which, under the name of "Holy Ghost", was consecrated by archbishop Tommaso Della Gharardesca.

With the suppression of convents, the convent buildings became State property (right now they are occupied by several private homes and the school of Military Health), whereas the church was secularised and its priest declared irremovable. Today it is run by the Christian orthodox Romanian community.

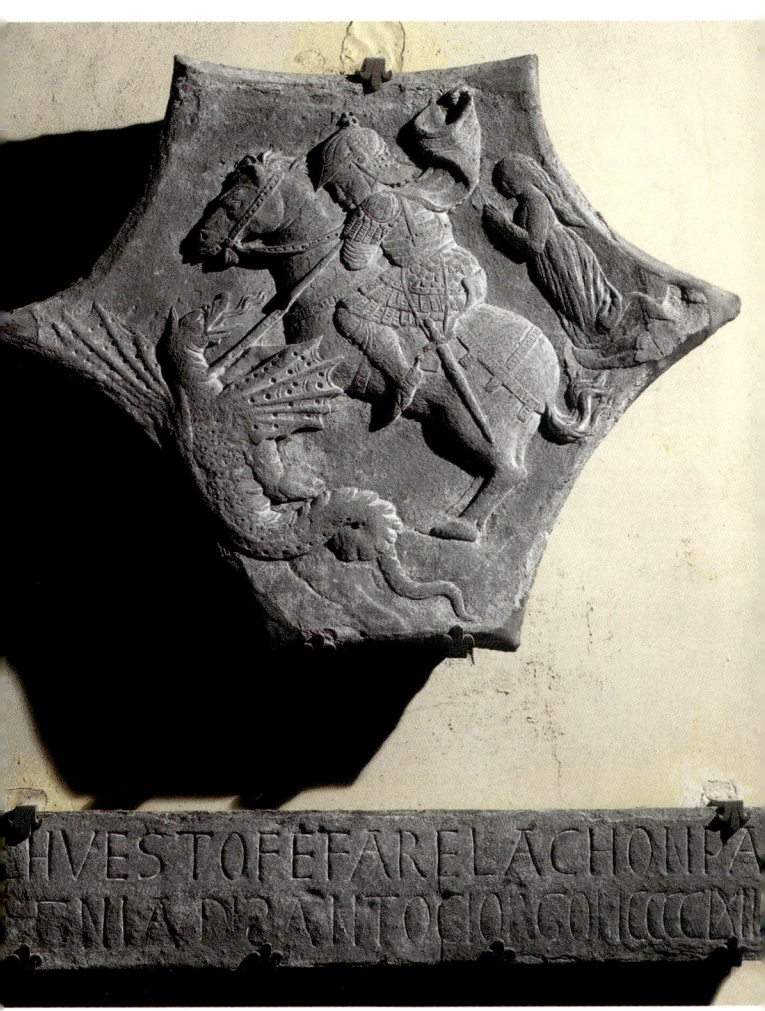

# San Remigio

*via San Remigio*

It was in the VIIIth century that the great Christian pilgrimages from all over Europe towards Rome began. Tuscany was affected by these crowds, even in centres not directly situated on the main via Francigena.

We can trace back to the IXth century – under Carolingian rule – a hospice with a next door oratory set outside the walls, by a postern. In several documents it is called San Romeo, maybe because the pilgrims directed to Rome were called "romei". The dedication actually points to the reference to France: Remi, who lived in the Vth century, baptised king Clovis with three thousand members of his court, contributing in a large measure to the Christianisation of the Franks.

Although not inside the city until walls were raised in 1172-1175 (when

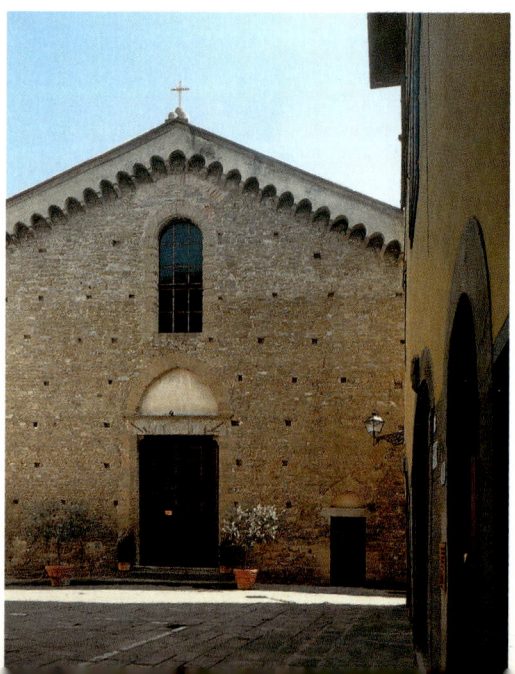

it probably became a parish church), San Remigio is defined as a "church" in a document dated 1040. In 1067-73 its patron was a certain Rodulfo, whose daughter Gisla gave the church to the San Pier Maggiore Benedictines in 1060, becoming its abbess, and to the connected men's abbey of San Salvi. It still belonged to them in 1265, when patronage passed on to the Bagnesi family. Gerardo Aldighieri's donation of a house in 1303 allowed the piazza in front of it to be enlarged. Around 1363 the Bagnesis' influence was replaced by rectors elected by the bishop. Towards 1350, probably after the flood of 1333, it underwent a thorough restoration, probably funded by ser Piero Del Bene Pepi who had a house in the neighbourhood and was buried in the church. The location of the church – lower than the nearby river – always exposed it to floods, this leading to frequent alterations. On what was probably a romanesque structure (evidenced by the single lancet windows recently come to light) were built side aisles

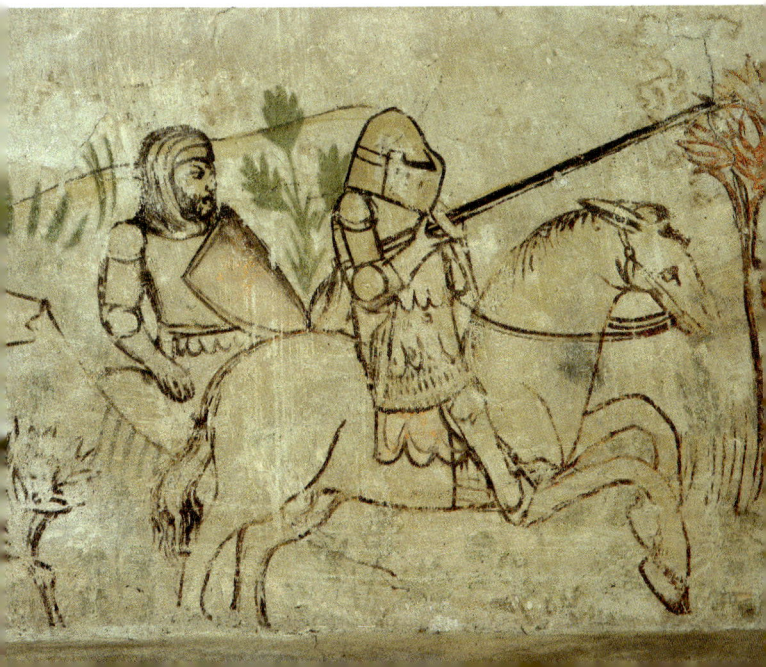

nearly as high as the central one, cross vault and pointed arches, similar to the Germanic gothic so-called "hall churches".

Between the fourteenth and the fifteenth centuries neighbourhood families, patrons of chapels or tombs, made various donations. The walls were frescoed as were the vaults, and important works of art were commissioned, partly lost or conserved elsewhere, such as Giottino's *Deposizione* (c.1360) which has been in the Uffizi since 1851, and the *Annunciazione* by Mariotto di Nardo dated 1842, now in the Gallerie dell'Accademia. In the early fifteenth century work involved the cloister, refectory and the new sacristy. A line and an inscription on the vault of the porch show the height the water reached in the flood of 1557. In 1568 the priory of San Pier Scheraggio, suppressed when the Uffizi galleries were built, was transferred to San Remigio. The new prior Francesco Falconcini promised various innovations, which can still be seen today, with the organ by the sacristy door and countless coats of arms. In 1589 the entire renovation was endorsed by the church being re-consecrated by Alessandro de' Medici, bishop of Florence and future pope Leo XI.

In the second half of the seventeenth century the side altars were done over in Corinthian style to give them a stylistic unity, with stone that Anton Maria Fabbrini, "Provveditore della Galleria di Sua Altezza Reale" (*Superintendent of the Galleries of His Royal Highness*) had brought from Rome. Among the patrons – the Bagnesi, Buini, Fabbrini, Beccuti, Totti, Fiaschi families – , several boasted very old ties with the church; Giovan Camillo Sacrestani and Francesco Morosini were the commissioned artists.

In 1818 Leopoldo Pasqui renovated the high altar; the painting *Battesimo di Clodoveo* is by Giuseppe Bezzuoli.

The flood of 1966 also seriously damaged San Remigio; a thorough restoration – to give back to the church its Gothic appearance – erased nearly all the later elements, bringing back to light fragments of fourteenth-century frescoes, but not enough to recreate the original ensemble.

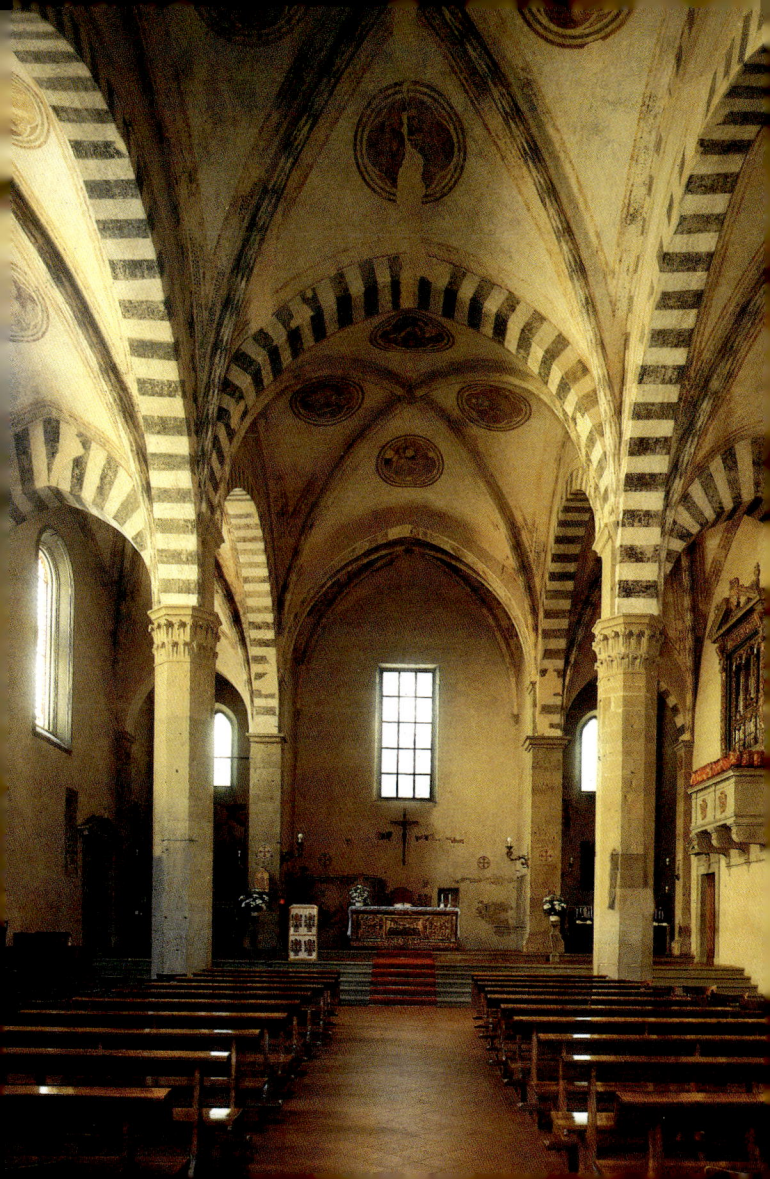

# San Felice in Piazza

*piazza San Felice*

The church owes its name to *Platitia*, or *Placza*, the flat area that in the XIth century went from the church of Santa Felicita to the present piazza Pitti, and which precisely towards the middle of that century was rapidly growing more populated along the road from ponte Vecchio to via Cassia in the direction of Siena and Rome.

Placed beyond the first commune walls, the church is mentioned in a document dated 1066 which reports its passing under the authority of the San Pier Maggiore benedictine women's monastery. November 6, 1221 it was re-consecrated by the papal legate cardinal Ugolino (which leads us to suppose it had been altered) in the presence of the bishops of Florence and Pistoia and the abbot of Nonantola.

At mid-century a second restructuring in Gothic style took place, evidenced by the arched windows still visible on the side of the nave and several fragments of frescoes. Between 1324 and 1334 the belfry with its three orders of double lancet windows was built.

In 1414, a brief of antipope John XXIII (that Baldassare Cossa whom Cosimo the Elder openly backed) endorsed the passage of the church and convent to the camaldolese order. Cosimo also exerted his influence in a clause obliging the abbot of San Felice to be a monk from the florentine abbey of Santa Maria degli Angioli. Cosimo's preference can also be seen in the great importance San Felice boasted throughout the XVth century as a theatre for evocative sacred representations, staged by young people of the society dell'Orciuolo. Brunelleschi's sets for the *Annunciazione* in 1439 were memorable. The church's single nave lent itself perfectly to a clear separation of the scenic area – the spatial volume of the apse – and the spectators' area. The trusses of the roof provided also an ideal support for theatrical machines, "devices", such as the "almond" wrapped in flames within which the angel came down from heaven to bear the announcement to Mary.

In the fifteenth century the old church underwent several major architectural and artistic alterations such as the new façade executed around 1457 and funded by Mariotto di Dinozzo Lippi who later had his and

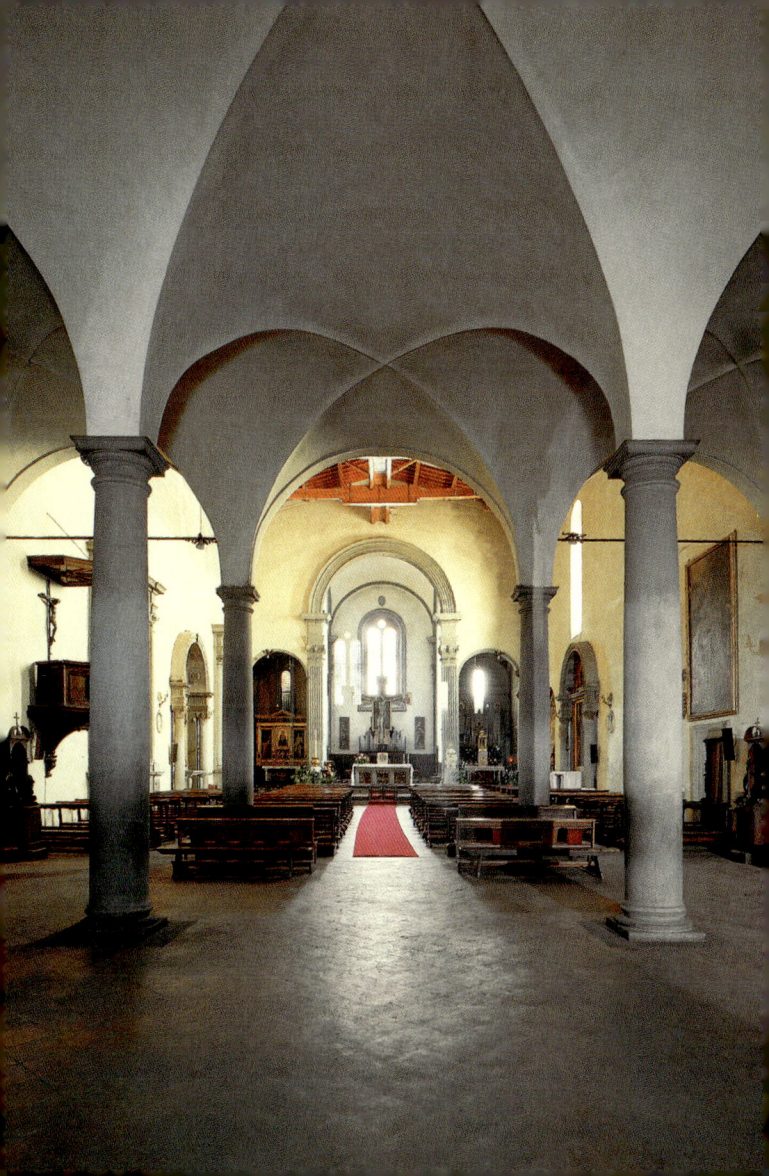

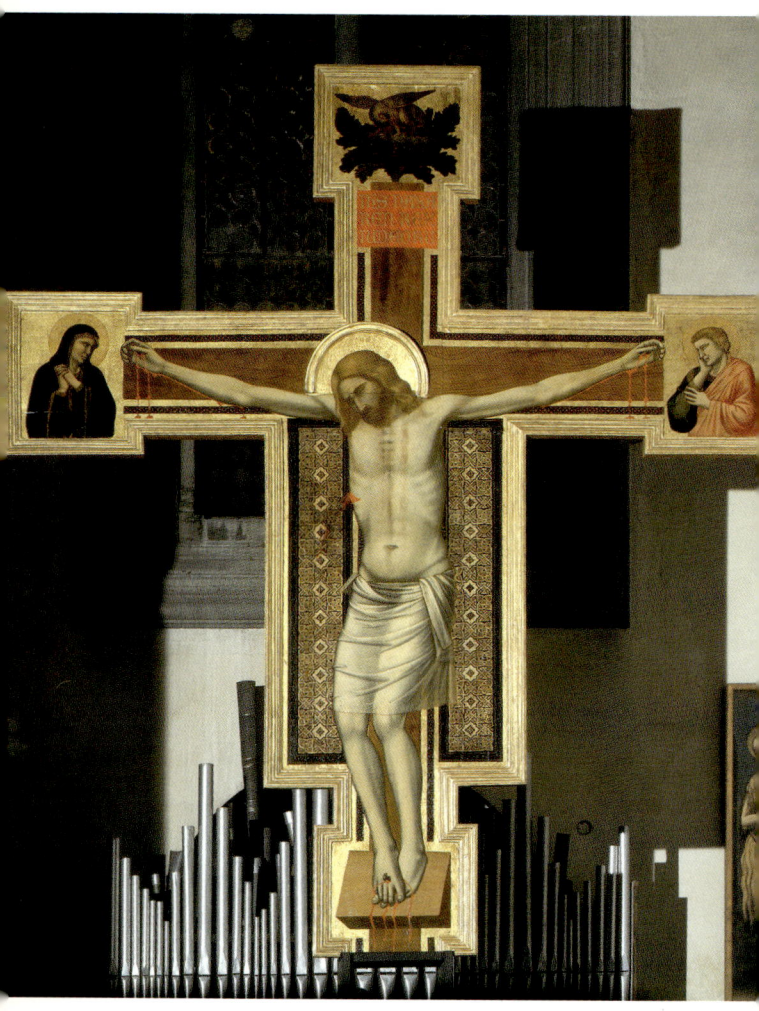

his family's resting place in the church.

The nave also was embellished by works by Neri di Bicci, and by the great frescoes, now mostly lost, by Maestro di Signa, Giovanni della Robbia's workshop and Filippino Lippi.

Around 1458 the main chapel (at the Ridolfi family's expense) and the two side chapels were renovated. Lacking documents explicitly naming the architect, several supposed attributions have been put forward. The most wide-spread is that of Michelozzo, supported by documents mentioning stone-cutters and workmen who collaborated with him in other yards and by resemblances with other works of his. Others prefer to suggest the name of Antonio Manetti Ciaccheri.

In 1553, once again the church belonged a women's monastery: the construction of the fortifications for the war against Siena, inside the fourteenth-century walls, had destroyed the convent of the San Pier Martire dominican nuns. Pope Jules III's bull dated November 8, 1553 granted them the complex of San Felice, where they moved four years later.

Returning to a cloistered order entailed large-scale works to adapt the church to a dual function, since it had officially become a parish church in 1115: work begun in 1553 lasted over fifty years, with the construction of the large choir raised on pillars allowing the nuns to attend functions with being seen by the faithful. In the rear part of it, above the entrance, furnished with carved wood stalls, a "work room" was also set up, completed in 1588, for the handiwork typical of monastic life.

Between the sixteenth and seventeenth centuries, in the nave – where the Gothic double lancet windows were reduced to rectangular windows – a number of new altars were built, in Counter-Reformation style, and works by artists such as Salvator Rosa, il Volterrano, Giovanni di San Giovanni, Ottavio Vannini were placed.

In the seventeenth and eighteenth centuries tombs of personalities, mostly artists and professional men connected with the grand ducal court residing in the nearby palazzo Pitti, like the architect Giulio Parigi, the painter Anton Domenico Gabbiani, the sculptor Giuseppe Piamontini and the court doctor Giuseppe del Papa, but also Marco Bogi, the grand duke's chief huntsman and chamber aide, were placed in San Felice. In 1700 the side entrance steps on via Mazzetta were rebuilt, with the portal bearing at centre the coat of arms of Cosimo Bordoni who funded the work. In 1742, after having torn down the Gothic belfry, the new bell gable with four bells was built on two orders over the main chapel. When Pietro Leopoldo di Lorena suppressed religious orders in 1785, San Felice too remained a mere parish church. The vicissitudes of the next decades aggravated the damage making restorations necessary, beginning with the reconstruction of the paving, and the removal of the tombs and plaques. A traumatic event led to new alterations in 1926 when a fire starting in the main chapel heavily damaged the apsidal part of the church. The engineer and architect Ezio Cerpi directed the restoration, seeking a style closer to the one it had in the fourteenth and fifteenth centuries: he removed the false ceiling of the nave, clearing the volume of the main chapel by removing the wooden choir with the organ placed there in the late seventeenth century, entirely reopened the double lancet window, created a new high altar in neo-fifteenth-century style and re-opened the arched windows on the side. He also restored the façade, using cement to replace even the carved stone elements that could not be saved. The apsidal chapels were decorated in the style of the times, in particular the right one, dedicated in 1880 to Our Lady of Lourdes. The frescoes combining floral and neo-Gothic style are works of 1928 by Rodolfo Fanfani. In 1935 a new neo-Renaissance style choir was built, with a nineteenth-century organ offered by the cathedral of Fiesole. In 1968 from the nearby oratory dei Bini in via Romana, owing to a restoration, several works of sacred art were transferred to San Felice and have become part of the church's furnishings, such as Leonardo del Tasso's *San Sebastiano* and the two Filippo Lippi panels with *San Giovanni* and *Santa Maria Maddalena*, presently in the main chapel. The architectural structures underwent a new restoration towards the end of the seventies, whereas in 1992 Giotto's great cross returned to its early splendour, and is now placed on the high altar.

Workshop of Giovanni della Robbia, *Deposition*, painted terracotta

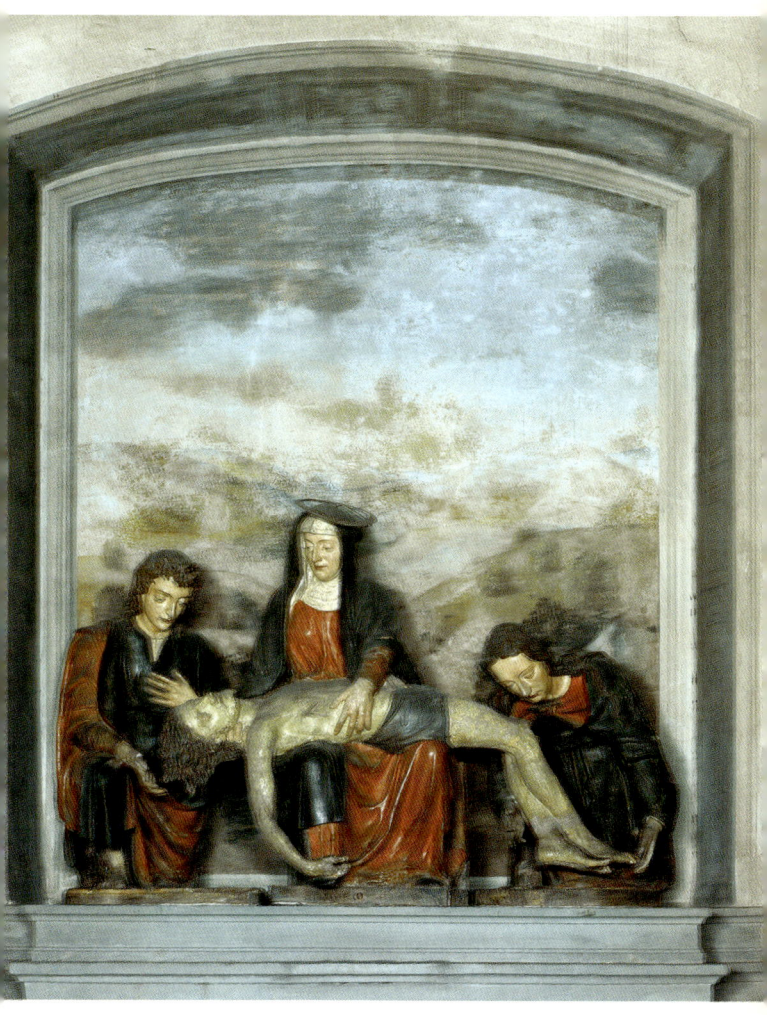

## Santi Apostoli

*piazzetta del Limbo*

The area where the church rises used to be on the edge of the Roman city, towards the bank of the Arno, where the river met with the upper course of the Mugnone and the aqueduct coming from the hills reached the city. There, from a bygone age, stood thermae, whose ruins would later be used as building material for the church. This area was also the burial ground of infants haaving died before baptism, a fact the present name of the piazza del Limbo evidences.

Medieval tradition has the church founded by the emperor Charlemagne and consecrated by archbishop Turpin in the presence of the celebrated paladins. This very distinguished birth certificate was soon refuted; however it had been largely sustained until quite recently, even with invented testimonies, like in the case of the plaque on the façade. The emperor's bust placed in the apse during the late XVIth-century restoration is purely commemorative. So although it is not of carolingian origin, the building's great age is apparent in the stone structure with nave and two side aisles with Prato green pillars and Composite and Corinthian order marble capitols – the first two coming from the demolished Roman thermae. The church can actually be dated to late XIth century, having a single semi-cylindircal apse and narrow curved single lancet windows; even if many of the elements giving it its medieval appearance are owed to a thorough restoration in 1930. The remnants of Donato Acciaiuoli's tomb, whose family was patron of a chapel until the XVIIth century, are fifteenth-century. In the early fifteenth century Paolo Schiavo's fresco *Madonna col Bambino* was on the façade of the church. Of this fresco, ruined by bad weather, the sinopite has been saved, detached and placed in the first chapel on the left. In the early sixteenth century the Altovitis, a family of rich bankers and merchants, funded several embellishments, like the Renaissance portal Benedetto da Rovezzano executed, on a design by Baccio d'Agnolo (in those same years author of the bell tower and the next door palazzo Borgherini, later Rosselli Del Turco).

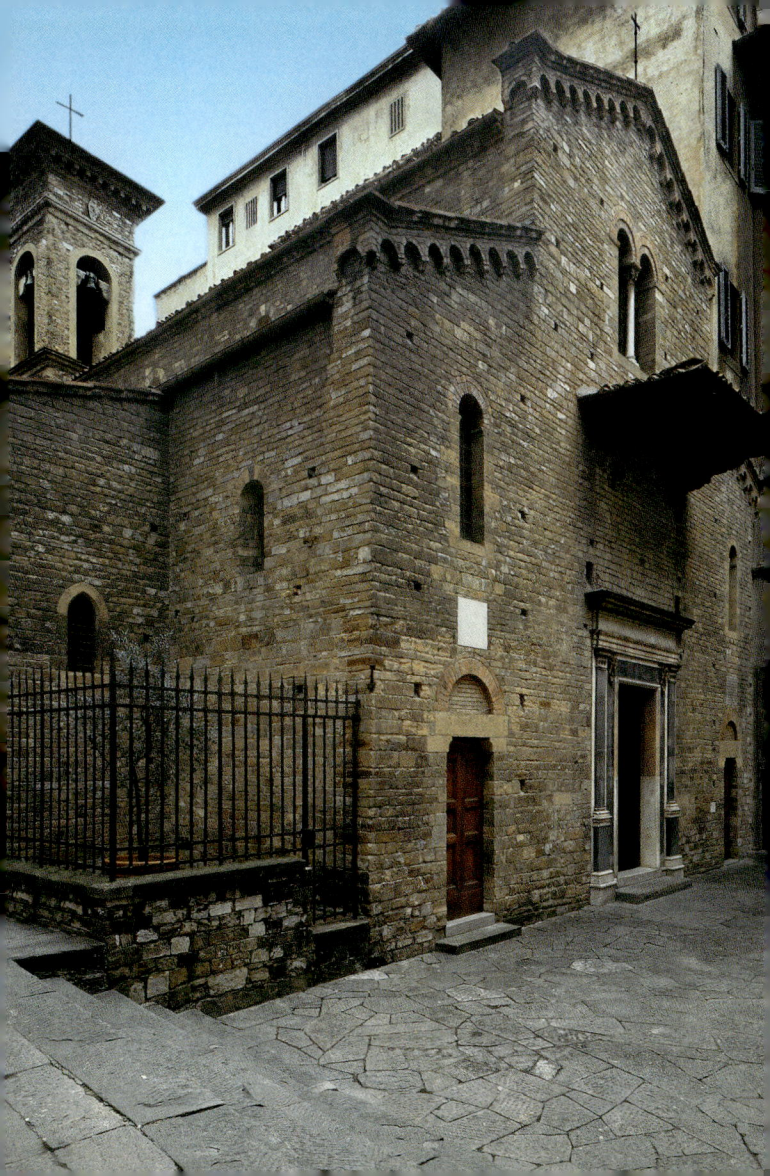

# Santa Maria nella Badia fiorentina

*via del Proconsolo*

La Badia, an ancient benedictine monastery dedicated to the Virgin, was built in the XIth century near the town walls by Willa, daughter of marquess Bonifazio di Toscana and Gualdrada, sister of Rudolph II king of Burgundy. On May 31, 978, in a solemn ceremony, the investiture of the first abbot took place. Willa married Hubert, margrave of Spoleto and Camerino, and from their union sprung Hugo, future count of Tuscany. Hugo indeed confirmed his mother's bequeath, bestowing countless privileges and gifts on the abbot and his monastery. By doing so Hugo won the monks' eternal gratitude: even today they regularly celebrate a mass for his soul on the anniversary of his death. The town authorities allowed the monks to lean their buildings on the wall, backing them against the small church – called Santo Stefano del Popolo – of the protomartyr Stephen, whose name was thus added to that of the Badia church. Despite the great prosperity accrued over the years by the privileges various popes conceded, the early edifice must not have been either particularly large or monumental since in 1284, to make it better suited to the cure of souls and the city's prestige, the Florentine republic charged Arnolfo with restoring and enlarging it. Work was still under way when in 1307 the town authorities levied a tax on the religious corporations, provoking a strong reaction of the Badia monks, who set to ringing their bells calling the people to their rescue. But when the citizens arrived, they turned against the monks, attacking and ransacking the convent. To punish the monks' rebellion, the commune decided to tear down the bell tower that was under way; it was raised again in 1330 by the pontifical legate Giovanni Gaetano Orsini's intervention, with the typical hexagonal form which has characterised it ever since. In the fifteenth century the Portuguese Gomezio Ferreira da Silva's abbacy, from 1419 to 1439, was particularly outstanding. During that period there were several major alterations in the ensemble, such as the construction of the cloister degli Aranci (1432-1438) commissioned

17th century chancel with Vasari's altar-piece depicting the Assumption of the Virgin Mary

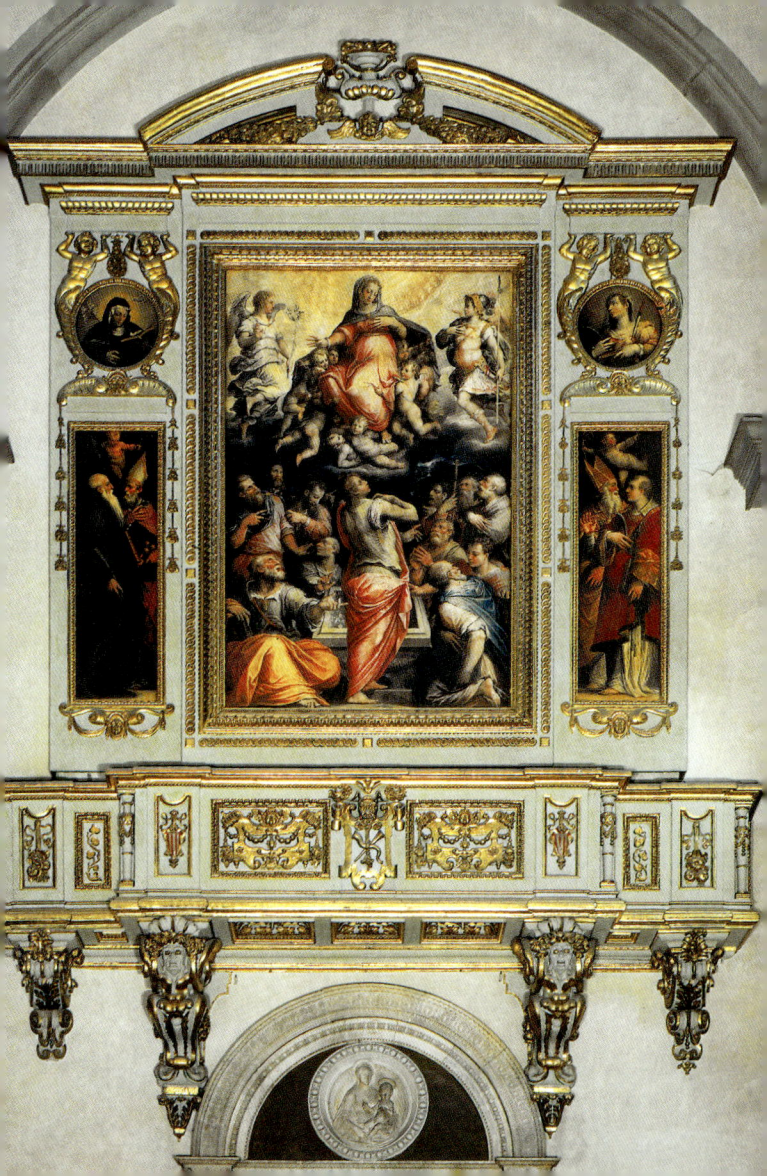

by Filippo Pieruzzi, attributed to Rossellino, and frescoed perhaps by a Portuguese named Giovanni di Consalvo. After 1436 Eugene IV had the monastery associated with the Montecassino congregation. In 1469 count Hugo's remains were solemnly entombed in the church in a monument directly planned by the monks and executed by Mino da Fiesole. After 1511 Giovanni Battista Pandolfini, whose family owned houses in the neighbourhood, carried out substantial new works. It was that same Pandolfini who had Benedetto da Rovezzano erect the new family chapel, building it partly over the old church of Santo Stefano. Between 1628 and 1631 abbot Casolani commissioned Matteo di Marco Segaloni, a practically

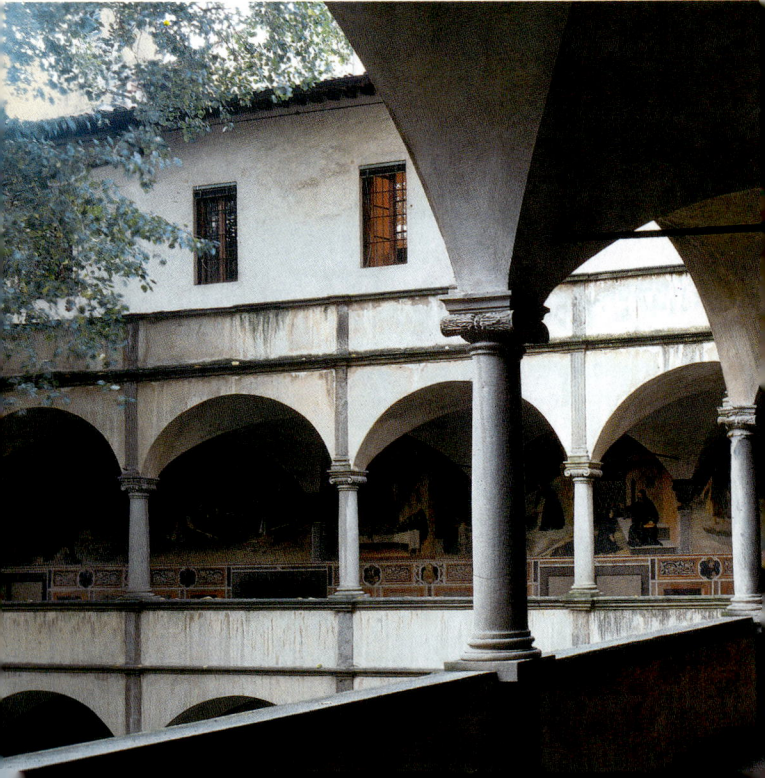

unknown artist, to radically alter the church, changing, aside from the decoration, the entire layout and creating, by the two new entrances thus formed, a special, organic relationship with the neighbourhood. During the next century Segaloni's baroque layout was enhanced by a deep, theatrical choir frescoed by Domenico Ferretti. In 1778 the Badia church was raised to parish church, thus inheriting the role that nearby San Procolo had played up to then.

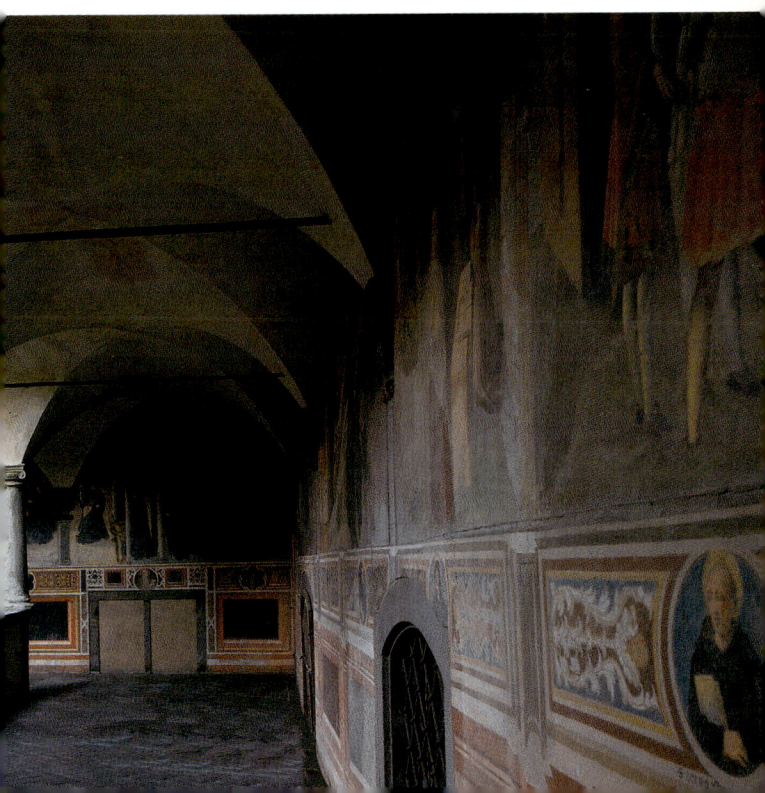

# Santa Trinita

*piazza santa Trinita*

This is one of the oldest Florentine churches. Its first structures actually go back to the XIth century; by 1077 its existence is documented, and its very first elaboration may go back to 1092. Santa Trinita arose on the edge of the old quadrilateral city walls where, after running along the present via Tornabuoni, they turned east to follow a parallel course with the Arno by Santi Apostoli. The original small romanesque church was therefore built in a space outside the old city centre, although very nearby, in a site where a chapel dedicated to the Madonna del Spasmo stood. But very soon the coordinates of its location were to change. In fact, between 1173 and 1175 the town authorities had the fifth city wall built (the first commune one, quite a bit larger than the preceding one) to contain the significant demographic growth. Thus Santa Trinita was absorbed in it, surrounded by large vacant spaces. Precisely in front of the church stood the tower-houses of one of the most important families in the city – the Spinis – who controlled the territory along the Arno exactly where the fourth Florentine bridge was built in 1252, the San Trinita bridge, named after the nearby church. During those same years, between 1250 and 1260, just when an important road connecting the church with the left bank of the Arno was being opened in front of it, the Vallombrosians – who had always had their Florentine premises in Santa Trinita and wished to somehow respond to the Mendicant orders' overwhelming expansion in the city at the same time – commissioned Nicola Pisano (according to Vasari's testimony) to nearly totally remodel the church: the result was one of the first examples of Florentine gothic, a building with an Egyptian-cross layout, divided in a nave and two side aisles by large pilasters crowned by lancet arches and cross vaults. Next to it was the convent, to which towards 1256, according to the religious orders' custom of assisting the needy and the infirm, a hospital was added, later moved to via del Parione in 1277. Thus Santa Trinita had a full claim on Florence's life and history: the town councils began to meet in its nave, not yet having their permanent premises (the palazzo della Signoria not yet existing); the most prominent local families began to compete to place therein the tombs of their most important

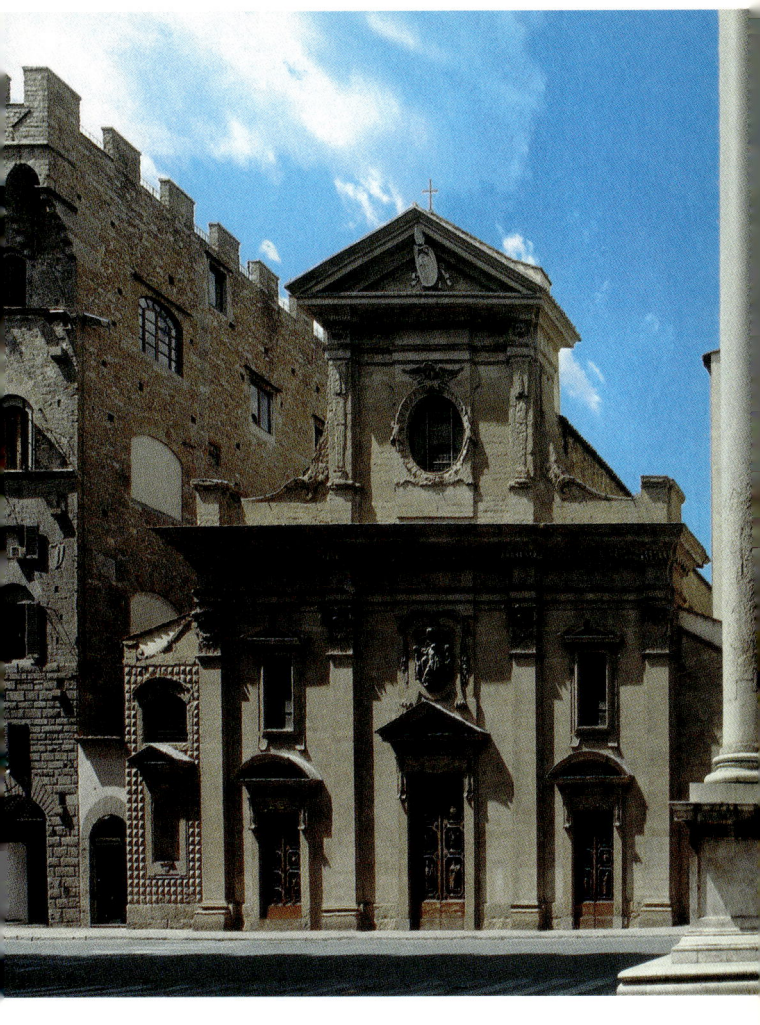

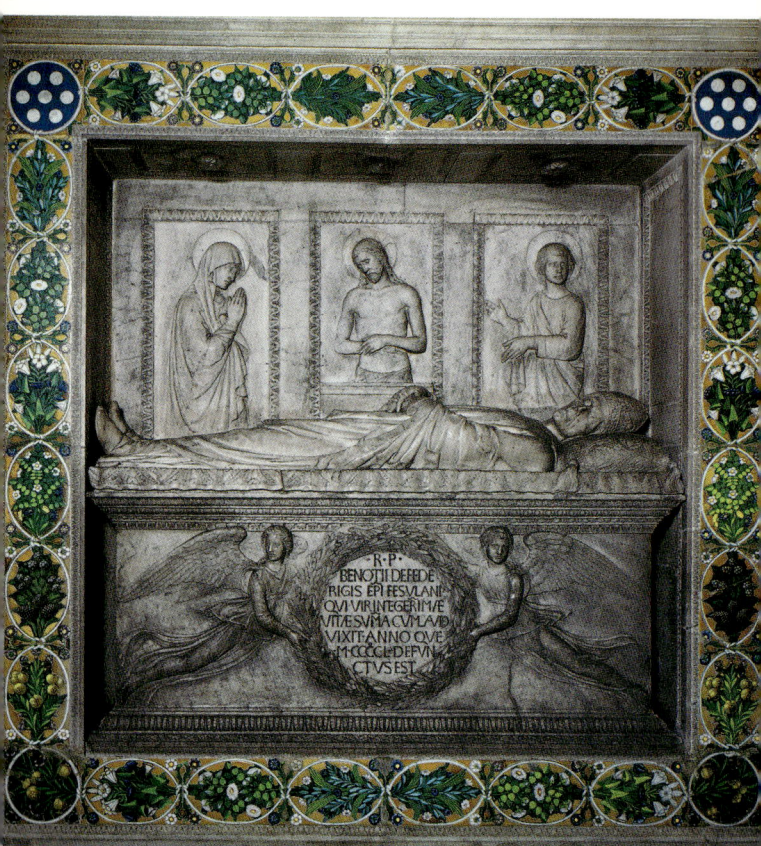

Luca della Robbia, marble tomb of Benozzo Federighi, Bishop of Fiesole

members (a prelude to the creation, in the XIVth century, of the many patrician chapels that contributed to enlarge the church); on the piazza in front celebrations and dances were beginning to be organised on the occasion of the most important events. It was precisely during the festivities for the Calendimaggio of 1300 that, in front of Santa Trinita, young men of the Cerchi family quarrelled with some of Corso Donati's supporters, thus writing a cruel chapter of the civil strife between Whites and Blacks. Soon later the flood of 1333 brought destruction to the entire district and seriously damaged the church. So the great restoration works began in 1340, with the building of the first three chapels left of the entrance. A very prominent architect of the times, Neri di Fioravanti, may also have taken part in this significant work. There are many names of famous artists connected with this church: including Cimabue, who executed for it a *Maestà della Madonna* today conserved in the Uffizi galleries; Giotto, the author of an alterpiece; Neri di Bicci, to whom is owed the fourteenth-century fresco representing the *Trinità*, some remains of which can still be seen today on the inner façade. But the most important mark was left by Domenico Ghirlandaio, with the fabulous cycle of frescoes on the *Storie di San Francesco* of the Sassetti chapel (1483-1486), and Bernardo Buontalenti who, in 1593-1594, executed the new mannerist façade, totally erasing the previous gothic one (which anyway the Strozzis, who owned a chapel in the church, had already altered in the XVth century). Buontalenti's work was somehow "completed" by Giovanni Caccini, author of the bas-relief with the *Trinità* on the central portal and of the statue of Sant'Alessio to the left of the same portal. This was one of the so-called "grand ducal façades"; the outer arrangement matched a parallel inner restructuring, introducing the monumental altar. On that occasion Santa Trinita assumed the appearance it still has today. Since then merely restorations have been recorded: the nineteenth-century one nearly exclusively regarded the frescoes (it was carried out, not always with felicitous results, precisely while the next door ex-convent was being turned into a secondary school); the one during our century was a necessity after the disastrous flood of 1966. More recent restorations have allowed a more exact chromatic interpretation of the pictorial cycles, thus remedying some mistakes and faults committed by nineteenth-century restorers.

# San Miniato al Monte

*Monte alle Croci*

Tradition reports the existence, at the top of the hill south-east of the Arno, of an oratory dating back to the IIIrd century, dedicated to Saint Peter. In the Vth century it would have been replaced by a larger edifice named after Saint Miniato, a IInd-century Florentine soldier martyr whom the emperor Decius decapitated near the porta alla Croce. According to legend, after his martyrdom Miniato miraculously climbed that hill carrying his head. Other legends mention a settlement of basilian monks and Charlemagne's visit. On the other hand archaeological traces on the hill attest a Longobard settlement. In 1018 bishop Hildebrand had a new church built there to venerate the martyr's relics, but especially to mark the greatness Florence had attained after the defeat of its perpetual enemy Fiesole, a city towards which the church of San Miniato turned its white façade, nearly as a sign of derision. Emperor Henry II and especially his wife Cunegond funded the work. The black benedictine fathers were charged with the service, but patronage was reserved to the bishop of Florence. Later it passed into the hands of the powerful Calimala or Wool Merchants Guild, so that in 1401 its symbol – the eagle grasping the batch (meaning a bale of 12 cloths) – was placed over the tympanum. In 1373, Pope Gregory XI passed the convent over to the olivetan monks. In the course of the XVth century the austere medieval church, with its frescoed nave and aisles, was embellished with works in the new Renaissance style. Among them the funeral chapel built for the Portuguese cardinal Jacopo di Lusitania, who died in Florence at an early age and was famed for his absolute purity, is particularly outstanding. In 1499 the old belfrey beside the church collapsed and was replaced by a new one built in the early sixteenth century on a design by Baccio D'Agnolo. Its particular position relative to the city below made this monastic complex especially important for the Florentine republic's defense when Charlemagne's troups descended in 1530 to back the Medicis' restoration. At the time San Miniato – although to no avail – was fortified with the Michelangelo's assistance. Cosimo I made the Olivetans leave and turned the convent into barracks. The monks, withdrawn in their monte Oliveto mother home, pretended for a long time to

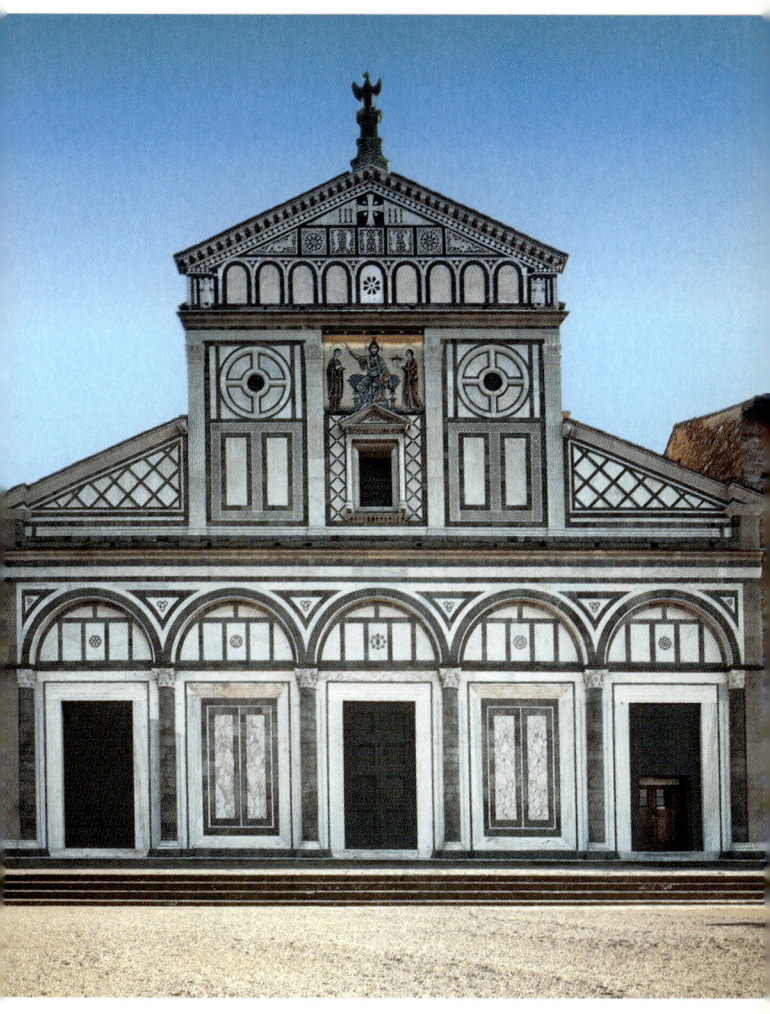

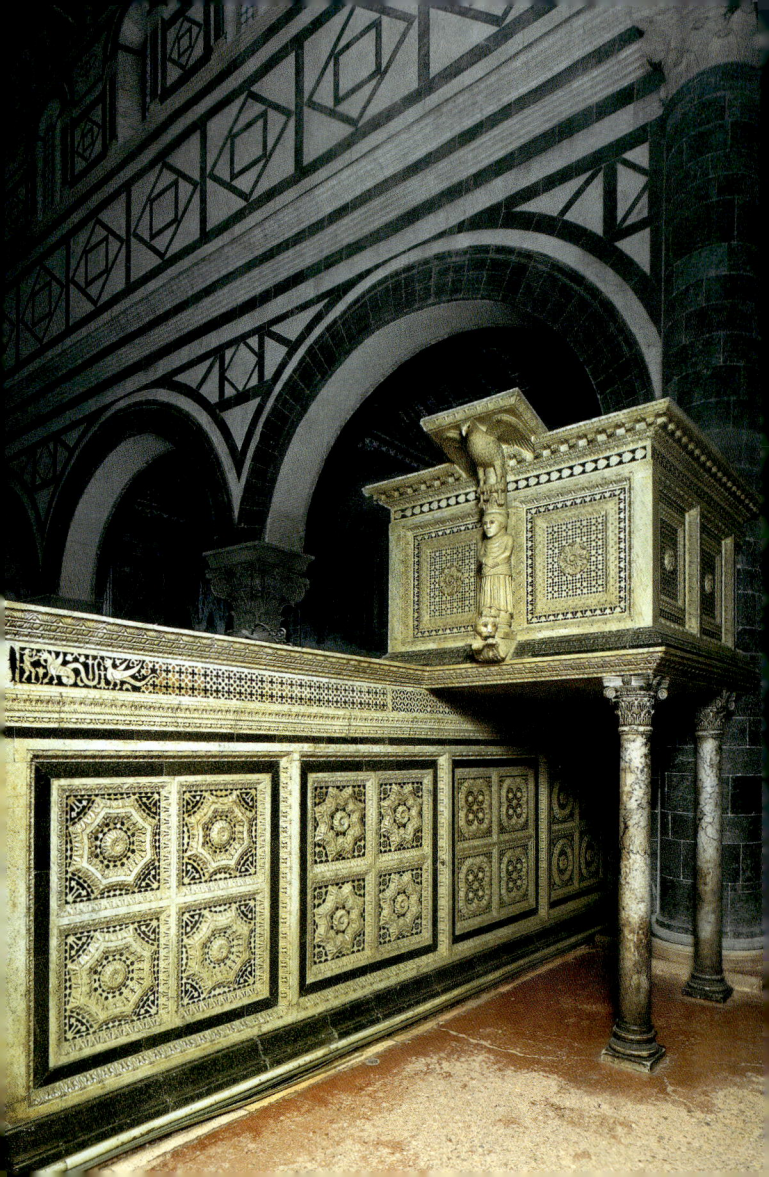

have taken the martyr's relics with them. In 1557 it lost its role as parish church, emphasising the decline of the ensemble. The plague of 1630 decimated even the soldiers; this time the barracks were turned into a thousand-bed lazaret. Once this use came to an end, a series of spoliations and large-scale removals ensued, like in the case of the crucifix which had belonged to saint Giovanni Gualberto that the vallombrosian monks – of the order created by the saint – were allowed to custody in their Florentine Santa Trinita church. Anxious about its increasing deterioration, the Calimala Guild proved, at the end of the seventeenth century, that – despite what the Olivetans had said – San Miniato's relics were still in the crypt. In 1703 Cosimo III passed the convent over to the Jesuits, who remained there officially until Clement XIV suppressed them in 1774. Actually, playing on Grand Duke Pietro Leopoldo's opposition to the pope, they pursued their spiritual activities masked behind an association of aristocratic Florentine believers, called the Opera. The Olivetans were allowed to return to San Miniato in 1784, but they only remained until the Napoleonic suppressions of 1808. However, the Opera, the institution behind which the Jesuits had hidden, had survived, taking over the custody and income from the monumental new cemetery, which Giuseppe Matas began behind the church in 1839, and then Mariano Falcini extended after 1865, and is universally known as the "cimitero delle Porte Sante" ("cemetery of the Holy Gates").

Enclosure and pulpit with marble inlays

# San Frediano in Cestello

*piazza del Cestello*

This church located on the left bank of the Arno, beyond the antique city wall and in a rather unhealthy district, is said to have sprung from a miracle blessèd Frediano da Lucca performed there. A first building would then have arisen thanks to gifts from the devout. The church was collegiate and priory, then tributary of the abbey of Nonantola and, in the early XIIIth century, of the Badia a Settimo Cistercians, who however retained the bishop of Florence's patronage. In 1514, cardinal Francesco Soderini (son of the Tommaso to whom the bishop had conceded that patronage), backed by pope Leo X and the bishop Giulio de' Medici, decided to appropriate it for some carmelite nuns devoted to the worship of Saint Joseph, moving the Cistercians to the church of Santa Maria Maddalena Penitente in Borgo Pinti. The Soderini family and the nuns ran the various institutional activities, including the election of the prior and the canons. This lasted until Paolo Antonio Soderini's exile towards mid-XVIth century, when the grand duke took over as patron. Meanwhile the area, by then absorbed in the fourteenth-century wall, had become densely populated and the building inadequate. At the end of the XVIth century devotion had sprung up for the Florentine Carmelite Maddalena de' Pazzi who, in the first half of the century, had lived in a small nearby convent dedicated to Saint Mary of the Angels, and been beatified in 1626 by Urban VII Barberini. Two other Barberini family nuns, Innocenza and Grazia, were also Carmelites. Since the area was particularly insalubrious, their powerful uncle – cardinal Francesco – provided them with better premises, in Borgo Pinti in stead of the old Cestello monks. When the Cistercians moved back to their earlier premises, they wished to restore them, keeping the veneration for the two saints in the decoration. Designed by Gherardo Silvani, it passed on, from 1680 to 1689, to the Roman architect Cerutti; in 1698 Antonio Ferri built the high dome, frescoed by Anton Domenico Gabbiani. After Grand Duke Leopold's suppressions, the Cistercians left the church; it became a parish church. Then it was once again collegiate, with a prior, canons and chaplains, until Pius X definitively closed the chapter.

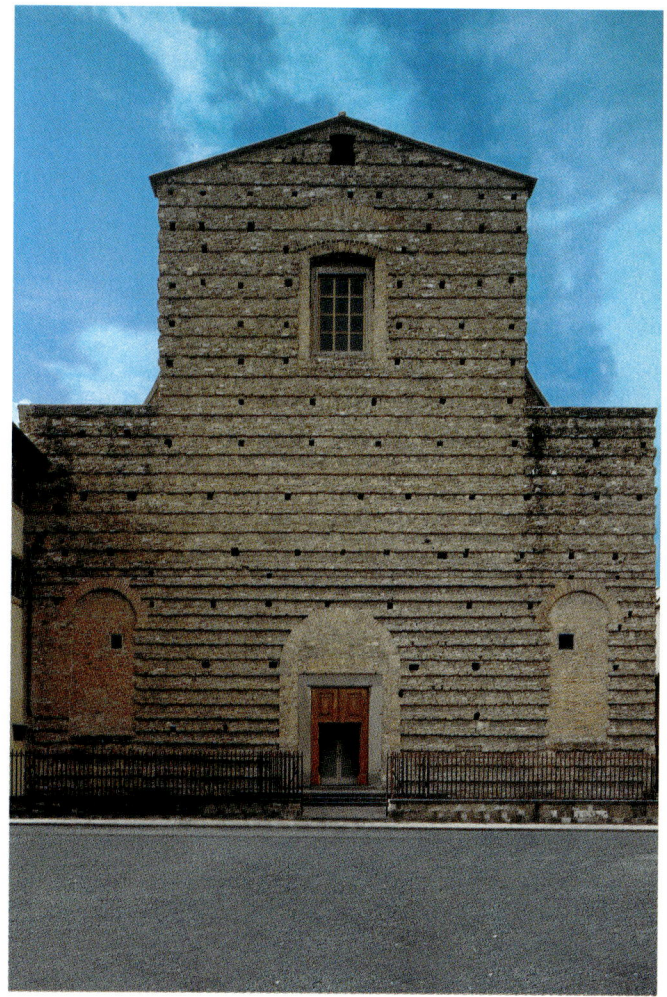

# Santa Lucia de' Magnoli
*via de' Bardi*

The church, located in via de' Bardi, on the left bank of the Arno, sup-posedly recalls a certain Magnolo, son of Uguccione Della Pressa, who may have completed the first building, begun by his father around 1080. It was under the jurisdiction of San Miniato al Monte until Gregory XI passed it over to the bishop. At that time the church had already been damaged by the famous landslide of 1284, which then caused the curious appella-tion "of the Ruins" to be added to the names of many buildings in the area, among which Santa Lucia. Then in 1421 its patronage passed from arch-bishop Amerigo Corsini to the Da Uzzanos – owners of the adjacent palazzo – as a token of gratitude for the large legacy left by Agnolo, later accrued by his brother Niccolò, who not only respected his brother's wishes by hav-ing the main chapel painted, but added the noteworthy sum of four hun-dred gold florins. Thanks to Ginevra Da Uzzano, both palazzo and patronage of the church were passed on as dowry to the Capponi family, which still in theory has them. Cardinal – and future pope – Alessandro de' Medici consecrated the church on May 3, 1584, and on that occasion it was pro-moted to priory. Substantially remodeled in 1732, Santa Lucia underwent further restorations over the next two centuries. Today it conserves a work by Empoli, *Madonna in gloria e santi*, and a *Santa Lucia*, a cuspidate panel by Pietro Lorenzetti. From the beginning, beside the church there was a hospital where, according to tradition, in 1211 the meeting between saint Francis and saint Domenic took place. Destroyed by the landslide of 1284, it was rebuilt where the palazzo Capponi Canigiani stands today.

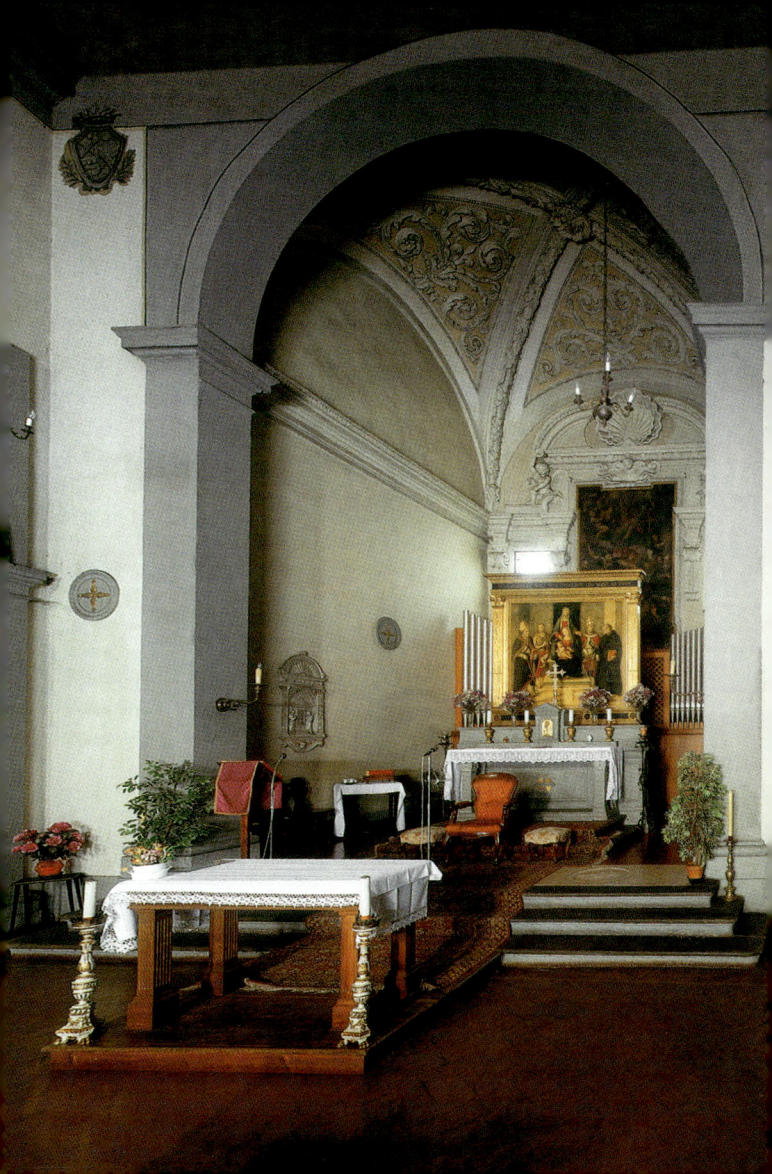

# Santa Maria Novella

*piazza Santa Maria Novella*

A small country oratory called Sancta Maria in Vineis, because of the vine-yards that probably surrounded it, rose during the Longobard domination outside the north-west Roman wall, in an area the waters of the Arno and the Mugnone made marshy, and which in the days of the barbaric invasions was abandoned for a long period, but was cultivated anew after the VIIIth century.

In 983 a document of the German emperor Othon II acknowledged the canons of the cathedral of Florence as its owners, a patronage later con-firmed by Beatrice countess of Tuscany in 1072 and four years later by pope Gregory VII. In 1090 the unsafe state of the building required it be entirely rebuilt. October 30, 1094 the bishop of Florence Ranieri, in pres-ence of the entire clergy and a large number of faithful, consecrated the new church which, to celebrate its renovation, was named Santa Maria Novella. The façade looked east and presumably the inside featured a pres-bytery raised over a crypt where the present sacristy stands. The nave would have extended to about the middle of today's main nave. Next to the small romanesque church stood the canons' houses and the rector's house; facing the entrance lay a small cemetery. November 9, 1221 cardinal Hugolin (future pope Gregory IX) had Santa Maria Novella ceded to a group of Dominicans sent to Florence two years earlier by saint Dominic himself, presided by blessèd Giovanni da Salerno. But the order's swift success soon made the new premises inadequate.

When, in 1244, one of the most renowned preachers of the times, Pietro da Verona, came to Florence (he passed into history as Saint Peter the Mar-tyr because he was killed in 1252 near Milan by followers of the Cathar heresy, the principal object of his invectives), the uninterrupted flow of faithful wishing to attend his sermons obliged the city authorities to cre-ate a large space in front of the church façade and spurred the priests to think about the advantages of a new sacred edifice. A pontifical bull of April 23, 1246 suggests that it was already under way, probably in the area of the present transept, alongside the pre-existing church. But its single nave once again may have proved unsuited for the prestige and the func-

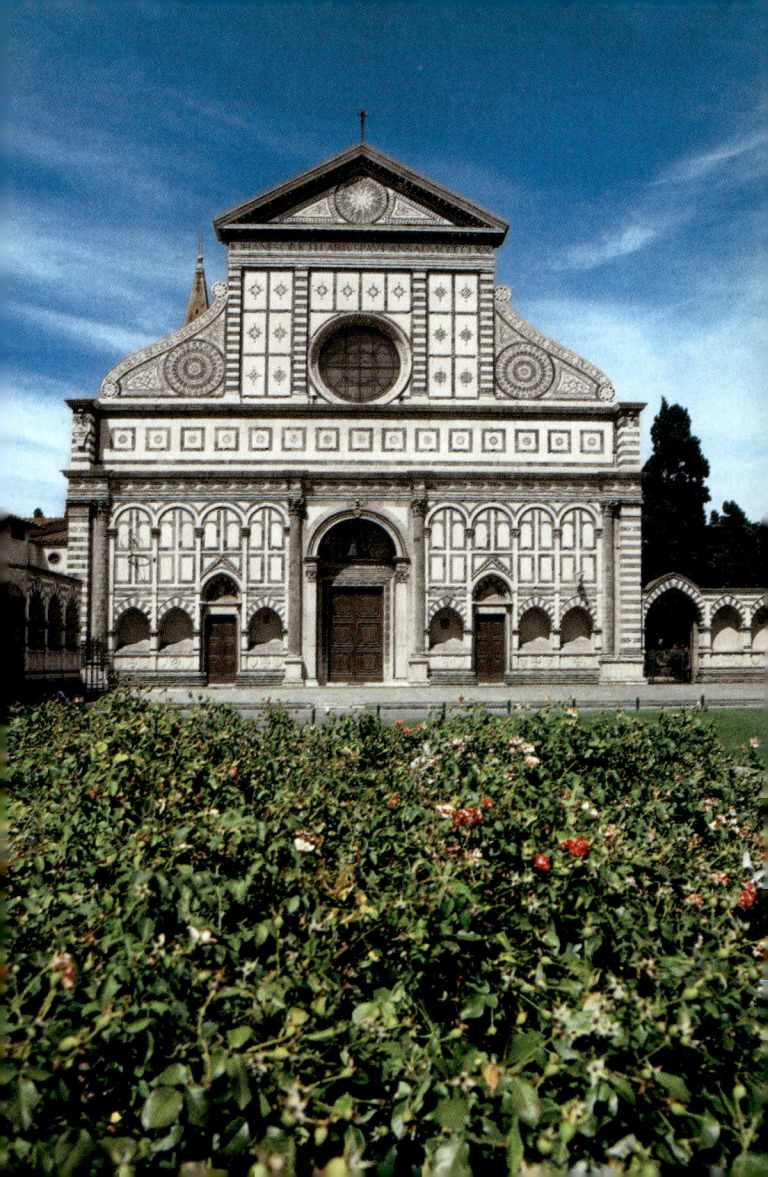

tions to which it was called. Thus construction of the next imposing edifice began, which was to absorb the pre-existing ones, designed with a nave and two side aisles and its façade turned south, as if to emphasise the transcending of the traditional east-west paleo-Christian orientation. After a complicated preparatory stage in order to gather funds and materials and purchase the surrounding land (a stage in which friar Aldobrandino Cavalcanti, uncle of the poet Guido, particularly distinguished himself), the foundation stone of the new church was laid, during an imposing ceremony on October 18, 1279, by the dominican cardinal Latino Malabranca Orsini, sent to Florence as mediator in an attempt to pacify the Guelphs and the Ghibellines. The design is perhaps the work of two dominican lay brothers, fra Sisto Fiorentino and fra Ristoro da Campi, who directed

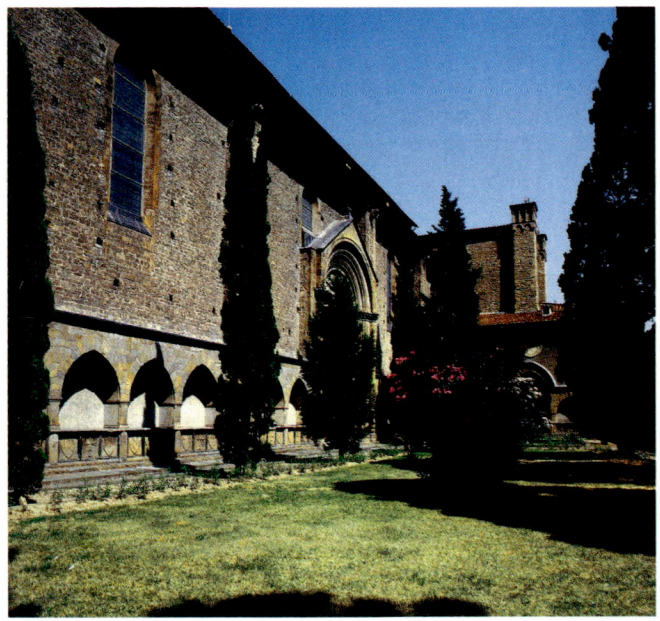

the first construction phase. In the next seventy years they were succeeded by five other master builders, all priests, up to fra Jacopo Talenti da Nipozzano who, directed by fra Jacopo Passavanti, in 1357 could claim the work completed. Thus the first great Florentine gothic Latin-cross building rose, divided in a nave and two side aisles covered with a cross-vault, with arches and ogival windows. The church was separated in two: below, from the entrance to the transept pilasters, with the pulpit in the middle, for the faithful; and above, a choir for the friars. Between the pilasters rose the "bridge" separating the two parts somewhat like an iconostasis.

The preachers' church was a constant point of reference for the history of the Florentine Church, like when in 1259 the Corpus Christus celebration was created with Santa Maria Novella at the end of the procession; a circumstance also benefitting from Santa Maria del Fiore being under construction and hardly suited for the purpose. The importance of the conventual role and its wide-spread national and international fame certainly enabled the new complex to be endowed with all the functions pertaining to the life of a major convent. As of 1294 it became – and it was to remain so past the mid-sixteenth century – an authentic *Studium Generale* according to the dominican tradition, meaning a university institution delivering academic diplomas. Beside the church the *Green Cloister* was erected in various stages after 1330 designed by Giovanni Bracchetti da Campi and completed after 1350 by Jacopo Talenti. Its south side backed up to the hospice built in 1319 to cater for important guests of the Florentine republic; on the other hand the north side backed up to the chapter-house, executed between 1345 and 1355 again by Talenti, funded by the merchant Buonamico de' Guidalotti and later richly frescoed by Andrea di Bonaiuto. Today it is more commonly known as the Cappellone degli Spagnoli (Spanish chapel), since in 1566 Grand Duchess Eleonore of Toledo (wife of Cosimo II) was granted it as a place of worship for the Spaniards who had come to Florence in her suite. The west side of the cloister backs up to the refectory built after 1350, once again by Talenti who forewent the gothic, going back to broader forms with rounded arches, just as the arches of the Green Cloister are broad and apparently lowered.

In 1425 Paolo Uccello and his workshop began frescoeing the walls with the celebrated *Storie della Genesi*, painted in several stages, and completed around 1448 with the *Storie di Noè*.

At the same time, between 1426 and 1428, Masaccio's extremely beautiful *Trinità* was executed. Painted on the wall of the third span of the left aisle, it represents, in a novel architectural frame – designed perhaps by Brunelleschi – the Crucifixion. In a very bold perspective, the cross is crowned by God the Father looming over it with outstretched arms; on each side the Madonna and Saint John. Just below, in a foreground at the viewer's level, we find the kneeling figures of the two patrons, occupying for the first time such an important position in the representation. In the refectory Alessandro Allori painted in 1590 the biblical scenes of the *Caduta della Manna* and *Le pernici nel deserto* (a scene incorporating a fourteenth-century fresco) and an *Ultima Cena*.

A passageway connects the Green Cloister with the so-called cloister of the Deceased which contained funeral chapels since the mid-fourteenth century and used to lead to the convent vegetable garden, destroyed in the last century to make room for the piazza in front of the railway station.

Here also the majestic bell tower stands, with its three levels of double and triple lancet windows, steeple and five bells. No doubt designed by Giovanni da Campi (c.1330), its base was a thick tower standing to the right of the primitive church and used as a lookout for fires. Blessèd Simone di Guido Saltarelli – archbishop of Pisa who had fled his city invaded by the imperial troups – funded the bell tower during his residence in the Florentine convent between 1328 and 1334. In 1358 fra Pietro Strozzi placed on the completed campanile a casket of relics to protect it from lightning that had often struck it, and some Florentines interpreted his gesture as a warning against the excessive pomp and wealth of the new convent. In 1380 donna Andreola di Jacopo Acciaiuoli wished to erect left of the church, using the south and west walls of the extremity of the little old church that was still standing, the chapel of the Annunciation where she solemnly buried her husband Mainardo Cavalcanti, grand seneschal of the kingdom of Naples, in a marble tomb. This large gothic hall with its soaring cross-vault later became a monumental sacristy, retaining at the entrance a copy of the Cavalcanti plaque.

The opulence of the ensemble and of its functional endowments caused it to be chosen as a privileged guest house for particularly important eccle-

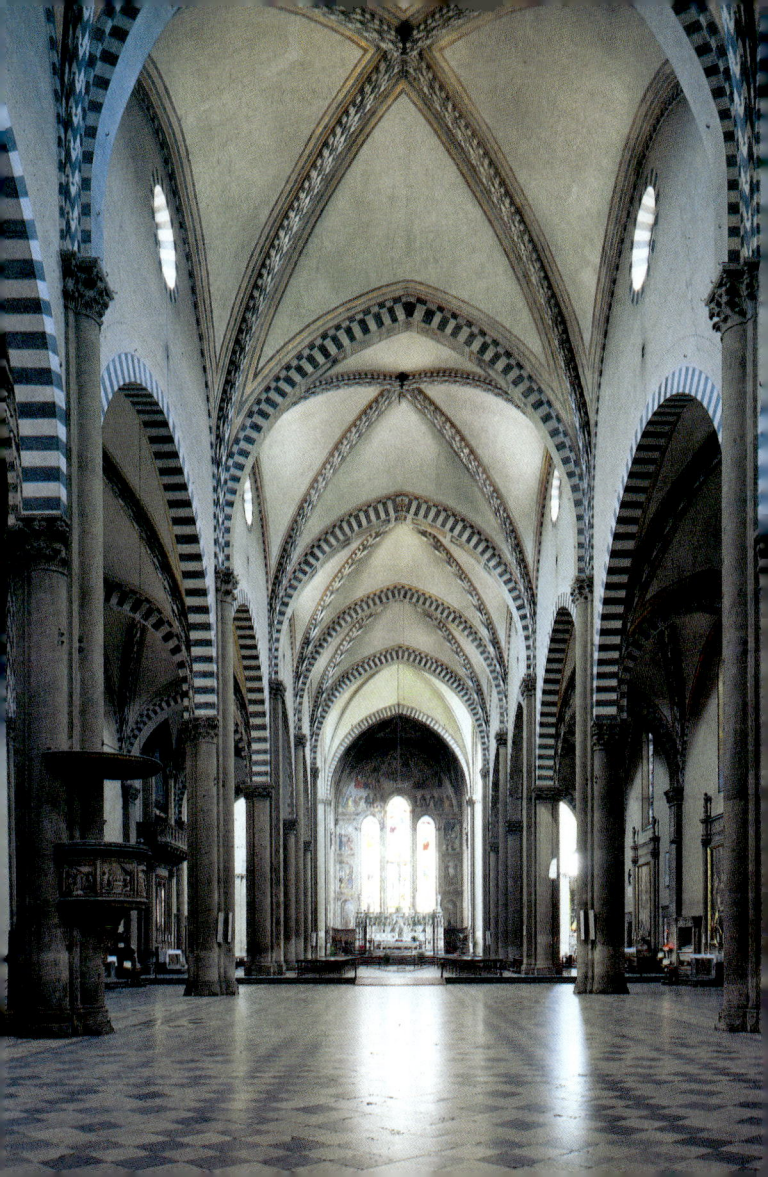

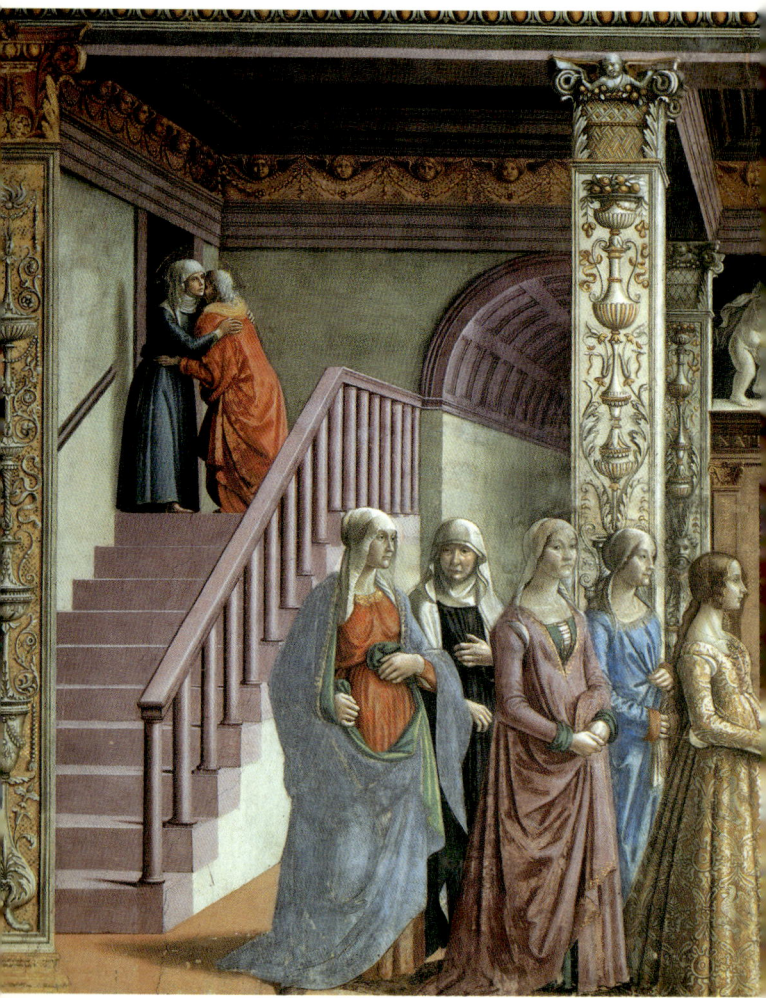

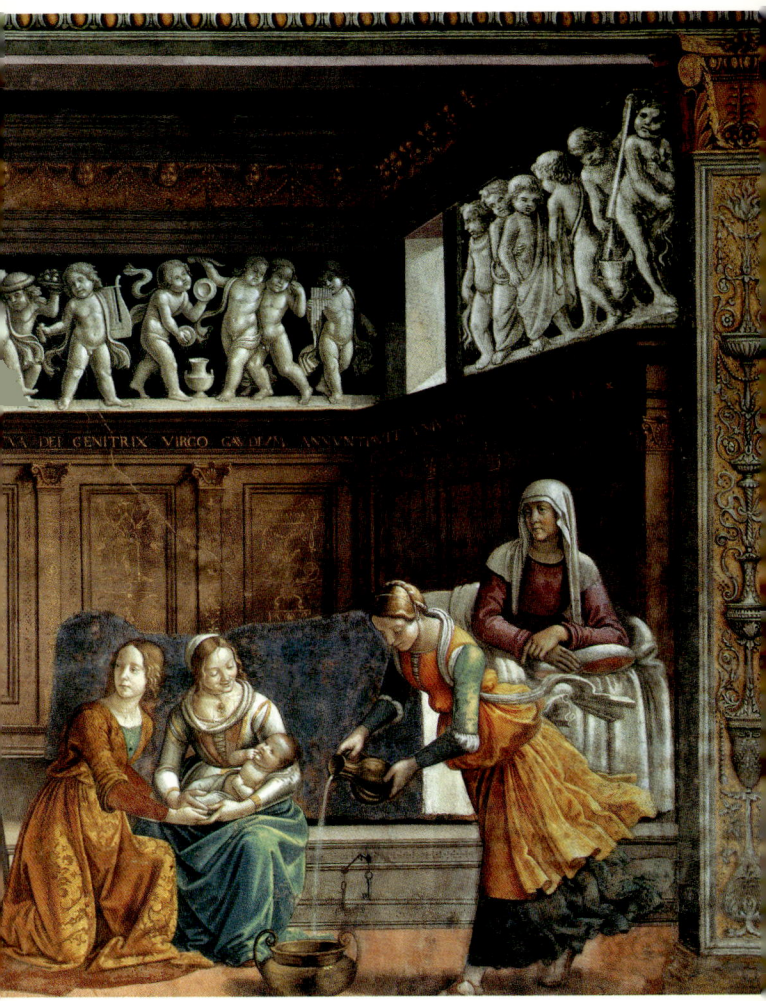

siastics, among whom pope Martin V on his way back from the Council of Constance, who stayed there for six months and in 1419 consecrated the new Santa Maria Novella; in 1434 pope Eugene IV, fleeing Cola di Rienzo's disorders in Rome, was greeted with great honours on June 23rd of that year in the convent of Santa Maria Novella. He led the solemn procession that, starting from the dominican church and progressing on a raised, richly decorated walkway allowing to cover the entire itinerary without being in touch with the crowd, on March 25, 1436 arrived at Santa Maria del Fiore to consecrate the new cathedral. In 1439, the council, which had been going on for several years in Ferrara (where a violent plague was raging), was moved to Santa Maria Novella: aiming at re-uniting the two great catholic and orthodox Churches, the council was the first step of the pope's policy, which he had also promoted during his Florentine residence, to bring the Christian Churches nearer to each another. Thus personalities from the East arrived in Florence, producing a strong impression on the entire population and the artists, as we can see in Benozzo Gozzoli's frescoes in the Medici palazzo chapel and even in the tomb of the patriarch of Constantinople who died during the council and was buried in the right transept of the church. Already on the occasion of Martin V's stay with his suite of cardinals, the Florentine republic had had built in the convent an apartment that could fittingly cater for such guests, located on the west side of the so-called Grand cloister, executed between 1335 and 1360. When Leo X de' Medici came to Florence in 1515 to restore his family's rule, he stayed in that apartment, and the chapel was newly decorated by Ridolfo del Ghirlandaio and Pontormo. The role of official guest house of the signoria was also confirmed by important lay guests, such as emperor Frederick III in 1452 and king Christian of Sweden in 1472.

Although at the center of such relevant events, Santa Maria Novella was still not entirely finished. As a matter of fact the façade had just a par-

*preceding pages*: Domenico Ghirlandaio, *Nativity of the Virgin*, fresco in the main chapel

Polychrome stained-glass window in main chapel made according to a design by Domenico Ghirlandaio, detail showing St John the Baptist

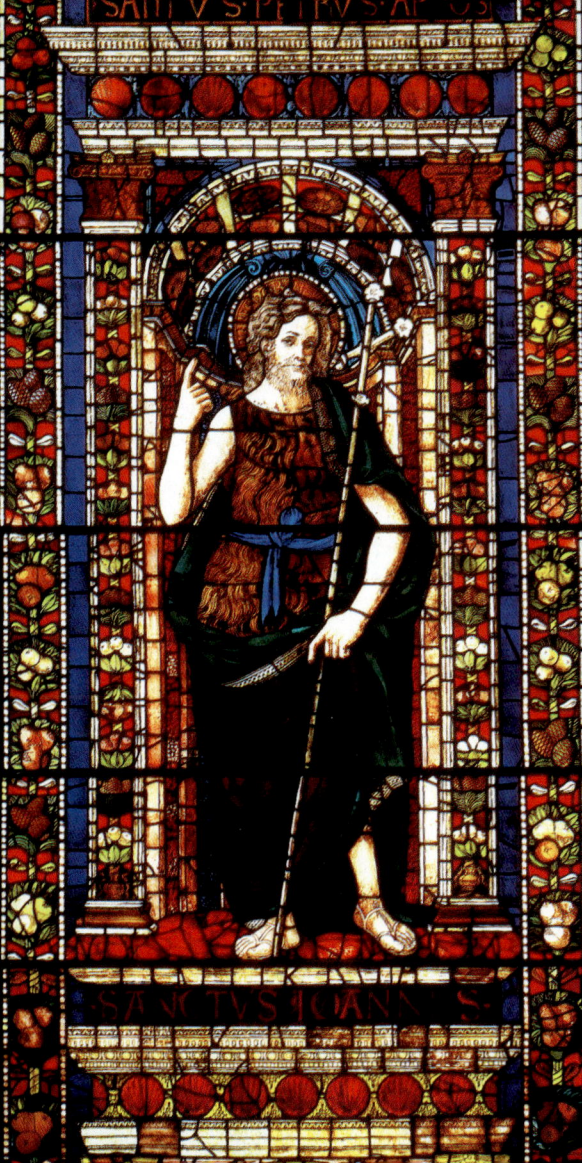

SANCTVS·PETRVS·AP·OS

SANCTVS·IOANNES

tial green and white Prato marble incrustation in the lower order, paid
for with funds specifically defined by Turino di Baldese's will in the scheme
of the major works during Jacopo Passavanti's priorship. We owe to
Tedaldino de' Ricci's bequeath the great central eye whose stained-glass
window, on Andrea di Bonaiuto's cartoon (c.1365-1367), figures the *Incoronazione di Maria* with the patron's portrait. In 1458, Giovanni di Paolo
Rucellai – whose name can be read under the tympan of the church – commissioned the great architect Leon Battista Alberti to complete the decoration of the façade in the new style, making Santa Maria Novella the only
great Florentine church to have a façade entirely completed before the four-

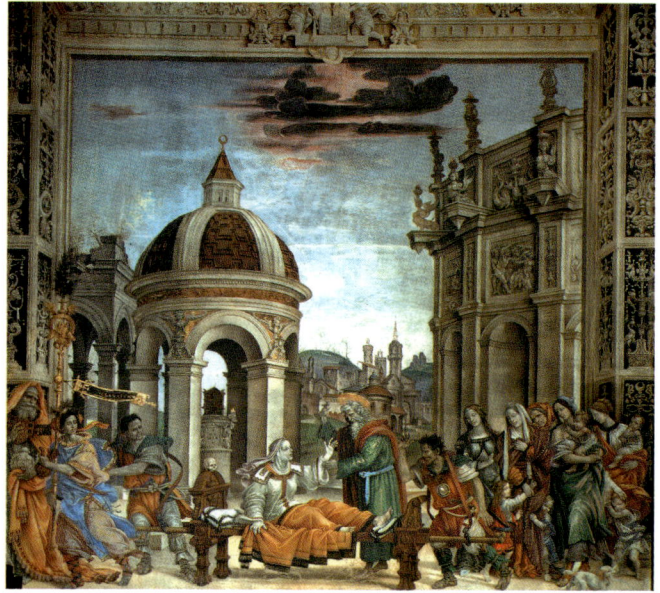

Filippino Lippi, *St John the Evangelist Resuscitating Drusiana*

Giovanni della Robbia, sacristy lavabo (1498)

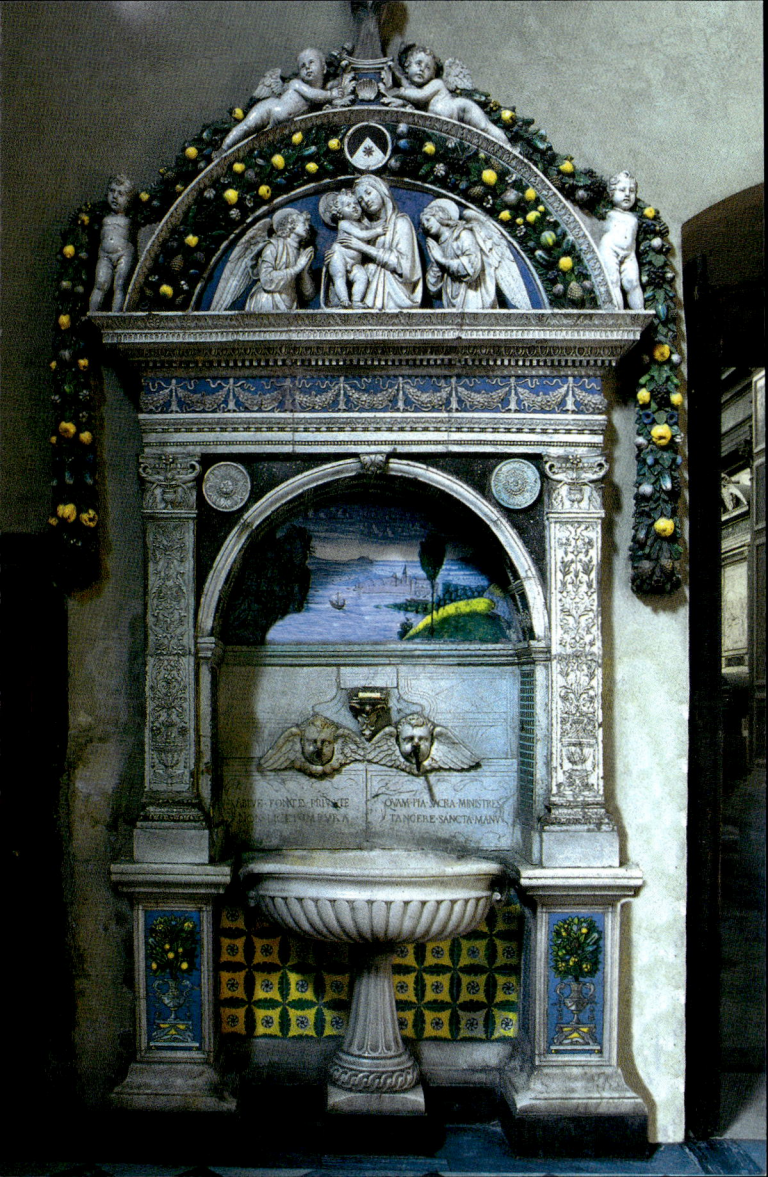

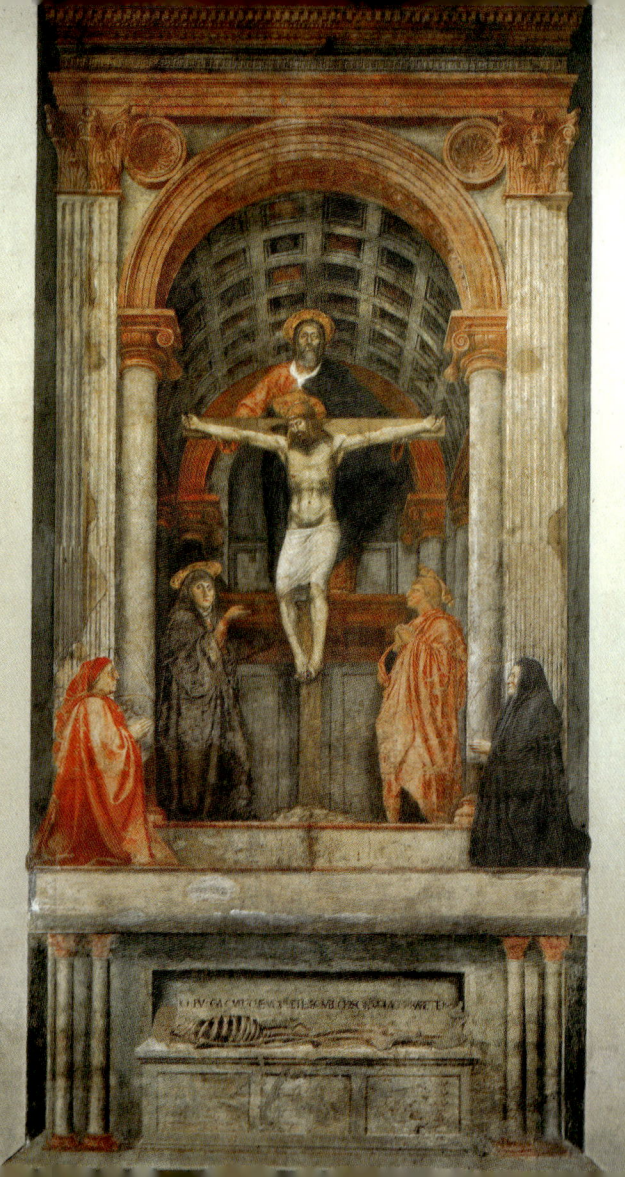

teenth century. Those were also the years of the miraculous event leading to the Ricasoli family's construction of the so-called della Pura chapel, with its entrance from the right side aisle. According to legend, the image of the Virgin, preserved in one of the tombs on the outer wall of the church, addressed two children asking them to be cleaned of the filth and the spider webs covering it.

In 1567, with Grand Duke Cosimo I's great restoration, under Giorgio Vasari the structure of the church underwent important alterations reflecting the ferments ripening in Counter-Reformation circles and which were to leave their mark on several Florentine churches. The "bridge" separating, according to the medieval custom, the presbytery from the area of the faithful was torn down, the nave and side aisles altars (one for each span) were added and made alike, frescoes were covered over and the gothic windows were changed to the Renaissance style.

Between 1857 and 1861 the church and convent underwent further alterations. The architect Enrico Romoli performed a neo-gothic restoration; the ogival windows were re-opened and provided with new polychrome stained glass, Vasari's altars were combined with gothic elements, the tombs were reduced to two parallel rows set between the pilasters of the nave and the side aisles, and the inside and outside bi-chromy was further emphasised.

During twentieth-century restorations, fragments of very precious frescoes were brought to light, such as in 1940-1941 the paintings by Orcagna found inside the Main chapel, and in 1951 the lower part of Masaccio's *Trinità*.

Masaccio, 1427 fresco of the *Trinity*, showing the Lenzi family in adoration

# San Niccolò

*via San Niccolò*

The church, already mentioned in a bull of Lucius III dated March 3, 1184, stood on the left bank of the Arno not far from the Ponte alle Grazie, on the slopes of the hill crowned by San Miniato al Monte, to whose abbot it was subordinate since its foundation. Later San Niccolò was absorbed in the new walls, where in fact the porta a San Niccolò was opened in 1324. Given the great increase of the population of the area, it became a parish church in 1374. The same year Gregory XI placed the olivetan monks in charge of San Miniato al Monte, which on the occasion lost several of its subordinates, San Niccolò being one of them. The jurisdictional transformation, which occurred at the same time as a gothic restructuring, soon led to many family patronages, a token of the population's deep attachment to the parish. The most important families who owned palaces and residences in the area, thanks to the chaplaincies they acquired in the

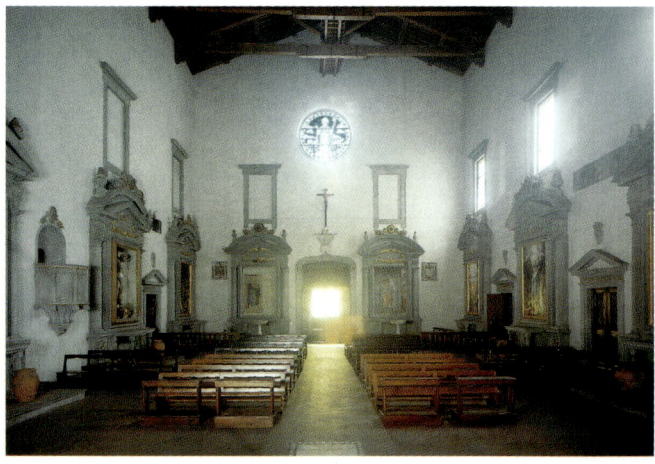

Fresco by Florentine maestro, first half of 15th century

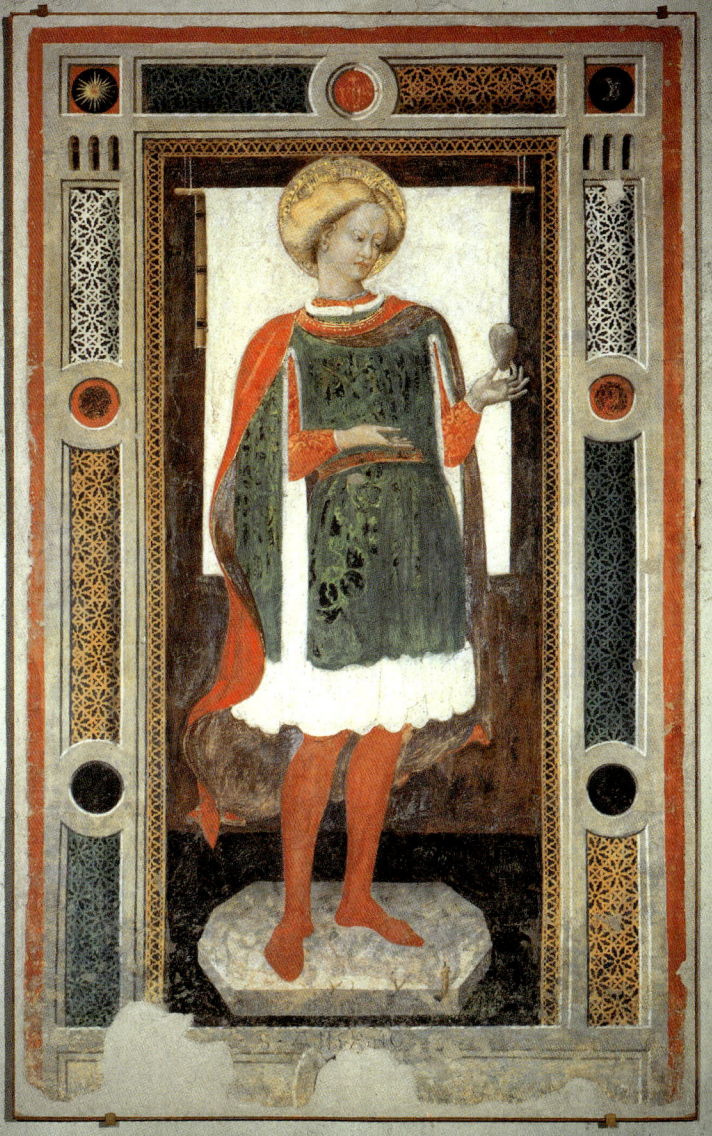

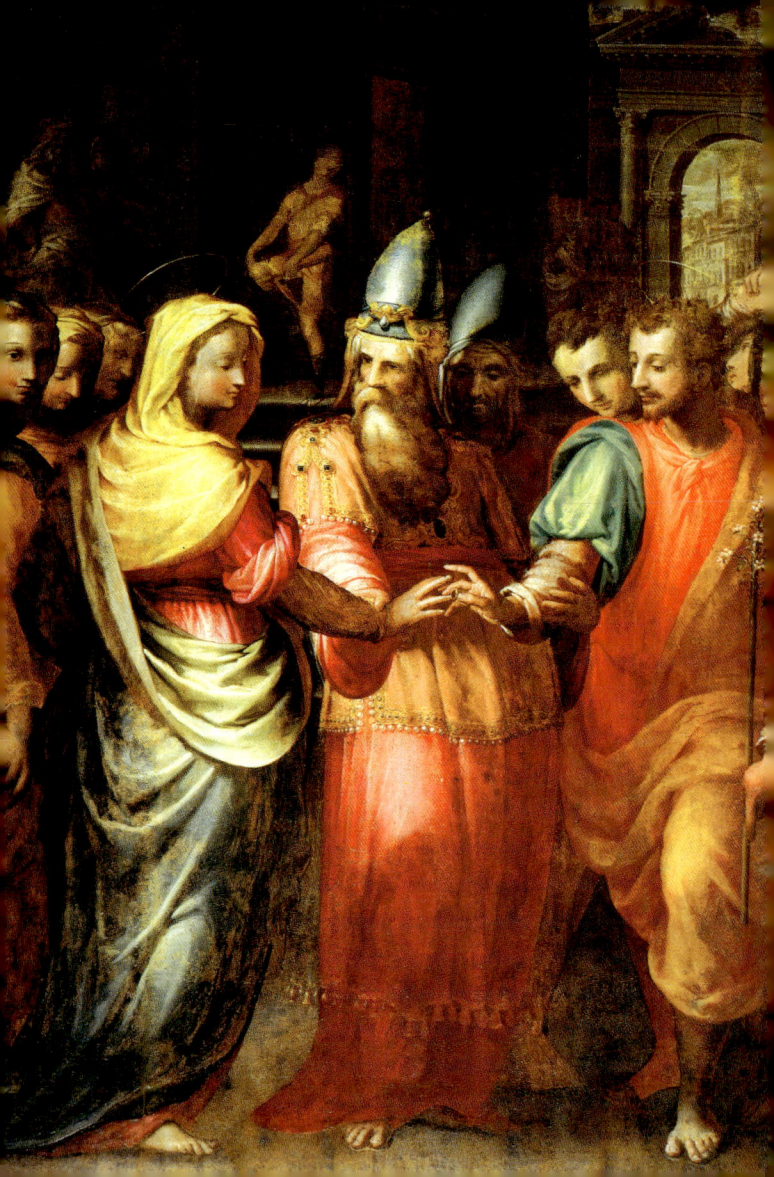

church, embellished it with altars and works of art. Outstanding among the main patrons were the Falconi della Zampa, Ugoccioni, Pieri, Guardini, Bianchi, Porcellini, Nasi and especially Da Verrazzano and Quarantesi families, the latter's coat of arms appearing on a handsome, pale blue-grey stone shrine in the style of Michelozzi. In 1525 San Niccolò became a priory. In 1530, according to tradition, Michelangelo, whom the Medici factions loathed for his deeds in defence of the Florentine Republic, found shelter in a small room at the base of the bell tower. During the XVIth century the entire church was further embellished; in 1582 Masseo de' Bardi re-consecrated it, perhaps after a renovation following the ruinous flood of 1557; in 1587 Vasari performed a radical decorative renovation. After the floods of 1966, restorations brought to light a number of gothic frescoes under Vasari's structure.

Francesco Morandini known as Il Poppi, *Marriage of the Virgin Mary*

# Santa Croce
*piazza Santa Croce*

The Franciscans' earliest contacts with Florence probably go back to the first decade of the XIIIth century, although their first Florentine residence was not officially established until 1218, with pope Gregory IX's endowment of the small hospice near porta a San Gallo where they had settled.

This same pope is also responsible for the first document mentioning the new church dedicated to the Holy Cross: a bull written in 1228, two years after saint Francis' death. Following the Franciscans' custom, the new settlement was located outside the walls, in a still sparsely-populated district, rather insalubrious owing to the presence of activities such as tanneries and dye-works. The original church must have been small and in a style in line with the order's institutional poverty. Throughout the XIIIth century the complex gradually expanded, while the district grew. The presence of a monastic settlement also contributed to the large-scale design of the city, both as regards roads, in the connection with the Rubaconte bridge (later alle Grazie) and in the construction of the adjacent walls, now become corso dei Tintori. Raised to protect the convent from the overflowing of the Arno, it was the first organised section along the banks of the Arno. The Franciscans' accrued role in the city led to enlarging the church. To that purpose the commune of Florence, April 8, 1295, decreed the impressive yearly allocation of one thousand two hundred florins "for the glory and the decorum of the city of Florence". The foundation stone of the new construction was laid the following May 3rd. A large contribution came from legacies and bequeaths of many faithful belonging to the leading local families: the Albertis, Spinellis, Benvenutis, Strozzis, Baroncellis and Mellinis. Whether or not the building should be attributed to Arnolfo di Cambio, the importance of Santa Croce in the city in the XIVth and XVth centuries can be clearly seen in the contributions of the many outstanding artists, Cimabue and Giotto, Taddeo and Agnolo Gaddi and Orcagna, Giovanni da Milano and Lorenzo Ghiberti, as well as the role played by Michelozzo and Brunelleschi in the convent. During the fourteenth century the church lost its original severe style; the powerful fam-

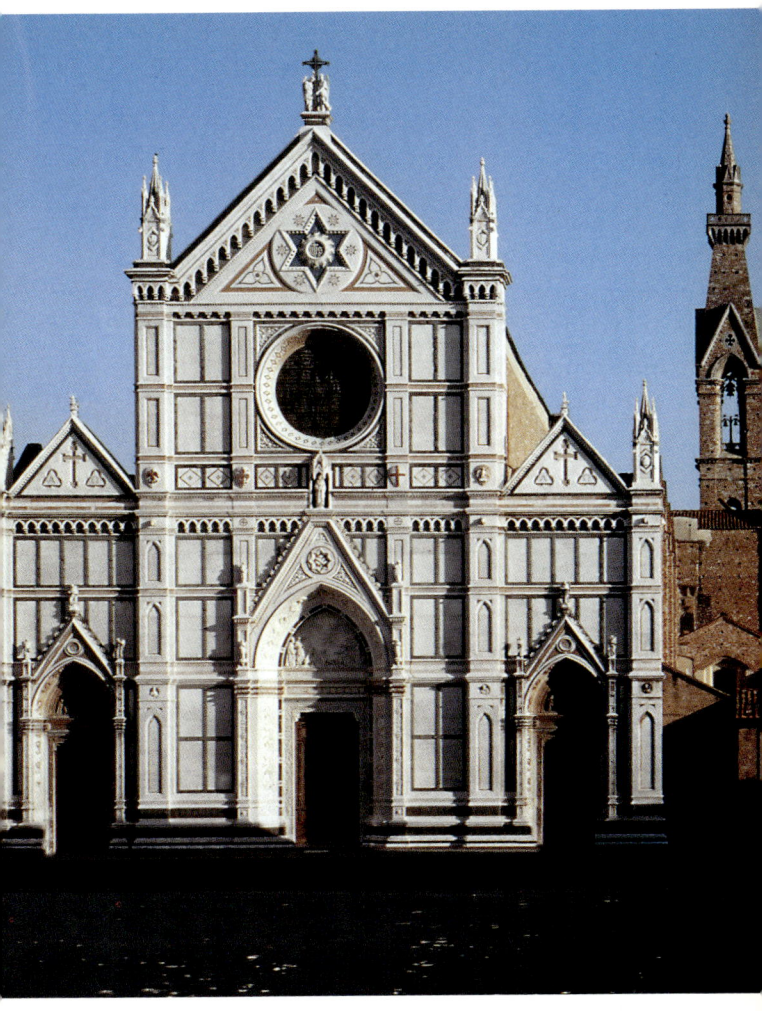

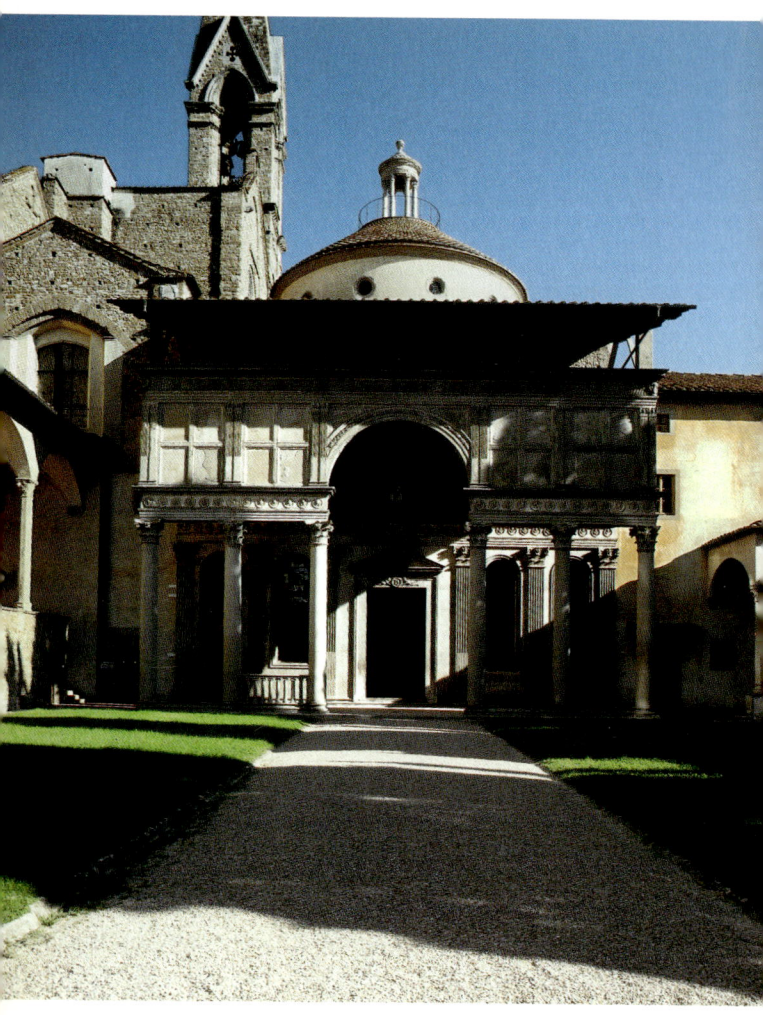

ilies vied in furnishing and decorating chapels and tombs, which would gradually cover the entire surface of the church. Work for the very modern chapel the Pazzi family commissioned of Brunelleschi began around 1430. Located in the first cloister adjoining the church, after various vicissitudes it was completed in the sixties, just before the family fell out of grace when the conjuration against the Medici family failed. Precisely towards the mid-fifteen-sixties, Cosimo I charged Vasari with a radical transformation of the church. The architect removed the gothic partition and arrayed the large niched altars along the nave and the side aisles, offering one of the first examples of the new conception of sacred space making headway in Counter-Reformation circles. At the same time – and by an odd coincidence just two centuries after an unheeded deliberation of the signoria dated December 22, 1369 deciding to assemble in this church the bones of the main standard-bearers of Florentine culture like Dante, Petrarch and Boccaccio – Santa Croce was seen as the pantheon of the elect spirits, with the construction of the monumental tomb of Michelangelo, who died in Rome in 1564 and was solemnly translated here a few years later. It is surrounded by illustrious tombs and cenotaphs that Ugo Foscolo in his *Sepolcri* celebrates in epic terms: those of Leonardo Bruni and Carlo Marsuppini, of Galileo, Vittorio Alfieri and Gioacchino Rossini, including the cenotaph dedicated to Dante in the last century. It may well be this aspect of its identity that saved the church from the radical purist re-inventions which the cathedral and Santa Maria Novella underwent towards the mid-nineteenth century. However, the taste of that period can be seen on the façade by Nicolò Matas (1853-1863) and Gaetano Baccani's imaginative bell tower (1847). The location of the ensemble below the level of the Arno, that had so worried the fourteenth-century Franciscans, entailed disastrous consequences with the 1966 flood, which damaged or even destroyed many works of art. Among these, nearly a symbol of the entire city, Cimabue's martyred *Crocefisso* which in its fragmentary recovery now hangs in the refectory, recalling the sad event.

# Santissima Annunziata

*piazza della Santissima Annunziata*

The Florentines' true sanctuary to Mary, the Santissima Annunziata's origin is closely bound to the story of the Seven Founders, the young scions of noble families who, after having withdrawn to a hermitage on monte Senario, in Florence built a hospital for pilgrims with its oratory. The site chosen for the construction, called Cafaggio – meaning an area featuring a luxuriant vegetation – was outside the walls near the porta di Balla, on the main road leading from the north to the cathedral. The founda-

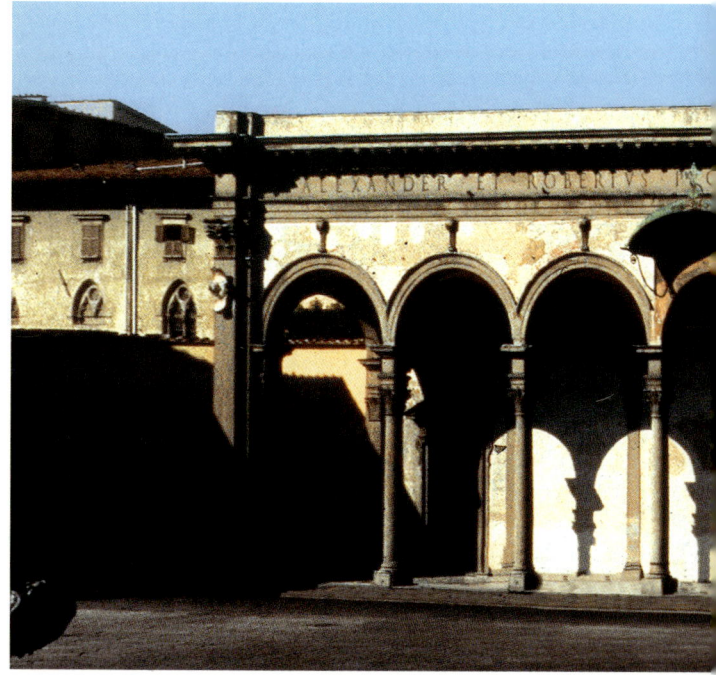

tion stone of the oratory was laid September 8, 1250. Only two years later an *Annunciazione* was painted on the wall, said to be by the hand of a certain Bartomoleo, who would have been helped – to portray the the Virgin's features – by no less than an angelic intervention. Precisely because of the prodigy said to be behind its creation, the image quickly became the object of great popular veneration. The oratory soon proved inadequate for its fame and, by the second half of the XIIIth century, it was enlarged thanks to the large sums collected, as well as to the indulgences popes Innocent IV and Clement IV promised to whoever would give to the work. Chiarissimo Falconieri, for instance, to repay his sin of

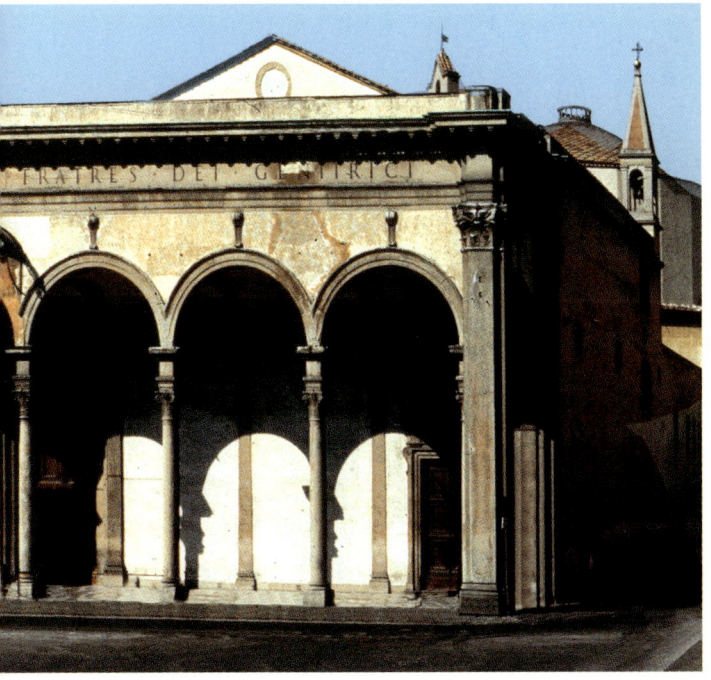

usury, became such a great benefactor of the church that in several documents he is even quoted as its founder. In 1288 Niccolò IV, and then Boniface VIII, placed the convent under the protection of the Holy See. The structure was radically transformed between 1444 and 1477, due to the Medici family's special favour, who owned extensive building land in this very area. It was at that time that the Chiostrino dei Voti – in front of the thirteenth-century façade – and the large apsidal tribune, designed by Leon Battista Alberti, were built. In 1448 the miraculous image of the *Annunziata* was placed in a chapel – a shrine commissioned by Piero, Cosimo the Elder's son – , consecrated January 8, 1452 by cardinal d'Estourteville. Then Antonio Del Monte, Leo X's legate, consecrated the renovated church January 17, 1515. In 1559, the Pucci family began building the great narthex portal on the piazza, finished in 1601, completing the portico system Brunelleschi had begun in the nearby Ospedale degli Innocenti. In 1600 the marble altar Piero de' Medici dedicated to the Annunziata was replaced by a rich embossed silver altar Ferdinand I commissioned to fulfil a vow for his son Cosimo's recovery. It was at that time that the great veneration spread, as evidenced by the success of the ritual procession connecting the Marian Impruneta sanctuary to the Santissima Annunziata, in front of which a fair was held and still is on that occasion. Popular devotion was expressed in countless life-size, gorgeously dressed wax statues, figuring the church benefactors, exhibited on solemn occasions. During the seventeenth century the church chapels, maintained by important families, were entirely refurbished. Adjoining the Santissima Annunziata lies the chapel of the Corporation of Saint Luke, a very old Florentine artists' association; in 1563, Cosimo I raised it to the dignity of Academy of Design, and its premises, where several art exhibitions were presented, remained here until 1784. In 1805 pope Pius VII celebrated a mass during which the church was declared basilical; the next year he bestowed on it the superior title of *Alma Basilica*, with further privileges.

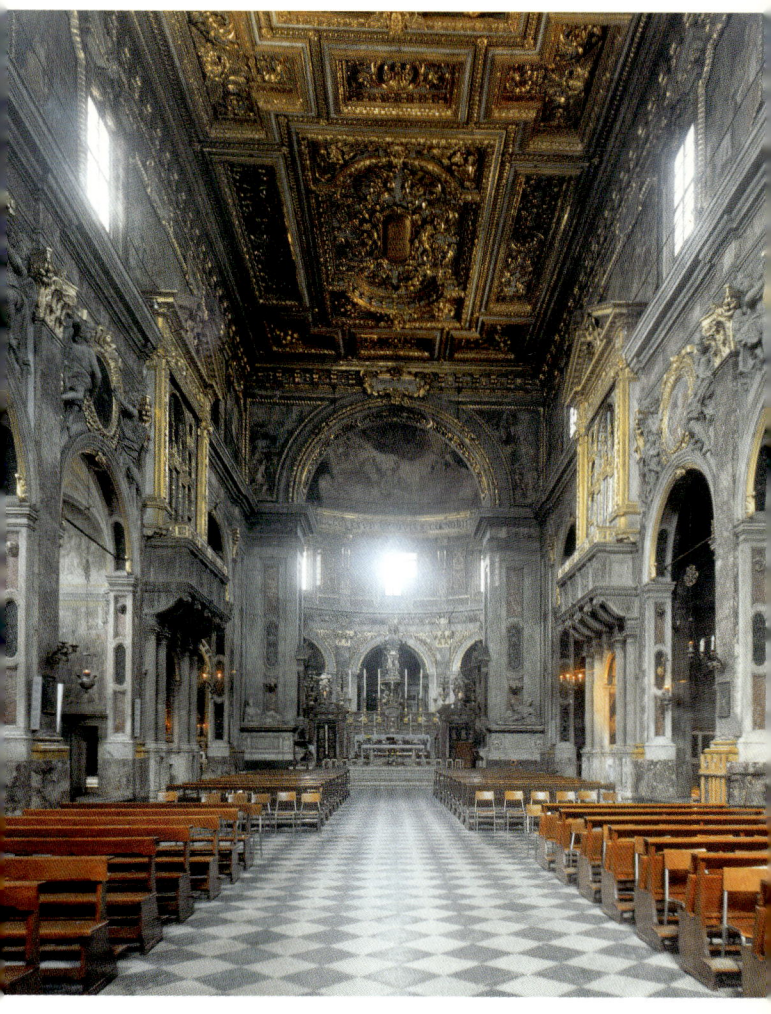

# Santo Spirito
*piazza Santo Spirito*

By the mid-XIIIth century, the left bank of the Arno was definitively enclosed by the walls the commune built between 1173 and 1175. Inside, in the most close-knit villages near the gates to Pisa, Siena and Rome, remained vast unbuilt districts having the kind of minor structures related to productive activities unsuited to the city centre, such as those connected with the wool industry. Nonetheless, important religious complexes like Santa Felicita, San Jacopo, San Felice had already been there for some time. The area between the roads to Pisa and to Siena, in reference perhaps to that type of building found there, was called "caselline". In 1252 the construction of the new Santa Trinita bridge would further promote a rather autonomous urbanisation compared to the city across the river, its point of reference and nucleus being, aside from the roads, the large conventual ensembles.

An act of 1250 documents the sale of houses with land and vineyards

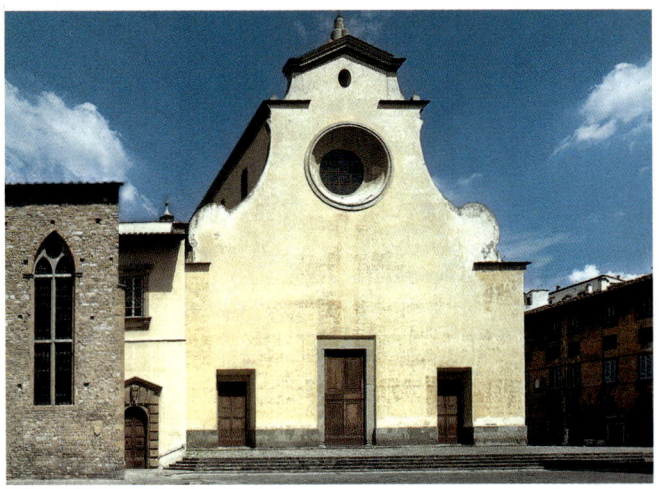

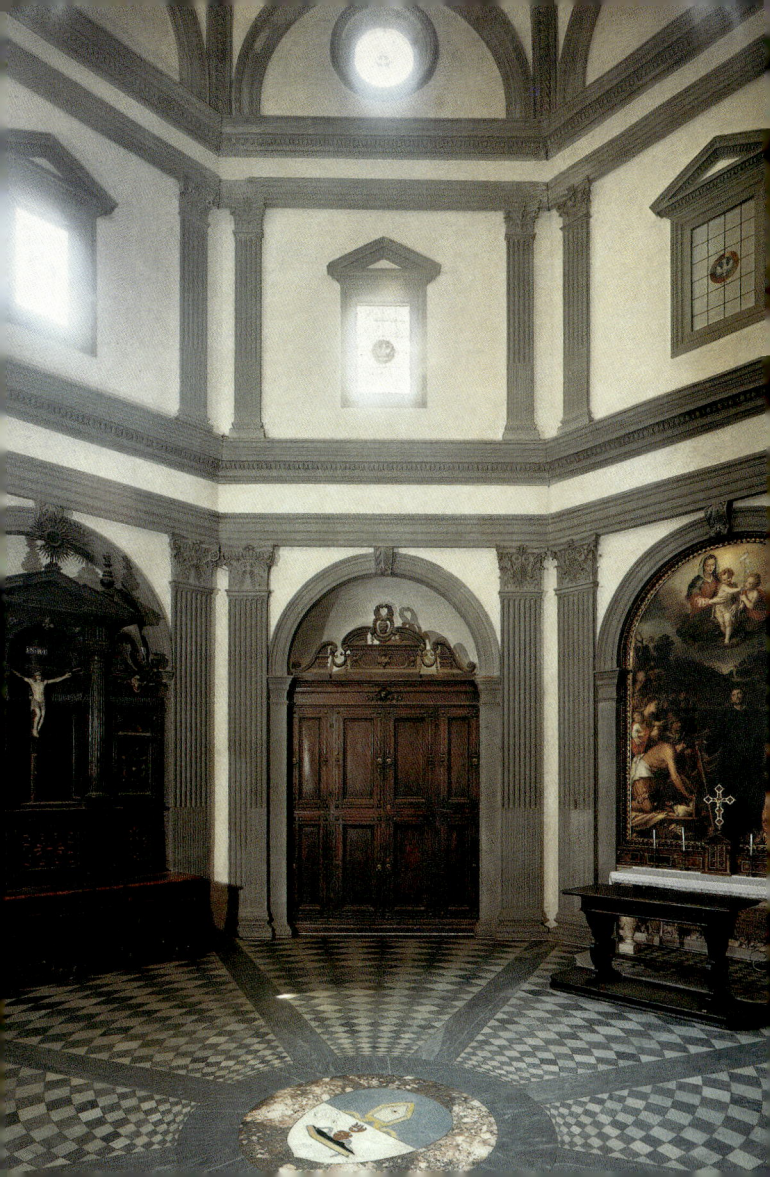

in the above-mentioned Caselline area, where there may already have been a small church dedicated to Saint Romulus. The sellers were Spinello Accolti and Omodeo di Guido Speziale, and the buyer fra Aldobrandino, an Augustinian of San Matteo a Lepore in Arcetri. The convent of San Matteo was the augustinian monks' first official settlement in Florence. Pope Innocent IV backed them, acknowledging them in 1243, and just a year later urged them to a more active apostolate, which may be why they decided to leave the hill of Arcetri for the city. The pope actually promised indulgences to anyone who would contribute to the building of the new church. By 1252 the first construction work on

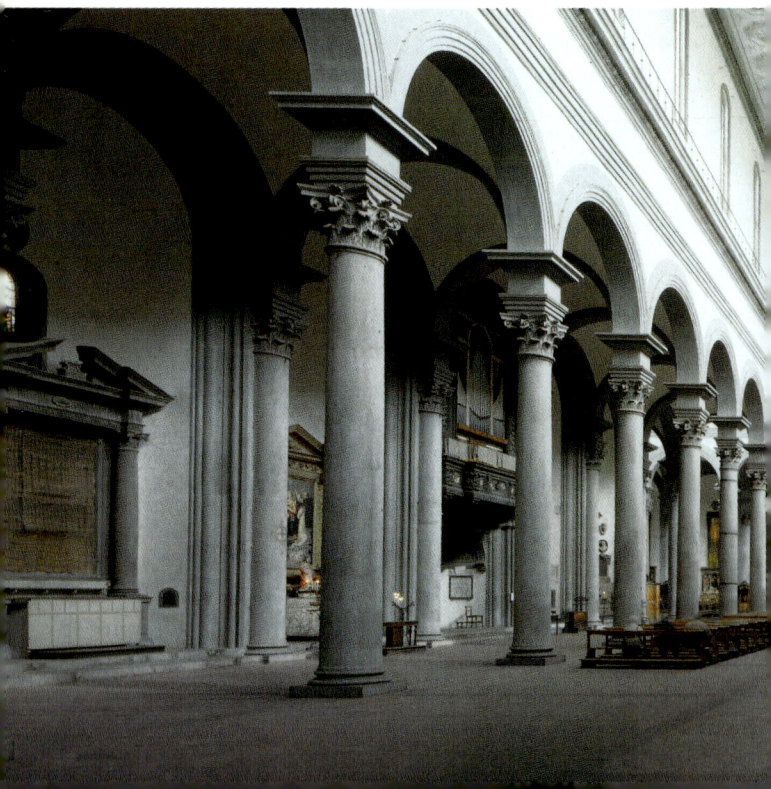

the recently purchased land and its dedication to the Virgin Mary, All Saints and the Holy Ghost are documented. The church – we can imagine it being in the severe Tuscan gothic style – was completed around the end of the next decade owing to further purchases of land. At the same time the piazza in front was being created which, like those of the greatest monastic orders, represented for centuries the only examples of defined city piazzas in Florence. The acknowledgement of its public role is proved by the secular use of the piazza of Santo Spirito as a market-place, as it still is today. The Augustinians' role in Florence was however essentially that of promoting since the late XIIIth cen-

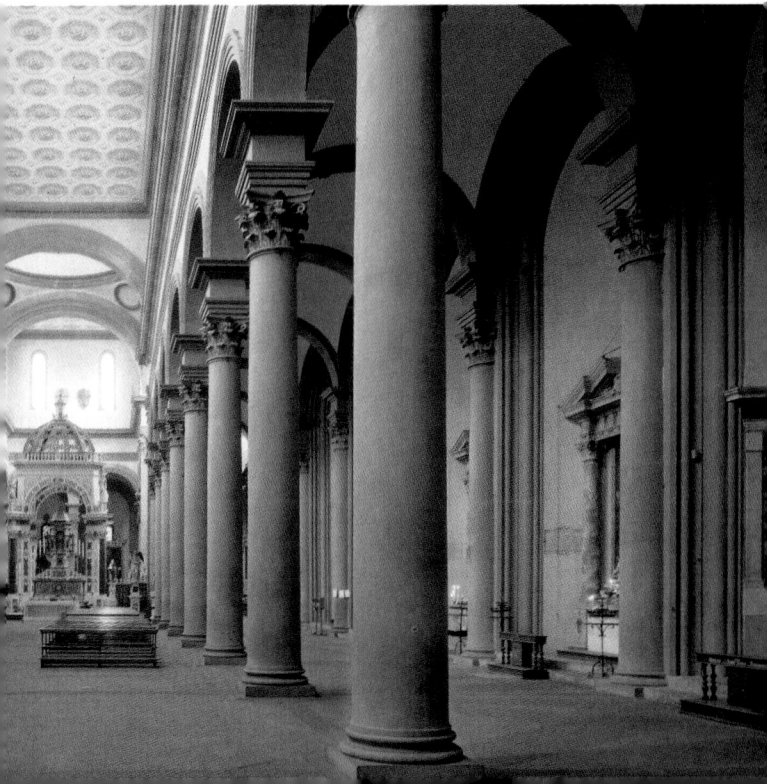

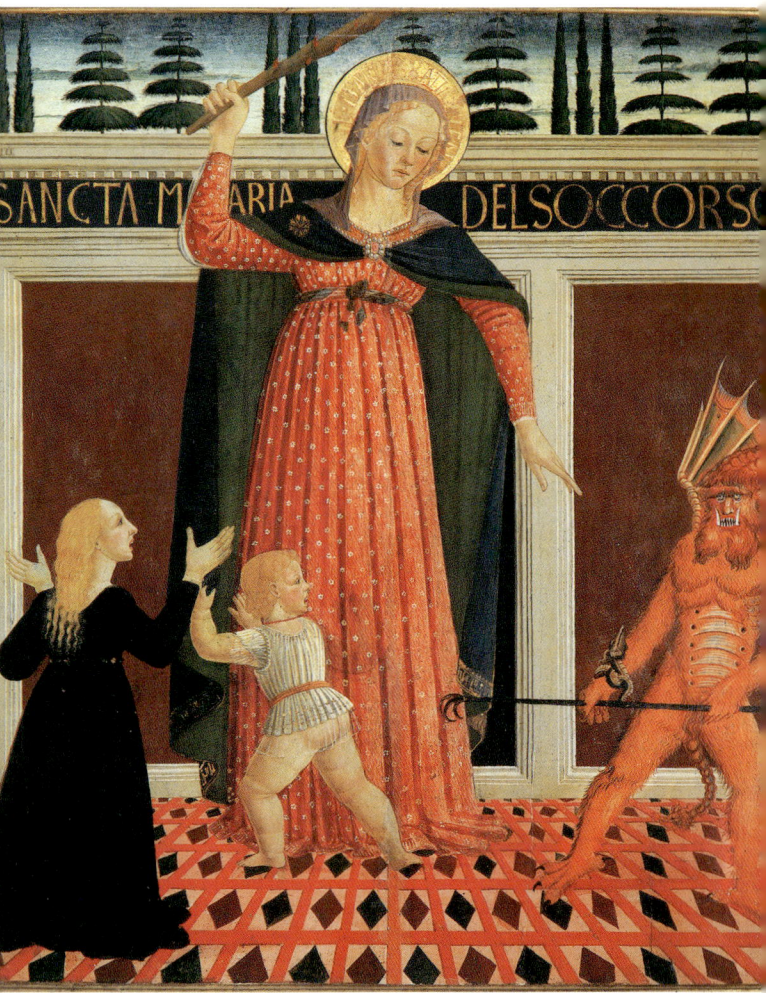

tury, by the institution of the "Studio Generale dell'Ordine" (*General Study of the Order*), theological and philosophical studies based on augustinian principles.

A great number of intellectuals were directly in touch with the Saint Augustine friars; From Petrarch to Boccaccio, to the politically-committed Humanists of the late fourteenth century like Coluccio Salutati, who had close ties with the erudite Augustinian Luigi Marsili. In the next century the presence of men of letters belonging to Lorenzo the Magnificent's circles was significant: it is not a coincidence if precisely at Santo Spirito on June 18, 1497 the excommunication of Savanarola, a Dominican of San Marco and an extreme exponent of anti-humanist rigourism, was publically announced.

In 1292 a further enlargement of the convent and the space in front was undertaken. In 1343 the district officially assumed the church's name and coat of arms, a white and gold dove on an azure field. Confirming the importance the augustinian church had assumed, as of 1397 the commune allocated a yearly amount for the construction of a new, larger sacred building. This was in thanksgiving for the victory won at Governolo by the Holy Alliance of Italian states over the Viscontis of Milan, precisely on Saint Augustine's feast-day. In fact, building did not begin until thirty years later, thanks to the tenacity of fra Francesco Mellini nicknamed "lo Zoppo" (the Lame) and his vehement sermons. Then in 1428 five "workers" were elected as well as a superintendent, Stoldo Frescobaldi, from the patron family of the main chapel in the old church. Filippo Brunelleschi was in charge of the project, presenting a first version in 1434. The most characteristic feature of the design – revolutionary in many aspects – was the reversal of its orientation, the façade being turned towards the Arno and connected to it by a large piazza, openly monumental in intention. The clash between the interests of the owners of the houses the execution of the plan would cause to be demolished, and delays in funding (in spite of a provision of the commune in 1435 imposing a tax on every left-bank family having a chapel in the old church) did not allow the building to begin, according to

Maestro of the Nativity Johnson (attr.), *Madonna del Soccorso*

the primitive orientation, until 1444. Brunelleschi, who died two years later, had probably begun one of the chapels in an angle of the right transept. At the same time, as usual, the old church was left standing so as to not interrupt litugical activity. In 1452 Antonio di Manetto Ciaccheri, already working on nearby San Felice, was put in charge of the works that had been interrupted, and he pursued them until his death in 1460, interpreting Brunelleschi's indications in a fashion that many considered irreverent. Work went on with other master builders until a traumatic event that in a way hastened it. On March 15, 1471 after the Sacred Representation in the old church, a fire broke out that seriously damaged it, destroying altars, paintings, paraments and codexes. The signoria allocated new funds both to repair the old building and to hasten the constuction of the new one on Brunelleschi's design. At the end of the eighties the church could be said to be completed, with numerous "betrayals" of Brunelleschi's conception, especially leaving apparent on the outside the cylindrical volumes of the chapels, even extending them on the façade by opening four doors, rejecting the traditional central door. At the same time, what was left of the original gothic complex was progressively eliminated, except the old refectory towards the piazza and the Corsini family chapel. In 1489 Lorenzo the Magnificent had the bell tower torn down also to make room for a new sacristy designed by Giuliano da Sangallo and not completed until 1495 by Antonio del Pollaiolo and Salvi d'Andrea. In the meantime Simone del Pollaiolo nicknamed il Cronaca, and the same Giuliano built the vestibule with its great antique-style lacunar vault favoured by Piero the Fatuous, who succeeded his father Lorenzo in 1492.

In 1503, designed by Baccio d'Agnolo, the construction of the new bell tower began: it would not be inaugurated until thirty years after the architect's death in 1571, with the installation of a bell Cosimo I donated, a confirmation of the Medici favour towards the augustinian church. It was inaugurated at last with a solemn ceremony November 11, 1573, although it had been served for nearly a century. In 1564 Bartomoleo Ammannati undertook the so-called Great cloister, completing the north side five years later. Here the alternating trabeations and curved arches recall Sangallo's cloister in front of the Santa Maria

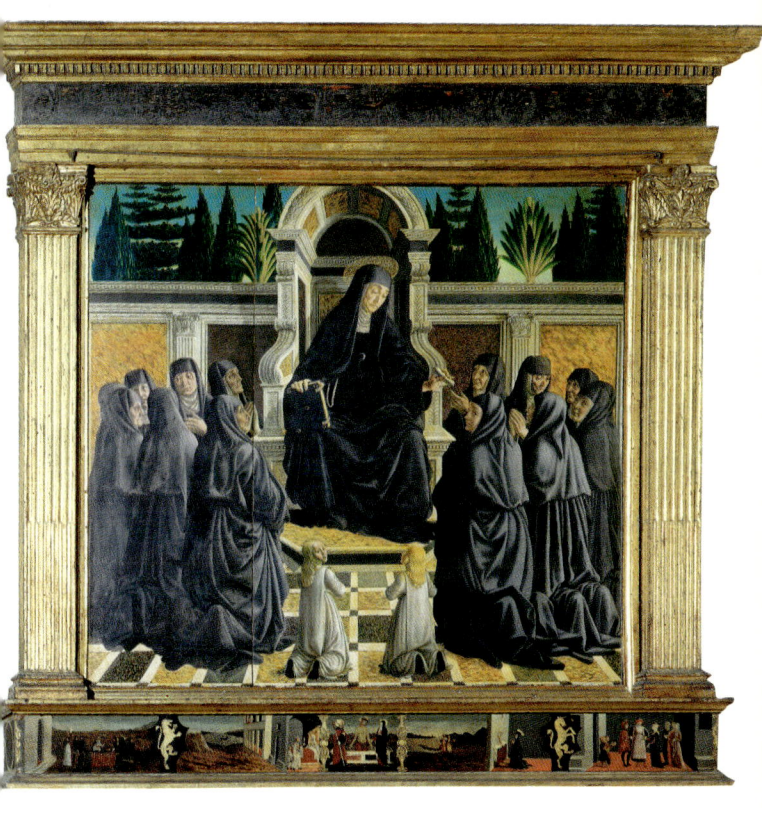

Francesco Botticini, *St Monica Founding the Augustinian Order*

Maddalena de' Pazzi church. Towards 1580 the large new refectory was built orthogonally to the gothic one, on a design by Alfonso Parigi the Elder (Ammannati's nephew), with frescoes by Bernardino Boccetti; after both of them died in the nineties, the other sides of the Great cloister were gradually completed. In 1620 Giulio Parigi, Alfonso's son, within the space already defined by the existing bodies (among which the chapter house built in 1560 in the place of the old one, beside the sacristy) undertook to build the so-called cloister dei Morti, in a rigourous neo-fifteenth-century style typical of many instances of early seventeenth-century Florentine architecture and art, a reaction to mannerist excesses. The cloister was completed around 1660, nearly twenty-five years after the designer's death. The lantern as well, crowned by the gilded bronze sphere mounted in 1602, is perfectly consistent with the dome above it which had been completed in 1482 on Salvi d'Andrea's design.

Between 1600 and 1607 the grandiose choir was executed under the dome, with the high altar in the centre and the monumental ciborium – obeying the dictates of the Counter-Reformation – , one of the most elegant examples of the Florentine art of working semi-precious stones. In its structure this choir perfectly illustrates the role of liturgical "machine" that Bernardo Buontalenti's choir in Santa Maria del Fiore must also have played in another form.

The chapels, thirty-eight in the final church, began being assigned in the fifties to the families having a chapel in the earlier church. A certain conformity was sought in the decoration – no doubt on Brunelleschi's indications – , so that it would somehow relate to the architectural layout. Yet by the end of the century a disparity in the choices appeared; over the two next centuries the interpretations of Brunelleschi's cylindrical surfaces were to greatly differ. The names of the families connected with the chapels of Santo Spirito are more or less those of the Florentine aristocracy settled at length on the left bank of the Arno: Frescobaldi, Ridolfi, Pitti, Capponi, Nasi. During the eighteenth century two lateral volutes were added to the unfinished façade and in 1792 it was painted with architectural elements, later removed in the nineteen-seventies' restoration. The Santo Spirito Augustinians saw the suppression of their own convent in 1808 and then, after a reintegration, once again in 1866 when Florence was capital. After various destinations, in 1900 a large part of the conventual complex was taken over by the military district, which still occupies it today, restricting visits.

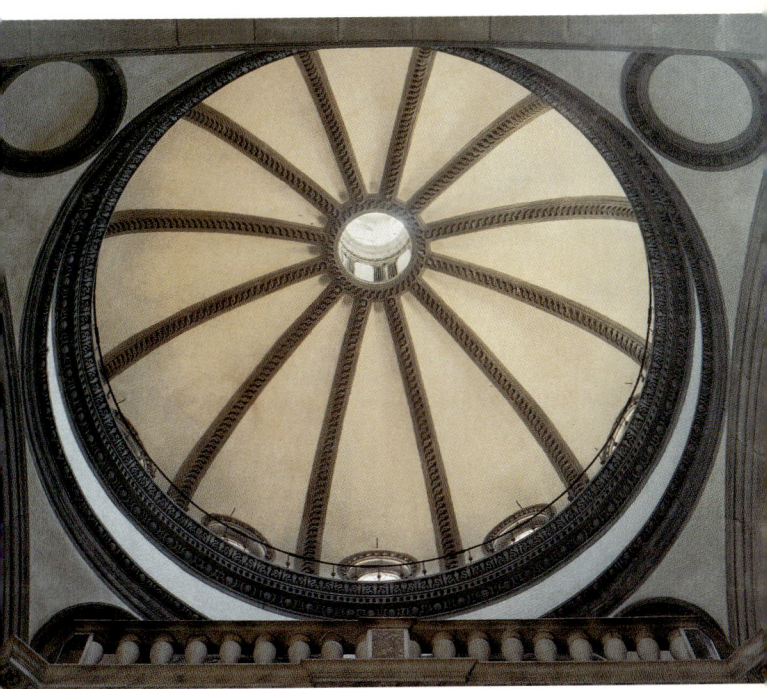

# Santa Maria del Carmine

*piazza del Carmine*

By the first commune wall, where it turns at a straight angle towards the Arno, next to the road between porta San Frediano and the homonymous camaldolese monastery, the Carmelites installed their Florentine premises in the late XIIIth century. The order, whose rule pope Honorius III acknowledged in 1226, could only boast a few other settlements in Tuscany, at Pisa since 1248 and at Siena since 1256.

They owed the opportunity to settle in Florence to a bequeath from Cione Tifa di Ranieri Vernaccia who, on April 30, 1267, left a large sum to his wife Avegnente for "Christ's poor". She hastened to give fra Matteo, the provincial prior of the Carmelites, a piece of land with houses near the Florence walls, committing herself to fund the construction of a church dedicated to saint Maria del Carmelo. After the bequeath was accepted, June 30, 1268, Giovanni de' Mangiadori bishop of Florence blessed the laying of the foundation stone, offering two relics: saint Cordula's head and saint Agnes' foot. Aside from these, there was a highly venerated image, held to be miraculous, called the *Madonna del Popolo*. It was said to have been brought from the East by a merchant, but instead recent studies have proven it to be a thirteenth-century work by Coppo di Marcovaldo, maybe at first placed on the high altar and after 1460 in the Brancacci chapel, at the rear of the right transept.

Soon the left-bank population showed its interest in the new church: important bequeaths were made allowing to pursue the work. The commune also played its part, re-opening in 1278 – on Ruggiero Soderini's insistence – an old door in the wall near the church and re-establishing the road connecting it with the church. Actually, lying outside the city nucleus the area had deteriorated, but in 1317 the friars were allowed to turn it into a piazza for the use of the convent. Nor did the authorities deny them the wide-spread custom of placing civil tombs in the church. After monna Tessa Biuzzi raised a funeral chapel for her husband Cambiuzzo in 1284, the chapter of the neighbouring San Frediano collegiate strived in vain to oppose the custom, as well as creating a controversy over the use of the bells. In fact the bell tower of the Carmine was not begun until 1396,

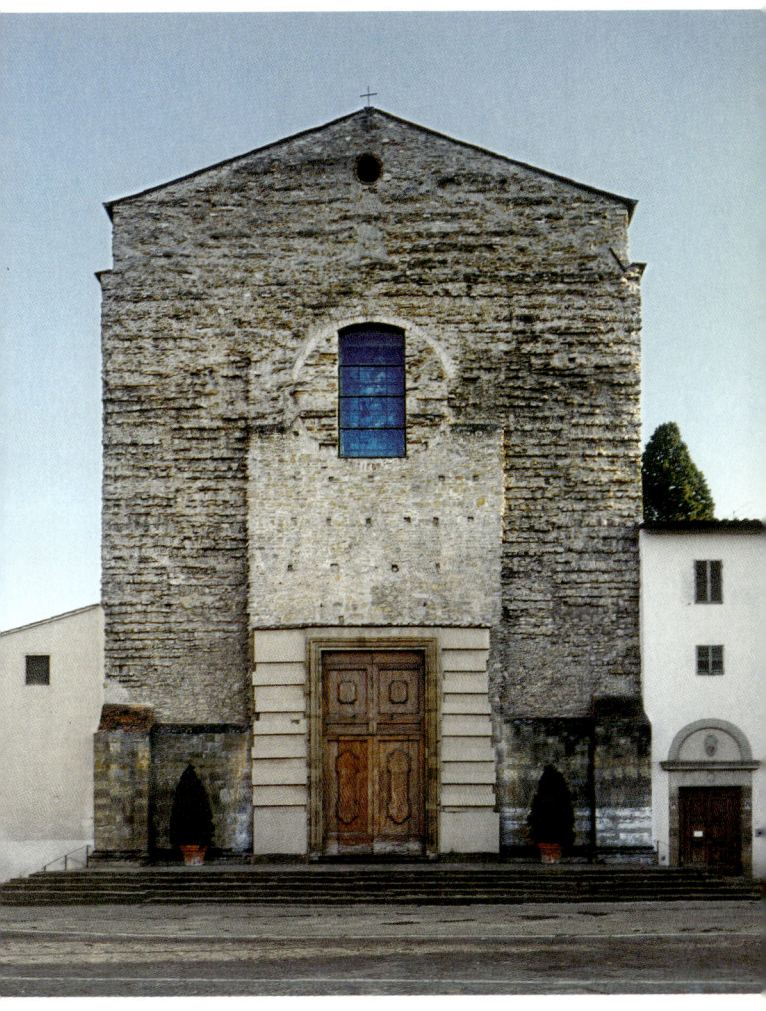

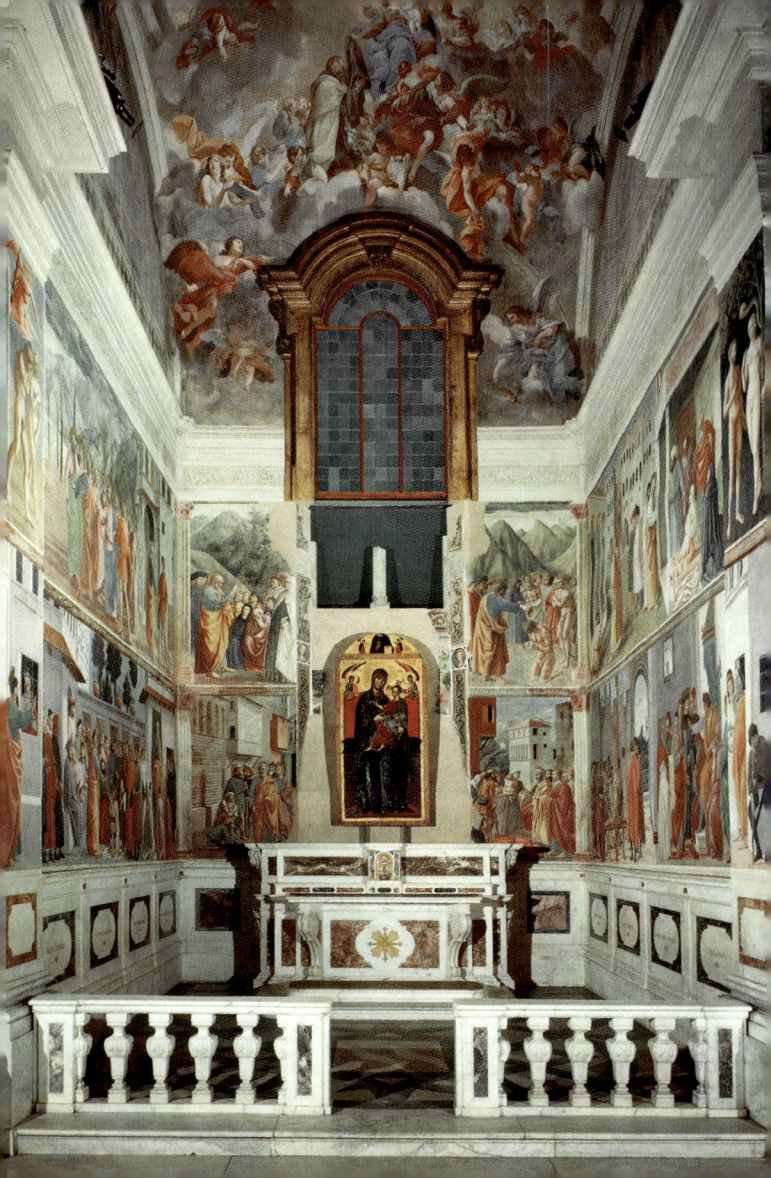

with the Alberti family's contribution, the work being completed in 1430. The attribution of the design of the church is uncertain, even naming Arnolfo or his disciple, a master Lapo, whereas we know that Francesco Talenti and the Carmelite Jacopo da Scopeto were in charge of the work during the XIVth century. In 1337 a cloister was built in the convent, in 1340 the new dormitory, in 1349 the library; even the church grew notably with the contributions of the greatest local families: Soderini, Serragli, Ardinghelli, Michelozzi and Brancacci. We owe to the wealthy silk merchant Felice Brancacci the commission to Masolino and Masaccio of the extremely famous cycle of frescoes in the chapel which by 1386 was under the family patronage. In time the importance of the convent had grown too: in 1324 a *studium* for the preparation to the carmelite rule was opened, and in 1333 it became the centre of the Tuscan communities of the order. In those years Andrea Corsini, of the noble Florentine family, was prior, and named bishop of Fiesole in 1349. His canonisation (in 1629) provided the Carmine with a gorgeous chapel where his remains were conserved, opposite the venerated *Madonna del Popolo*.

On April 19, 1422 another Corsini, Amerigo, bishop of Florence, finally consecrated the church, which was only completed in 1475. This solemn ceremony figured in a fresco by Masaccio in the portico adjoining the church, where there was a kind of portrait gallery of eminent Florentines, including Brunelleschi, Donatello, Giovanni di Bicci, Niccolò da Uzzano, and Lorenzo Ridolfi. These works could be seen until 1612, when they were covered with whitewash during the construction of the new cloister.

The single-nave church with an Egyptian-cross transept separated by a partition (also used as a stage for sacred representations) and a paving layered with funeral plaques had a raised choir and three chapels on each side of the main one. It was lit by ten large gothic double lancet windows, later reduced in a late-seventeenth-century re-structuring (1690-1704), but of which traces are still to be seen on the outer walls. The stone façade was embellished by a rose with a decorated stained glass window

View of the Cappella Brancacci

*following pages*: on the left, Masolino, *The Temptation of Adam and Eve*; on the right, Masaccio, *Adam and Even Driven from the Earthly Paradise*

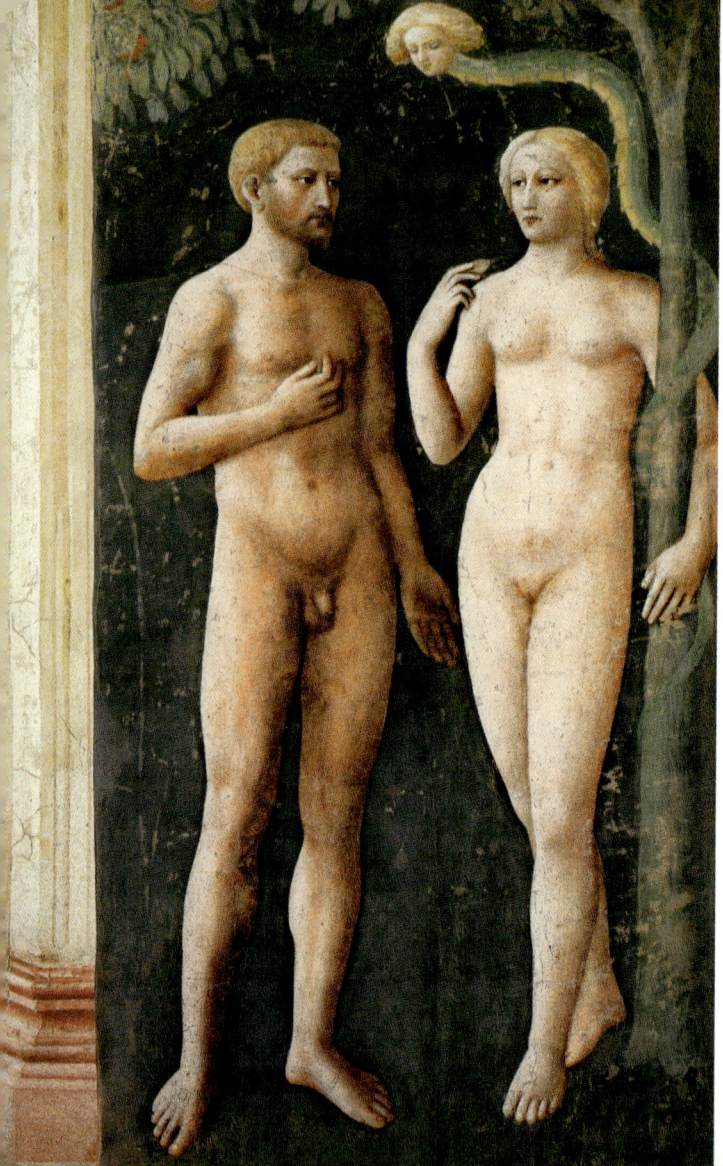

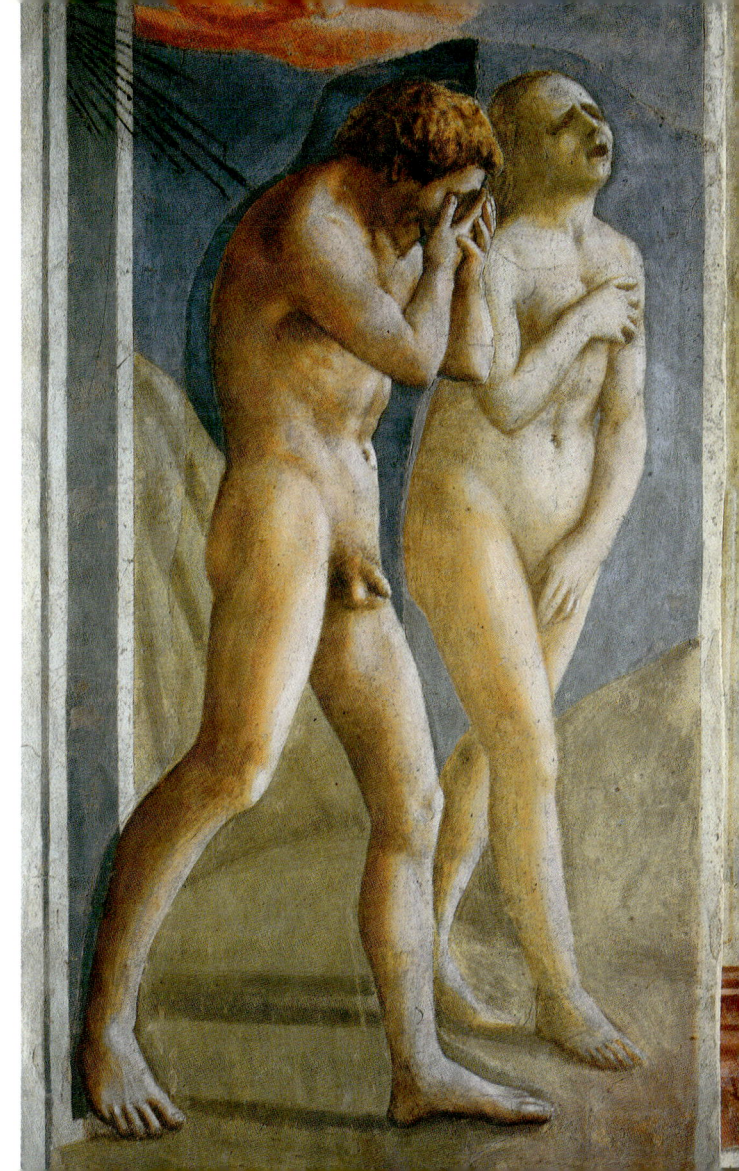

commissioned by the Micheluzzis, and whose outline surrounds the present rectangular window. The inside was rich with frescoes, separated by the main patron families' shrines.

As of 1568, in Cosimo I's renovation of Florentine churches, Giorgio Vasari significantly altered the church. The partition was torn down, the choir moved to the back, the layout and appearance of the chapels along the nave were unified and increased in number, sacrificing a large part of the frescoes. The patrician altars were enhanced with decorations and pictorial works, while – on a new symmetrical pattern – the figures of the *Apostles* were painted on the walls of the nave by various artists, including Passignano and Poccetti.

During the XVIIth century the embellishments and transformations of the church and the convent reached their climax with the Corsini chapel.

In 1763 the friars commissioned Zanobi del Rosso to design a carved wood ceiling with painted inserts to cover the fourteenth-century trusses. The expense and the features of the work provoked harsh criticism. Thus, when on the night of January 28, 1771 a violent fire, perhaps owed to an attendant's neglect, damaged the church and its furnishings, even some of the friars were suspected. Valuable works were lost, like the miraculous fourteenth-century wooden *Crucifixion* of the Compagnia del Chiodo, venerated as a protector against Arno floods and often carried in processions. The altarpieces, removed during the work, and the Corsini and Brancacci chapels were saved.

Owing to Grand Duke Pietro Leopoldo di Lorena's concern, all the dangerous structures were torn down – including the bell tower – and in just a few months the reconstruction of the church on a design by Giuseppe Ruggieri began. A narrower nave arose, in which five large niches were carved out on both sides, containing altars of the same dimensions separated by sections of walls (on a Jesuit architectural scheme), set between corinthian pilasters. Above, twelve niches with curved tympans to hold the statues of the apostles replacing the lost frescoes. Below, doors in walnut and confessionals executed in 1779 by Pietro Pertici.

The transept also was entirely altered, reducing the chapels next to the high altar from three to one, and creating large angular pilasters to support the pendentives of the vault, completed at the same time as the bell tower in 1772. The nave was covered with a barrel vault with windows corresponding with the altars, just like the arms of the transept. Giuseppe Romei's scenes, set in Domenico Stagi's bold perspectives, formed the pictorial decoration. In 1775 the church was considered completed and was consecrated September 15, 1782. The façade kept its severe, rough unfinished appearance. The chapels returned to their old splendour with the altarpieces saved from the fire and new paintings. Among the first we should mention the *Crocefissione con Vergine, Maddalena e San Giovanni* painted by Giorgio Vasari between 1561 and 1563 (now in the third chapel on the right); the *Cristo che risana il servo del centurione a Cafarnao* by Giovanni Maria Butteri dated 1584 (now in the fourth chapel on the left); the *Annunciazione* by Bernardino Poccetti dated 1601 (now in the second chapel on the left); the *Esequie di sant'Alberto carmelitano* by Bernardino Monaldi dated 1613 (now in the second chapel on the right), and last the *Visitazione* by Aurelio Lomi dated 1618 (now in the fourth chapel on the right).

Over the past two centuries large parts of the convent passed on to other uses. In 1966 the flood caused a great deal of damage, requiring important restorations. The last ones, executed as of 1989, were those of the Brancacci chapel.

# Ognissanti
*piazza Ognissanti*

The area along the north bank of the Arno beyond the antique centre – which today looks largely nineteenth-century – , by mid-thirteenth century still lay outside the walls built in 1173. Like in other outlying areas, the abundance of water and ditches encouraged the installation of artisanal activities and the close-set social fabric connected with them.

More or less across from where the church of Ognissanti would rise, the bed of the Arno was divided by a small sandy islet jokingly named the "Sardigna" which formed a sort of canal. The commune reserved the meadow along the river to the public for promenades, the livestock market and events such as horse races.

The construction of church and convent turned out to be decisive for the entire neighbourhood.

In 1239 the humiliated friars had come to Florence from the convent of the Bormiola of San Michele in Alessandria (Piedmont). Created as a lay movement of poverty, their lives were characterised by extreme moral and evangelical rigour, and were based on manual work, in particular the production of woolen fabrics and the working of glass. After first settling in the cistercian monastery of San Donato in Polverosa, whose small romanesque church still survives amidst the constructions of the Novoli district, in 1251 they were allowed to move closer to the city and especially to water, essential for their manufacturing activities. Previously the friars had purchased in the area of the meadow a piece of land and an oratory near a chapel dedicated to Santa Lucia; this enabled them to begin to build the new church and the convent, already completed by 1260.

The new church was dedicated to the Madonna and All Saints – precisely Ognissanti – and probably from the start was a parish church; it had a large nave covered with polychrome trusses and lit by tall arched windows – in part still visible from the outside – and ending in a T-shaped apse. During those years the manufacturing role of the order led to an increasingly closer relationship with the florentine commune; by 1278

Sandro Botticelli, *St Augustine in His Study* (1480)

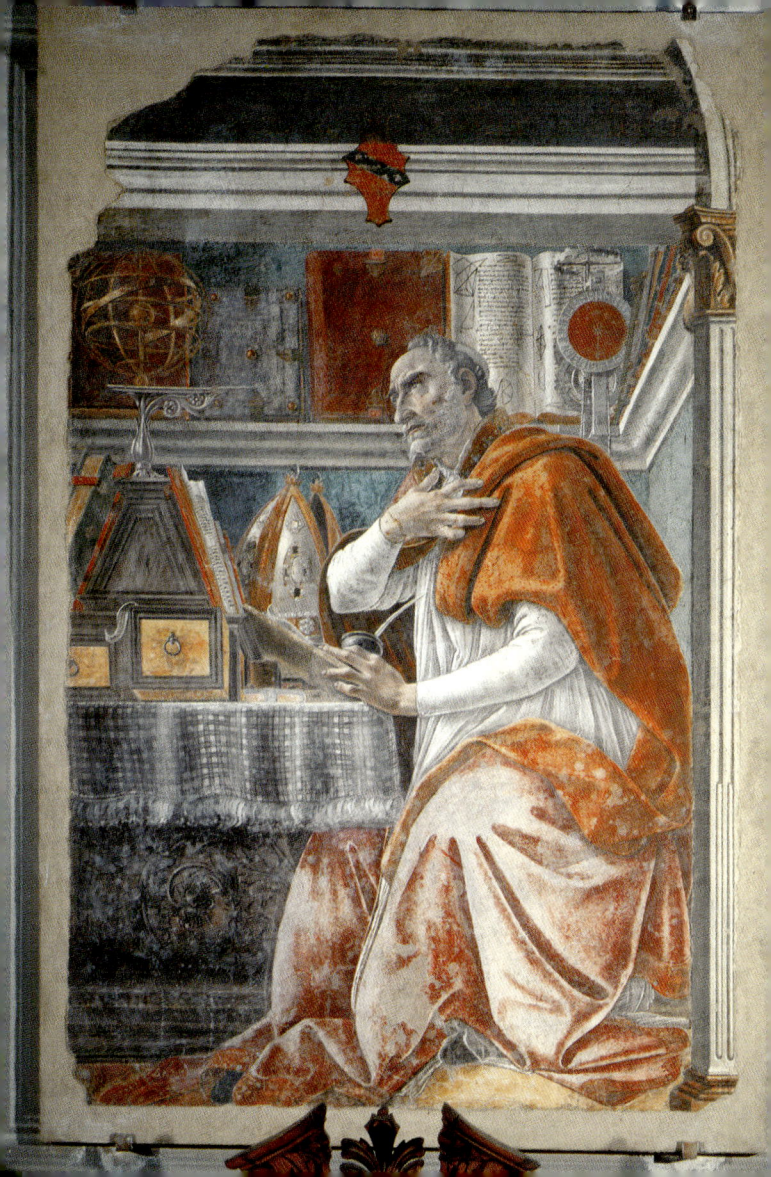

the Humiliated claimed they were willing to undertake in the neighbourhood the construction of housing for craftsmen, of a millpond and related mills, of a small port and of a postern of the walls by the river for their own use and that of the entire city. The commune entrusted them with prestigious public commissions.

The extensive conventual complex and its connected activities therefore influenced the appearance of the area and especially of the vast parvis of the church going down to the river, along which was performed processing requiring alot of space, like pulling bolts or certain stages of dyeing. The size of the piazza, even with slight architectural alterations, still today is more or less like the original owing to a decree of the commune establishing its dimensions.

After the Medici rule, important families came to settle in the neighbourhood, such as the Vespuccis and the Lezis who had the palace that still stands on the piazza built in the fifteenth century. Also artisans and artists arrived, like the goldsmith Maso Finiguerra and Sandro Botticelli's family – the Filipepis –, patronages and works of whom are to be found in the church. In the early sixteenth century the order began its decline, which suddenly was accelerated – in 1571 pope Pius V even decreed its canonic suppression – when a milanese Humiliated tried to kill Carlo Borromeo archbishop of Milan.

Already in 1561 the florentine Humiliated, greatly reduced in number, had been replaced by the minor friars of saint Francis of Assisi who, in those times of dissidence and reform within the franciscan order, had taken the name of minor observants. In Florence they owned the church of San Miniato al Monte alle Croci and the convent of Santa Caterina d'Alessandria which was given to the Humiliated in exchange for Ognissanti. The new tenants found the church and the convent in wretched condition and for twenty years performed restoration work and new costruction, largely supported by Eleonora da Toledo, grand duke Cosimo I's wife. The renovated church was consecrated August 1, 1582 by Masseo de' Bardi bishop of Chiusi, who had been a minor friar of the first community settled there.

That was when the two cloisters were built: the smaller one, with monks' cells, chapel, library, infirmary on the upper floor, and guest house, lodgings for families, service areas including the barber and, a curiosity, rooms used as prison cells on the lower floor; the large cloister – entirely rebuilt on the one the Humiliated had built – was used for official and collective functions, such as Chapter, refectory and apothecary's shop. Both were frescoed in the early seventeenth century.

In the large cloister, not subjected to clausure, episodes from saint Francis' life were represented. The medallions painted on the cells of the small cloister were on the other hand dedicated to franciscan saints and blessèds. The franciscan rule substantially altered the cultural and functional features of the convent: the parish remained, the cure of souls was enriched by theological and humanist studies supported by a rich library, to which was added a sector devoted to the study of Arabic and another to botany. The wool activity was partly maintained in the structures inherited from the Humiliated and a large vineyard was added to the extensive vegetable garden. The embellishing of the complex continued until the seventeenth century; in 1627, it was perhaps the architect Sebastiano Pettirossi, commissioned by Giovanni Battista di Ambra, who executed the cornice inside the nave that, with the upper windows separated by pilasters, entirely erased the memory of the Gothic construction. In 1635-37 the façade was done over on Matteo Nigetti's design. The new pictorial decoration, medallions with franciscan saints between the windows of the nave, is also seventeenth and eighteenth-century.

In 1769-1770, to cover the old trusses, the trellised false ceiling was made and painted during the next decade with *Gloria di San Francesco e di San Pasquale Baylon* by Giuseppe Romei; his also are the monochrome *Virtù cardinali* on the tympans. The architectural trompe l'oeil were the work of Giuseppe Benucci. When the paving was rebuilt, most of the sepulchral plaques were removed in 1744, except Antonio and Vitale de' Medici's, placed in front of the entrance, they having been the ones to fund the reconstruction of the façade.

*following pages*: Domenico Ghirlandaio, *The Last Supper*

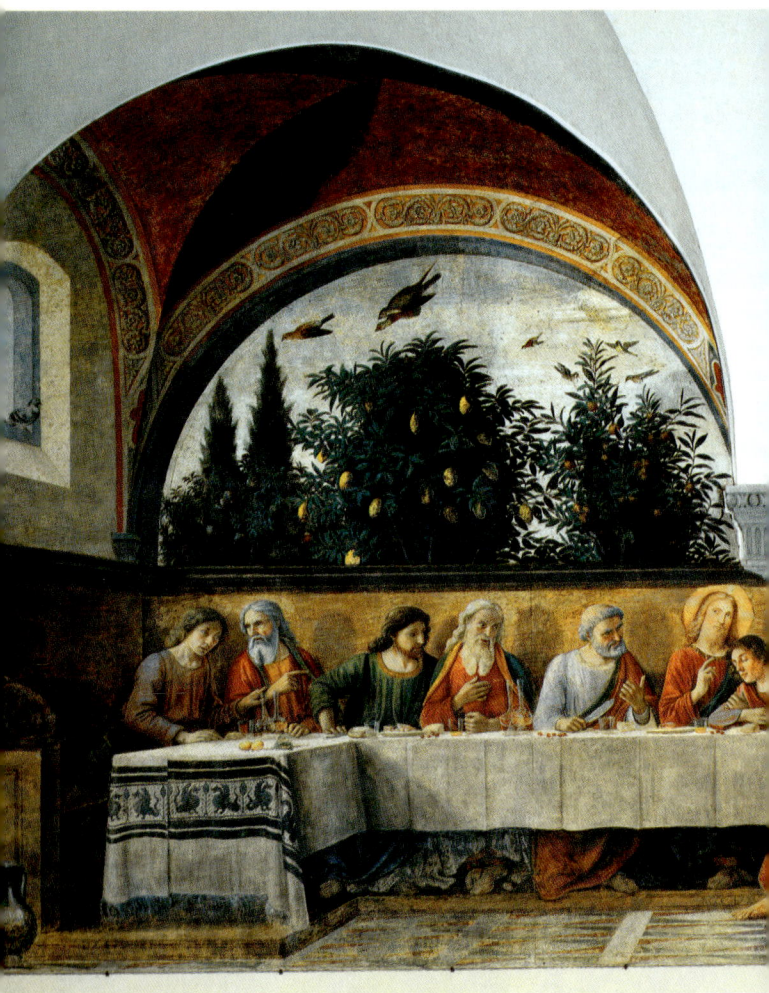

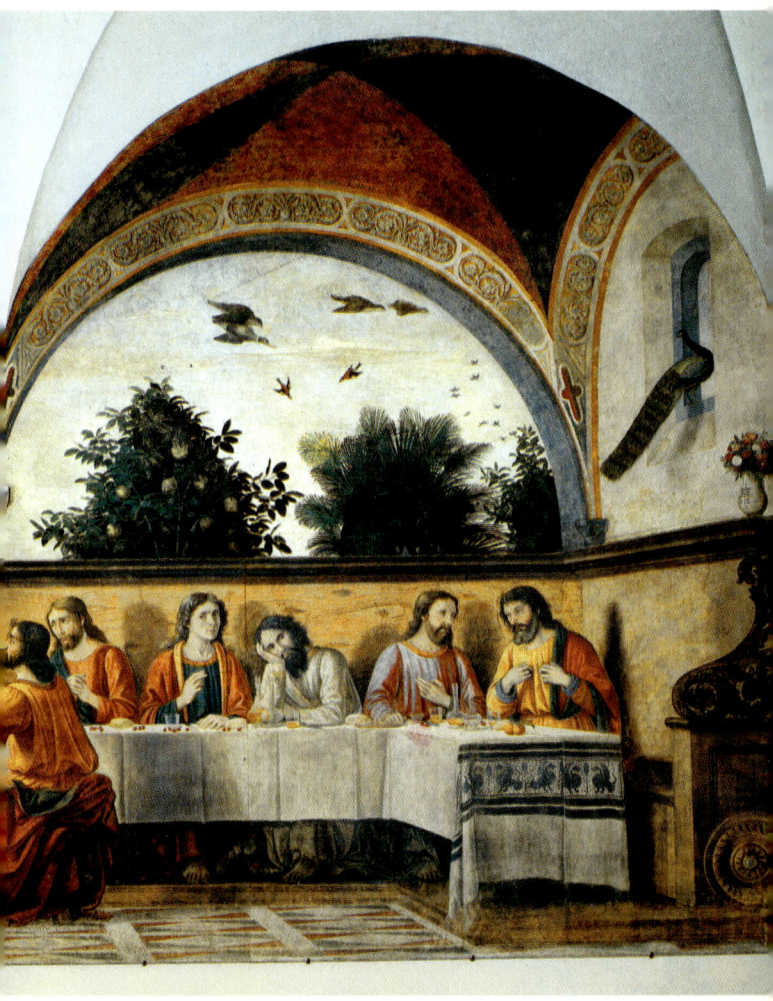

# San Marco

*piazza San Marco*

A monastery, probably the work of vallombrosian monks, rose in an outlying area by the North gate, perhaps upon an earlier small oratory. In 1290 the ensemble was given in concession to the Silvestrines who brought radical changes and considerable enlargements, officially sanctioned when bishop Francesco Monaldeschi laid the foundation stone, on May 8, 1299. Thanks to this bishop it immediately became a parish church. The new monastery was built and decorated with a wealth of means, as documented by the few elements still to be seen going back to those times, such as the works of Pietro Cavallini and Lorenzo di Bicci. The Silvestrines' fortunes lasted about a century and a half, until they were accused, first to Martin V and then to Eugene IV – both popes being ever-present in Florentine life – of manifest moral and spiritual decadence, as well as of misappropriation. Owing also to Cosimo the Elder's interest, who was consolidating the family's power and presence in the area (the same as the great Medici palazzo), the Silvestrines were then replaced by Dominicans from San Giorgio alla Costa. March 15, 1436 they made their solemn entry in San Marco. Only a year later Cosimo, after pope Eugene IV's penitential suggestion regarding a rather unorthodox acquisition of funds, commissioned his favorite architect, Michelozzo, to reface the convent. On his own initiative Cosimo added to the pope's suggestions the care of all the furnishings, including the prestigious library, thus quadrupling the advised investment. The restored church was solemnly consecrated January 6, 1442 in presence of Eugene IV, the celebrants being cardinal Acciapacci – who consecrated the surrounding walls – and fra' Bartolomeo Lapacci, who consecrated the altar dedicated to Our Lady of the Assumption. Outstanding figures for Florentine spirituality and culture stayed in the convent of San Marco, including Antonino Pierozzi, who ran the convent before becoming bishop of Florence in 1466 and was canonised barely sixty-four years after his death, becoming an important symbol of Florentine spirituality. More controversial but equally important was the figure of the Ferrarese Girolamo Savanarola who – until his death at the stake, May 23, 1498 – upheld moral exigencies that finally led him to

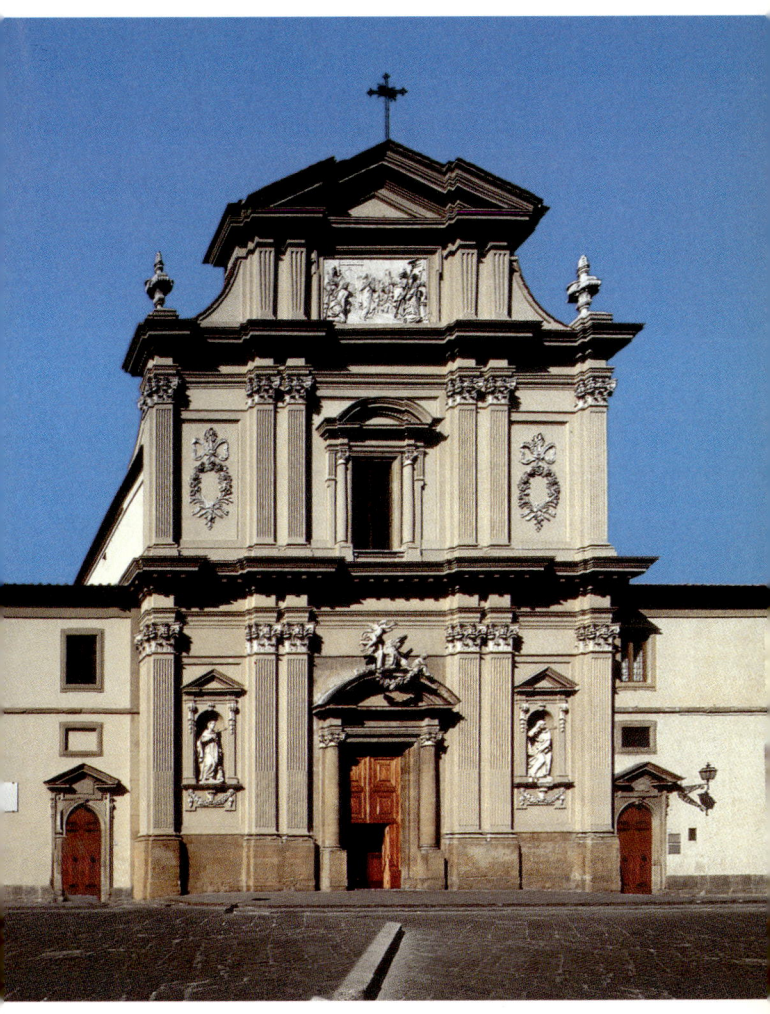

an irreconcilable clash with the Medici family and the Magnificent in particular. Savanarola voiced the opposition, announcing and sanctioning the end of what can be considered the first phase of the Medici hegemony. The role the convent of San Marco played in artistic commissions was not less important; the works of Beato Angelico, Filippo Lippi and his son Filippino conferred on it great value. This cultural relevance can also be seen in the tombs the church contains: outstanding personalities like Agnolo Poliziano, Giovanni Pico della Mirandola (1494) and Girolamo Benivieni (1592). The clash with the Medici dynasty continued during the next century: when Cosimo I was restored and took power after becoming duke, the Dominicans were removed, on May 31, 1545 and replaced by the Augustinians, more appreciated by the ruling household. But only six months later, owing to pope Paul III Farnese, the Dominicans were re-integrated. In 1580 Giambologna entirely renovated the church. That same year the artist built the adjacent Salviati family chapel, dedicated to saint Antonino. The façade was done over between 1777 and 1780 by the carmelite friar Gioacchino Pronti. In 1866 a good part of the convent was withdrawn from the friars and successively turned into a museum devoted mainly to Beato Angelico's works. In 1942 San Marco ranked as basilica minor.

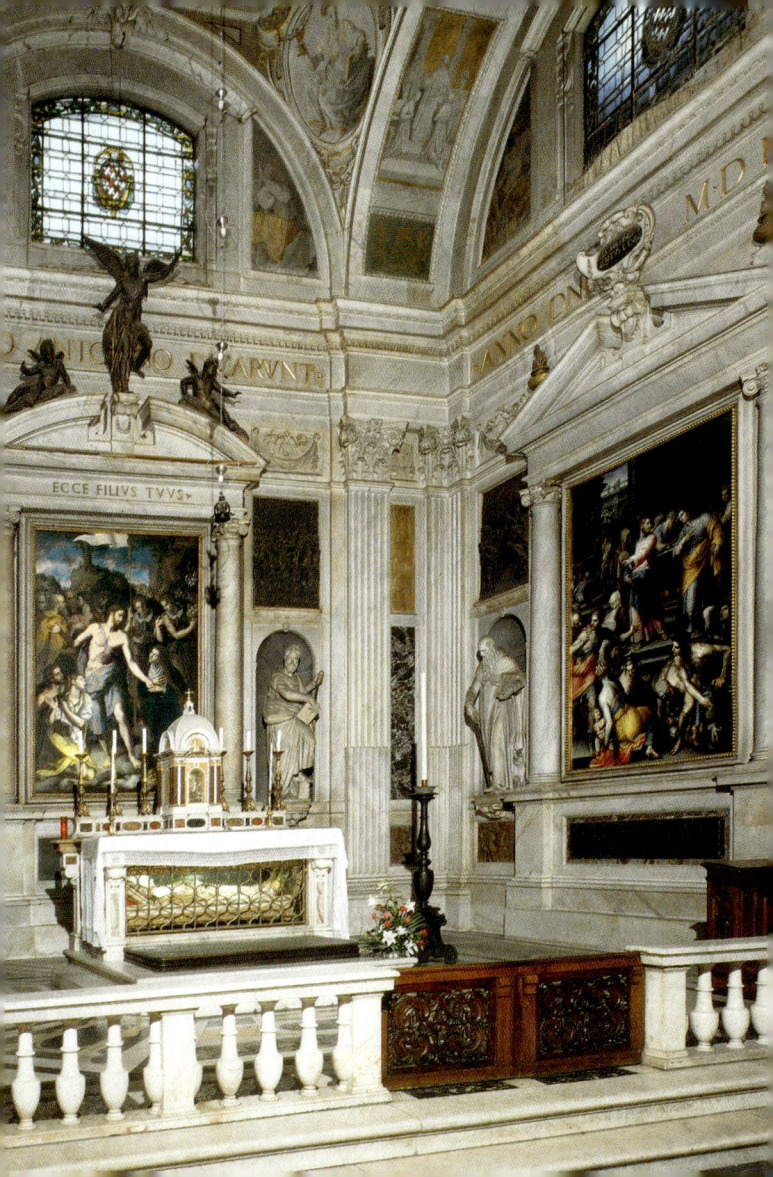

# Santa Maria Maggiore

*via de' Vecchietti*

Regarding the foundation of this church tradition may go rather too far back in time; a plaque refers it to pope Pelagius, on April 17, 580. Instead the first documents date to the early Xth century, when the church appears in a rental contract. At the time it must have been small, with apse and porch, a cemetery and living quarters of the canons who served it. Pope Lucius III, with a bull dated May 6, 1184, and two years later Urban III extended their protection to the church. It was perhaps in those years that Santa Maria Maggiore assumed a romanesque style, which lasted until the XIIIth century, when the most important families of the area – Cerretani, Barucci, Manovelli – had it radically altered in the new gothic taste. Spinello Aretino's great cycles of frescoes, which today have been partly recovered, and the bell tower, replaced in 1630 by the present one, should be attributed to the gothic period. After 1515 when Leo XI moved the canons to the cathedral, a secular priest was put in charge of the church, followed by the carmelite fathers of the Observance in 1521. Backed financially by the Cerretani family, they charged Bernardo Buontalenti with its restoration which, with the new frescoes of the chapels and Cigoli's wooden choir (1607), meant whitewashing the medieval frescoes. In 1630 the gothic arches of the nave were altered, while the old double lancet windows were abandoned for new windows. During those years the neighbourhood was partly transformed, with the creation of palaces and the placing of Giambologna's famous *Centauro* at the center of the crossroads then overlooked by the church. In the nineteenth century the area underwent further substantial changes. After being withdrawn from the Carmelites in 1808, Santa Maria Maggiore was assigned to a diocesan priest for eight years and then, as still today, to the friars of the order of San Camillo de' Lellis.

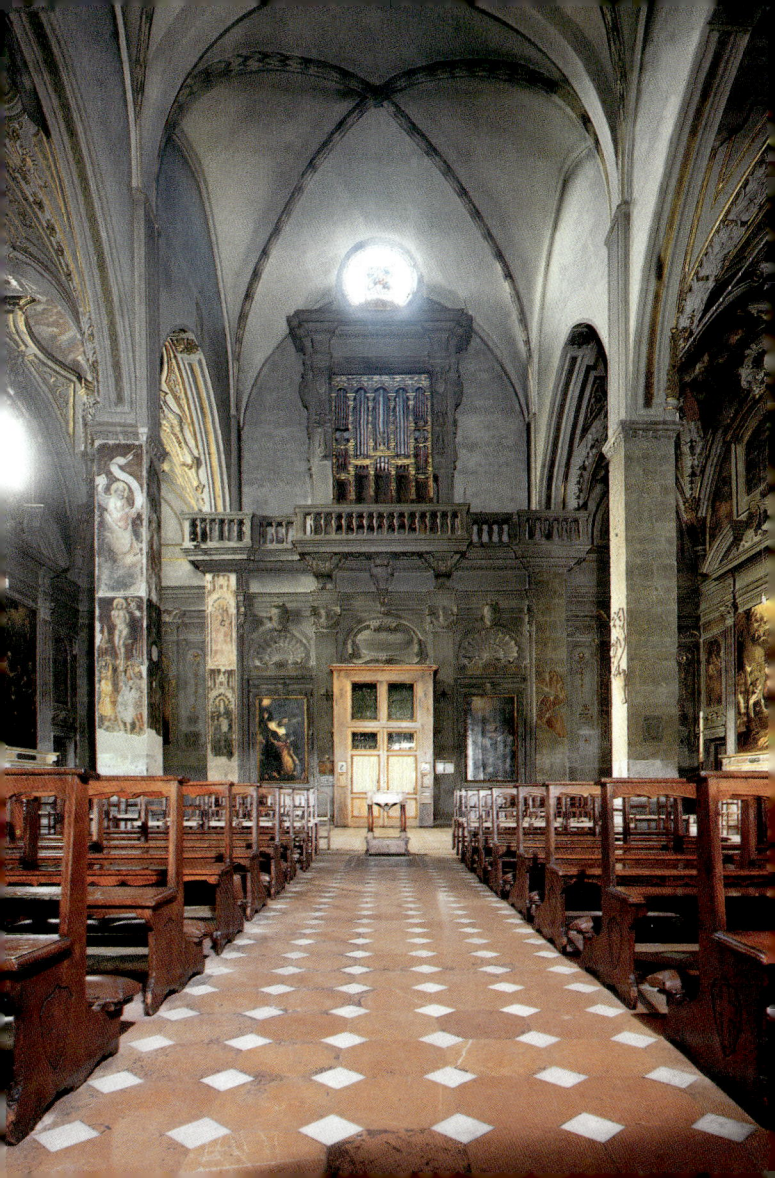

# Santa Maria Maddalena de' Pazzi
*borgo Pinti*

Borgo Pinti is one of the streets – although contained in the fourteenth-century wall – that still have the curves of their previous suburban meandering towards Fiesole.

In 1256 a monastery of converts of the benedictine rule, dedicated to saint Mary Magdalen Penitent established itself here. At the time the church had plain Gothic forms, with a single nave and maybe two side aisles, high

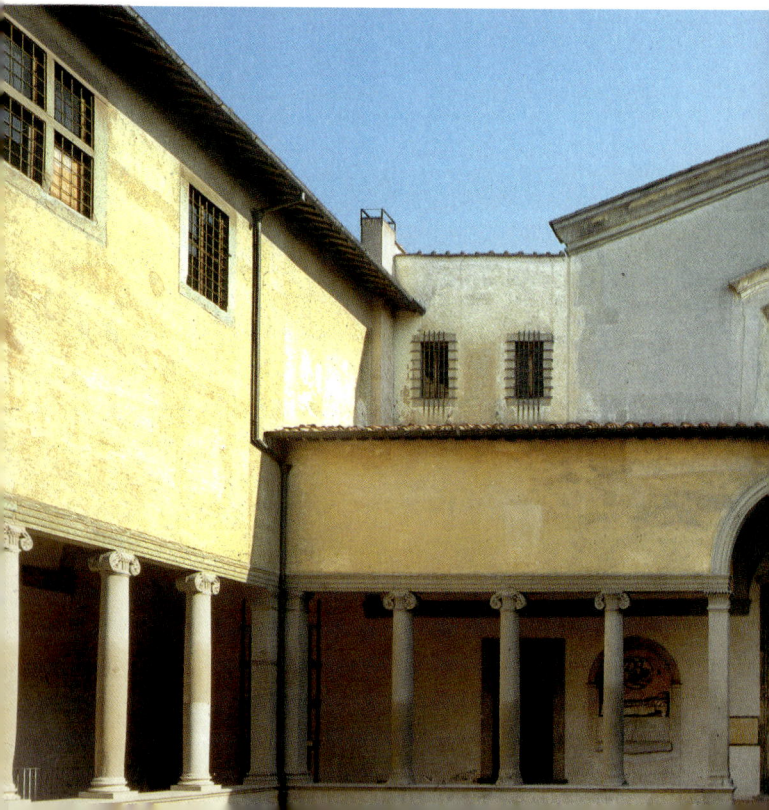

Gothic windows the tops of which can be seen on the south wall.
In 1321 the monastery was passed on to cistercian nuns who changed
the name to Santa Maria Maddalena di Cestello, remaining there for over
a century, in the claustral isolation of their rule. In 1442, cardinal Domenico
Capranica and abbot Timoteo di Giannaino had the nuns replaced by
monks, Cistercians too, from the Settimo abbey.
For Santa Maria Maddalena the second half of the fifteenth century was
a time of radical transformation and further major enlargements. The architectural changes designed by Giuliano da Sangallo were substantial. In

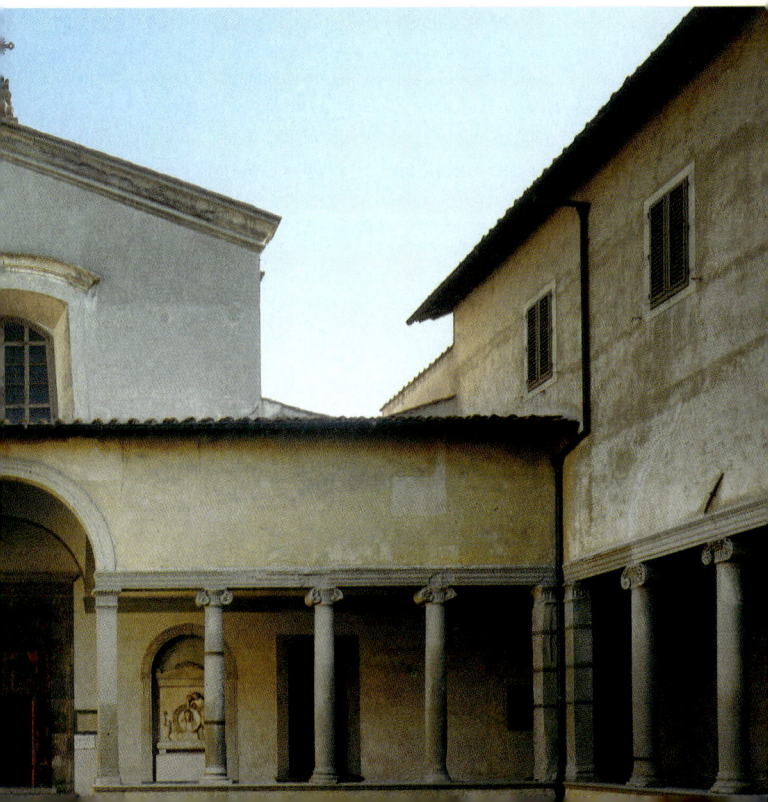

1492 building began, never to be completed, of the cloister in front of the church, the only one of its kind in Florence: it has a trabeation resting on Ionic pillars, the capitols being directly copied after an antique Roman capitol discovered in Fiesole in the fifteenth century and conserved today in the Casa Buonarroti museum.

The interior of the church was turned into a large hall covered by trusses, with six chapels on each side, executed between 1488 and 1562, the mouldings of which – for the most part attributed to the stone-cutter Piero di Giovanni della Bella from Settignano – form a very rich catalogue of late Renaissance decorative motifs.

The patrons of the chapels came from the most important families in the city – Salviati, Tornabuoni, Albizi, Del Pugliese, Nasi, Serristori, Pepi, Pucci, Rucellai, Neri, Strozzi –, whose members belonged to the society of San Benedetto Bianco that met there. The patrons' wealth determined endowments of works by the main artists of the times, including Perugino and Botticelli, Lorenzo di Credi and Domenico and Ridolfo del Ghirlandaio.

During the hundred and fifty years in which the cistercian monks were present, the chapels often changed patrons, and sometimes decoration. In 1505 by the Borgo Pinti entrance a chapel had been built for the Del Giglio family, then passed on to Neri de' Neri, Ferdinand I's doctor. The chapel was frescoed by Bernardino Poccetti. A further alteration occurred in 1628 when the Cistercians had to leave the convent, trading their premises with those of the carmelite nuns (now San Frediano in Cestello, then called Santa Maria degli Angioli). The convent on the banks of the Arno was found to be too humid and unhealthy for pope Urban VIII Barberini's two nieces, sister Maria Innocenzia and sister Maria Grazia who were cloistered there and who arrived at Santa Maria Maddalena accompanied by grand duchess Maria Maddalena of Austria and Cristina di Lorena. The monumental epigraph with the Barberini coat of arms placed on the present street corner between Borgo Pinti and the nineteenth-century extension of via della Colonna recalls the event.

The new premises were called Santa Maria degli Angioli and that same year the architect Luigi Arigucci began to restructure and enlarge them. In 1699 the florentine Carmelite Maria Maddalena de' Pazzi was canon-

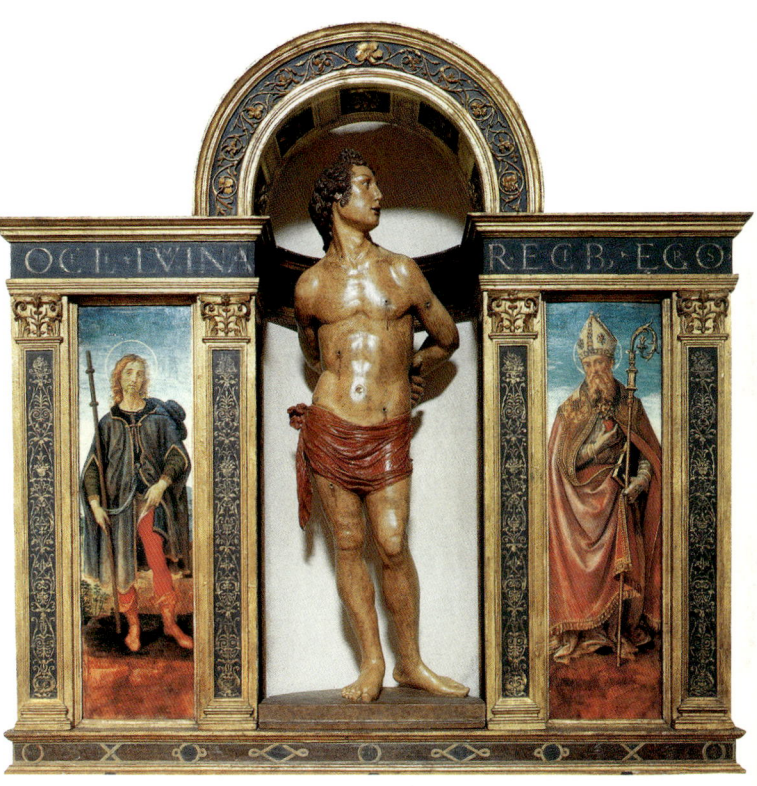

Aedicule with St Sebastian in polychrome wood (workshop of the Del Tassos)
and two paintings by Raffaellino del Garbo

*following pages*: Pietro Perugino, *The Crucifixion with Saints Magdalene, Benedict
and Bernard of Chiaravalle*

ised: a mystic having lived between 1556 and 1607, ever since her death and the discovery of the miraculous incorruptibility of her remains, she had become the object of devotion in Florence and elsewhere. The saint's relics were transferred to the new premises and placed in the monumental apse built in 1685 – in stead of the main chapel of the cistercian church – , designed by Ciro Ferri, Pietro da Cortona being in charge of the construction. A flat false ceiling was made, where Jacopo Chiavistelli, with Marco Antonio Molinari called il Lombardino, painted in bold perspective *Santa Maria Maddalena de' Pazzi presentata alla Trinità*; in the upper part of the outside walls ten paintings illustrating the *Storie della santa* by Cosimo Ulivelli were placed. The Napoleonic requisitions deprived the church of its most important works of art, which for the most part never

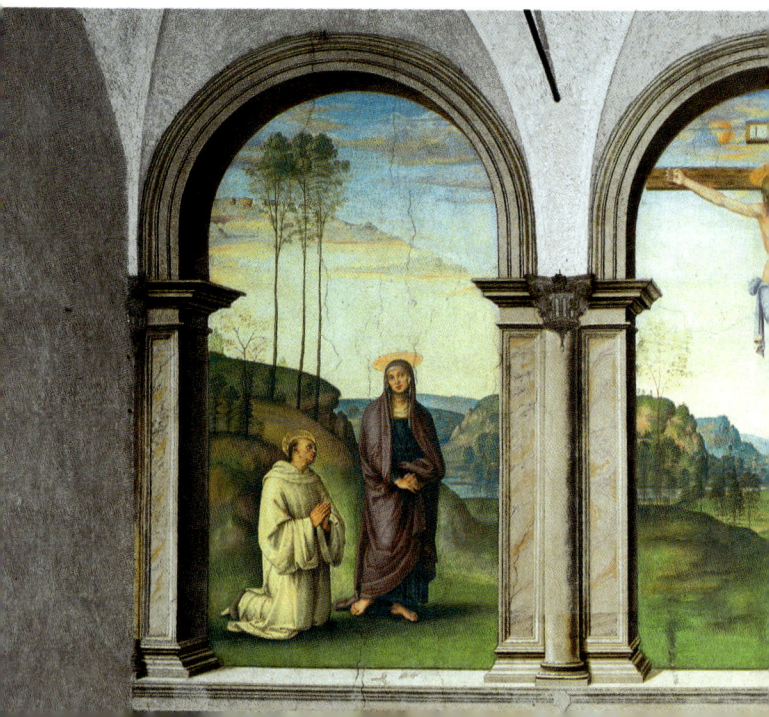

returned. Between 1865 and 1870, when Florence was the capital of the new kingdom of Italy, part of the convent was torn down because of the new city needs, and the rest of the building was turned into a school. In 1888 the Carmelites left the part of the monastery they still had, which was adjoined to the nearby barracks of the carabinieri. The church passed on to the secular clergy until 1926 when the augustininan fathers of the Assumption, of French origin, settled there, Santa Maria Maddalena de' Pazzi becoming the official church of the French community in Florence. When in 1966 the flood ruined the church, the French government and the France-Italy committee largely contributed to its thorough restoration. It was at that time that Sangallo's cloister was finally completed.

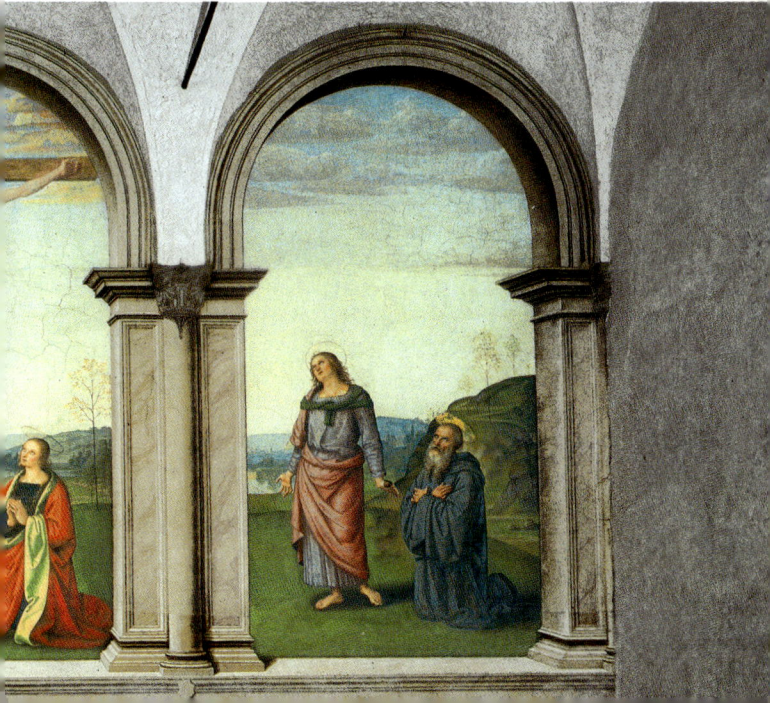

# San Giovannino degli Scolopi

*via de' Martelli*

In 1351, a gothic oratory dedicated to Saint John the Evangelist, aligned on the homonymous street, was raised; it was called dei Gori, because it was built on land – in part already owned by the Medicis – bequeathed by Giovanni di Lando Gori, who died of the plague in 1348. Its appearance was that of a secular rectory, under the Goris' patronage, and boasted outstanding personalities as rectors, including, in 1450, Gentile de' Becchi, teacher of Cosimo the Elder's children. At San Giovannino, Giovanni, the Magnifico's second-born and future pope Leo X, served as prelate when he was only seven years old. Over the centuries the area underwent sweeping changes, turning the nearby via Larga into the fifteenth-century city's most elegant street, especially after the Medici palazzo was built. Rectory until 1554, the oratory passed over definitively to the Jesuits, openly backed by duchess Eleonora, Cosimo I's wife. After 1579 the complex was thoroughly restructured on a design by Bartomoleo Ammannati, in a mannerist style, severely influenced however by Counter-Reformist rigour. The architect and his wife – the Urbino poetess Laura Battiferri – devoted personal funds to the work, later receiving together a worthy burial and commemoration in the renovated church. San Giovannino was the object of a number of donations, contributing to the building of the large college next door. In 1773, with the suppression of the Jesuit congregation, the church was assigned to the Scolopis, who since then have been the main religious educators of the population. However, after Italy was unified, a large part of the complex was turned into a public school; the Scolopis continue to custody the church, as well as part of the convent.

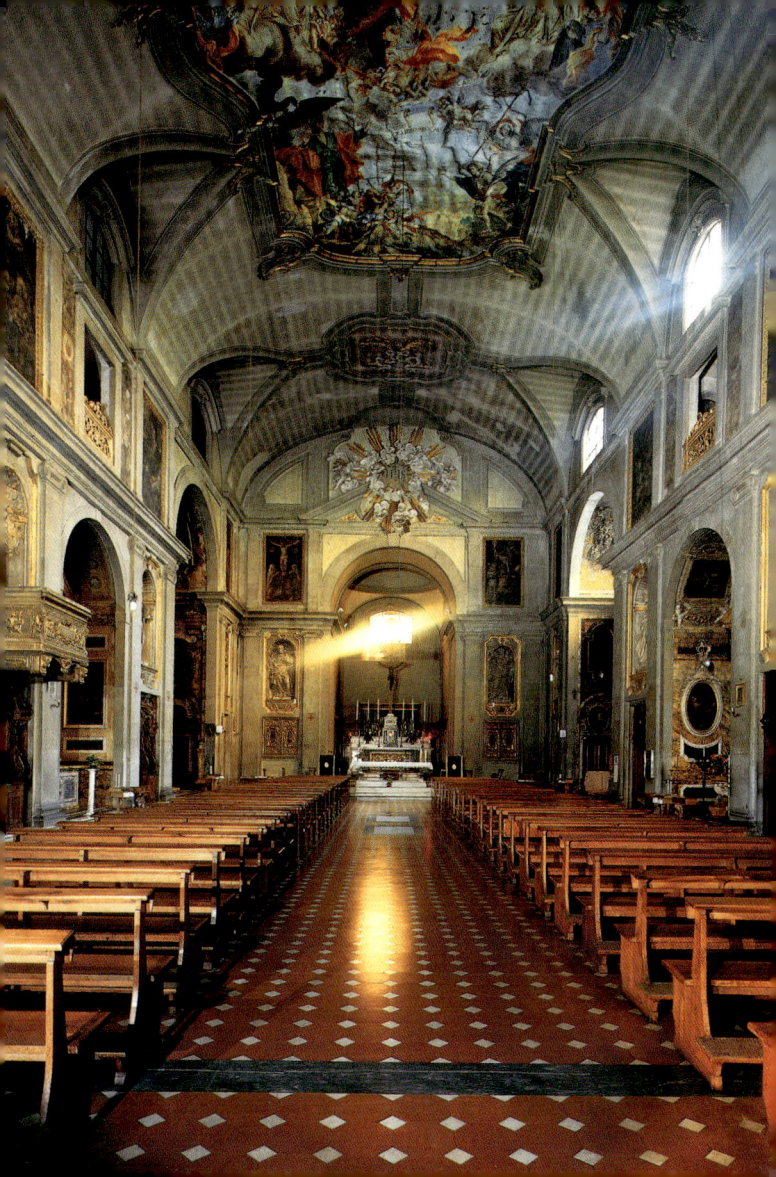

# San Firenze

*piazza San Firenze*

The church of Sant'Apollinare is mentioned in several documents of 1605: probably of Byzantine foundation, it was located – just beyond the commune walls – between via dell'Anguillara and via della Giustizia. In the adjoining block (where the Mancini and Magalotti families' towers also rose), after 1220 however documents mention a church dedicated to saint Firenze, giving onto a piazzetta facing outwards. A saint of uncertain identity, saint Firenze (or else Florenzio or Fiorenzo) is identified with an old bishop of Orange. Between 1240 and 1250 the rector's election was highly contested, resulting in armed warfare between factions backing rival candidates. In 1640 Urban VIII gave the church to the order of the Philippines, founded in Rome nearly a century earlier by Saint Philip Neri, who devoted particular care to children's education. In conformity with

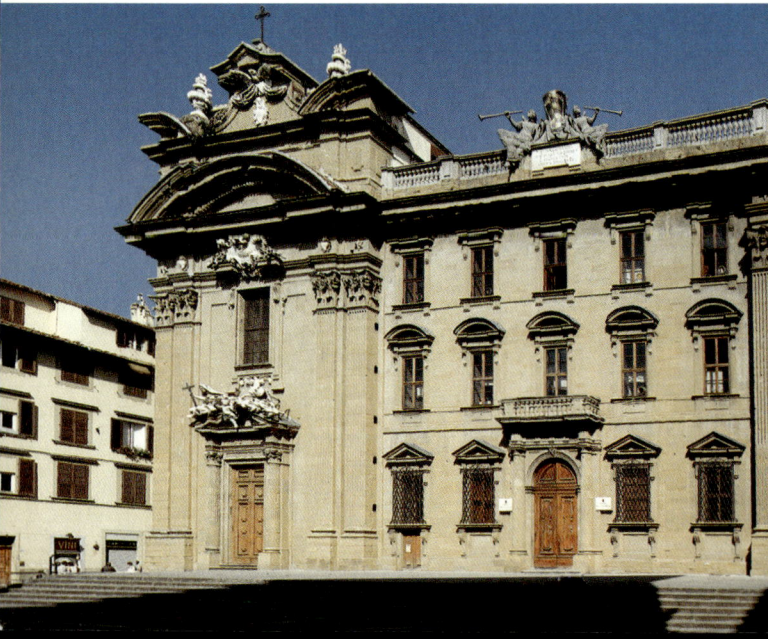

the rule, an oratory for traditional musical performances was to be associated with the actual church. In 1643, to make room for the new complex, several medieval buildings were torn down, including the Magalottis and the Mancinis' towers: a concession that gave those families the privilege of having several masses in their memory celebrated in the new church. Piero da Cortona – in Florence at the time for the construction of palazzo Pitti – made a first design but, perhaps owing to a lack of means, it never went beyond the laying of the foundation stone. In 1645 Pier Francesco Silvani was put in charge of the works, beginning what became the oratory. But in 1648, Giuliano Serragli, at his death, left the Philippines a large bequeath, which allowed them to ask Pietro da Cortona for a new design for the church. But his plan was held to be too grandiose and nothing came of it. So the old church became the oratory while the oratory Silvani had begun building became the new church, also dedicated to Saint Philip Neri. But it would only be completed much later, when Antonio Maria Ferri built its apsidal gallery (1688), Gioacchino Fortini its lacunar ceiling and Ferdinando Ruggieri the façade in late-mannerist style in 1715. Next to the church, and occupying the block behind it, Giovanni Filippo Ciocchi built the Philippines' new convent between 1745 and 1749. In 1772 the new oratory replaced the old san Firenze which was demolished. The orientation of the old church was also reversed, thus creating, with its new façade, a symmetrical plan with that of the new church, with the convent in the middle. Thus the notion of symmetry imposed, in early neo-classical style, the nth interpretation of Florentine late-mannerist stylistic elements and taste. And in memory of its past benefactor, at the centre of the façade, a large Serragli family coat of arms was placed, still to be seen. For over a century now the expropriated spaces of the convent have been the seat of the court of law (making it nearly impossible to visit), the superb old oratory is used as a court room, open only during audiences. Instead the church has retained its original role, as has the part of the building still occupied by the Philippines' convent.

# San Salvatore al Monte

*viale Galilei*

The view of Monte alle Croci, rising from Porta a San Niccolò to the San Miniato hill with a stairway set out as a *Via Crucis* for Holy Week processions, ends at the top with the façade of San Francesco or San Salvatore al Monte alle Croci, belonging to the reformed franciscan friars' order. By 1419 the friars had a small oratory here, dedicated to saints Cosmo and Damiano, given them by the Della Tosa family. The present building however was executed thanks to Castello Quarantesi's bequeath: he died in 1465, and his will was carried out by the Calimala Guild. After a first construction, that went on from 1490 to 1498 on a design by a friar named Leone, they called upon Simone Del Pollaiolo said il Cronaca, who between 1499 and 1504 designed and executed the great single-nave church with its classical proportions, which soon became the favorite place for high-ranking tombs and prestigious artistic commissions. The building is distinguished by semi-precious stone architectural elements outlining the windows, both inside and outside, niched with alternating triangular and curved tympans. In the right-transept double chapel were buried Tanai de' Nerli, an important statesman and patron who died in 1495, and Marcello Virgilio Adriani, the chancellor of the republic who signed Savanarola's death sentence in 1498. The preacher is figured in a bust on the counterfaçade executed by Andrea Ferrucci in 1522, a year after his death.

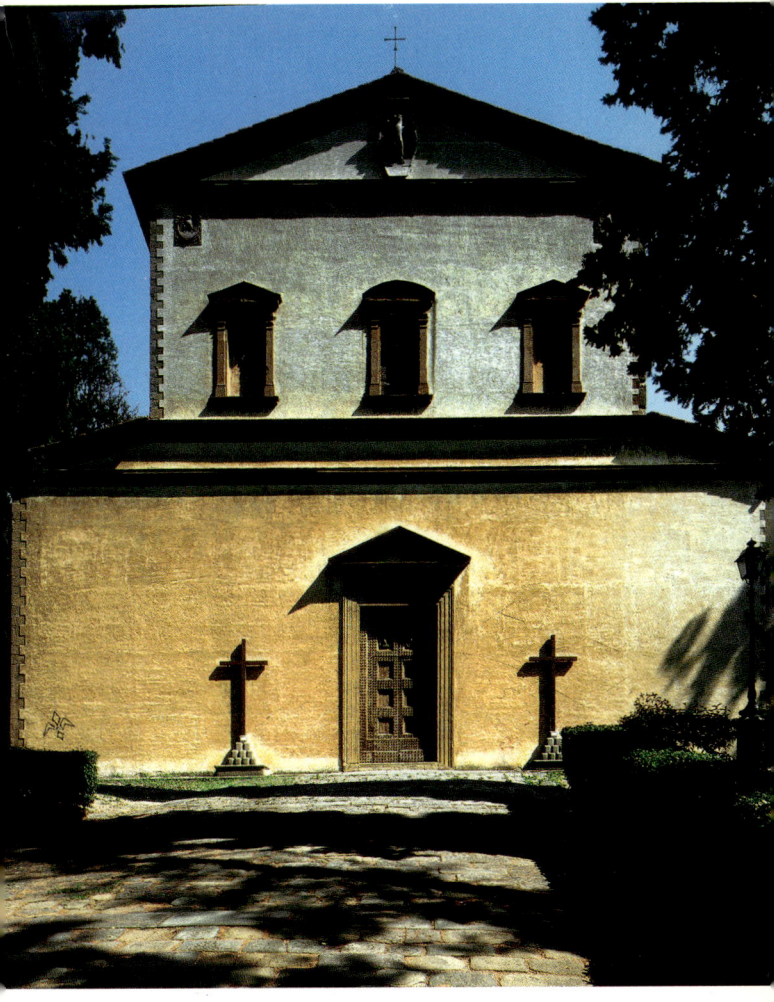

# San Giovanni Battista all'autostrada

*Autostrada del Sole*

In the late fifties the plan for the big freeway axis connecting Italy from north to south under the suggestive name of autostrada del Sole (*the Sun freeway*) was completed: it was one of the symbols of the boom in an Italy governed for years by the party that openly claimed its roots in the Catholic faith. Florence, the first exit after the ridge of the Apennines, seemed a particularly important intersection for automobile itineraries.

In 1959 the Autostrade company decided to build a church, near the connecting road between the autostrada del Sole and the Firenze-Mare state road, in a service station by the north access to the Florence area. There were two purposes for a religious building far from an urban centre: on the one hand to commemorate the victims of accidents during the execution of this great road network, on the other to respond to its users' spiritual needs. The architect Giovanni Michelucci, one of the protagonists of the architectural renovation of Florence and Tuscany since the thirties, was chosen for the design. For the entire Catholic Church those same years – with the Second Vatican Council promoted by John XXIII – would be the last great moment of a broad revision of its history. The attempt to be in touch once again with a deeply changed social and cultural reality, also meant an extensive revision of liturgy and spaces of sacrality. Michelucci's design partly reflected the evolution taking place and expressed it, even before its most striking effects had been codified, thanks to the freedom the specific context provided. The fact of being outside any defined ecclesial community, the celebrative and symbolic function, the novelty of the surroundings, allowed him entirely new expressions, through an interiorisation of faith materialised in a precise study of trajectories, in the gradual impregnation from outside to inside marked by a scheduled series of iconographic themes, which the international Institute of liturgic art commissioned of several contemporary artists. You enter from a kind of parvis partly closed by a large stone wall, through Pericle Fazzini's majestic bronze door (representing two great journeys narrated in the Old and New Testaments: the *Passaggio del Mar Rosso (The Crossing of the Red Sea)* and the *Viaggio dei Magi (The Journey of the Magi)*, into a

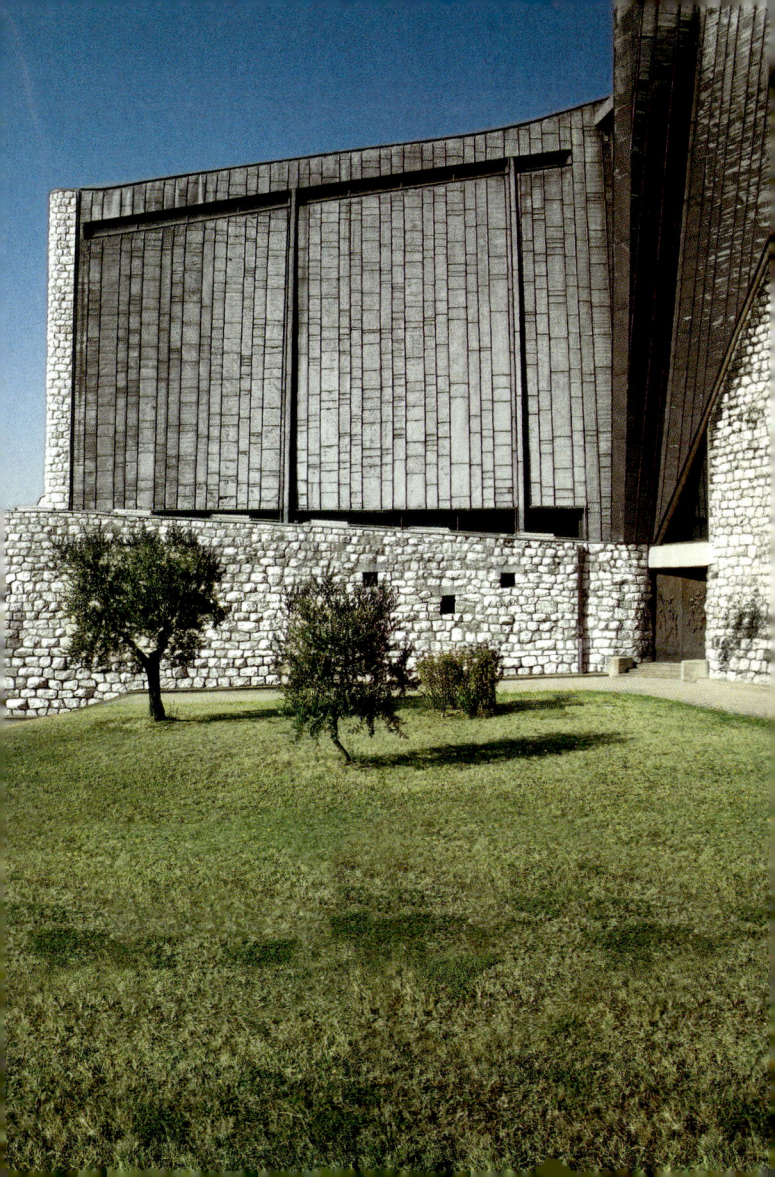

vast gallery running along an inner courtyard. The gallery – which serves as narthex – is rhythmed by cement walls with bronze reliefs dedicated to the patron saints of the cities the new freeway reaches between Milan and Naples. From there you enter the ecclesial hall shaped rather like a Greek cross, somewhat extended by the structure that connects the different-shaped and sized partitions to the huge concrete covering, like a huge tent upheld by intricate supports apparently defying constructive logic. This theme – one of the architect's main inspirations – is based on a rich harvest of Bible references inspiring the church's entire ideal structure. They heighten the symbolic value of finding shelter in faith, perfectly clear to a civilisation for which tents were a part of its nomadic tradition. The quest for analogies between the meaning of this church and the Christian believer's experience, in the architect's own writings, included the direct reference to Jesus' words: "I am the Way".

The work was carried out between 1961 and 1963, with interventions up to 1968. Another functional and at once symbolical element of the ensemble is constituted by the baptistry which you enter from the outside, and is connected with the narthex gallery. The baptismal font in porphyry is placed within a space where the stone walls determine a spiral-shaped trajectory, both a connection and a point of observation, which bestows on the Sacrament the dimension of an intense and responsible awareness, fully explicited by the archaic-styled reference to the baptismal space of the first centuries of Christianity.

The baptismal font

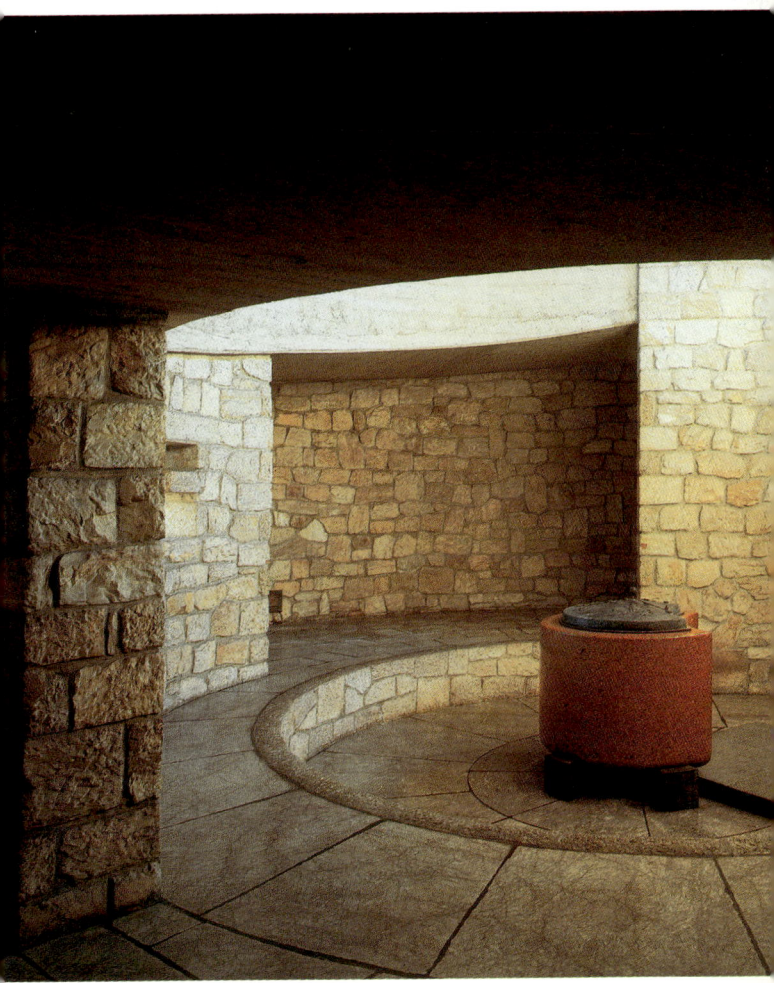

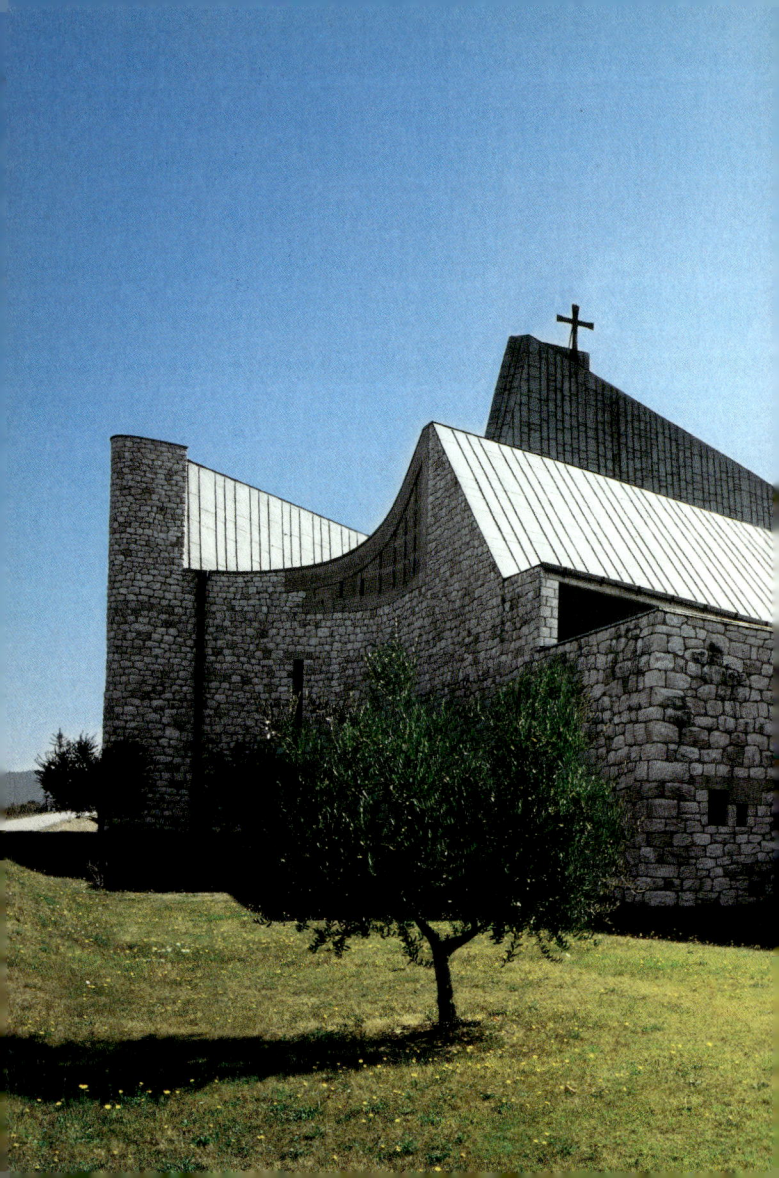

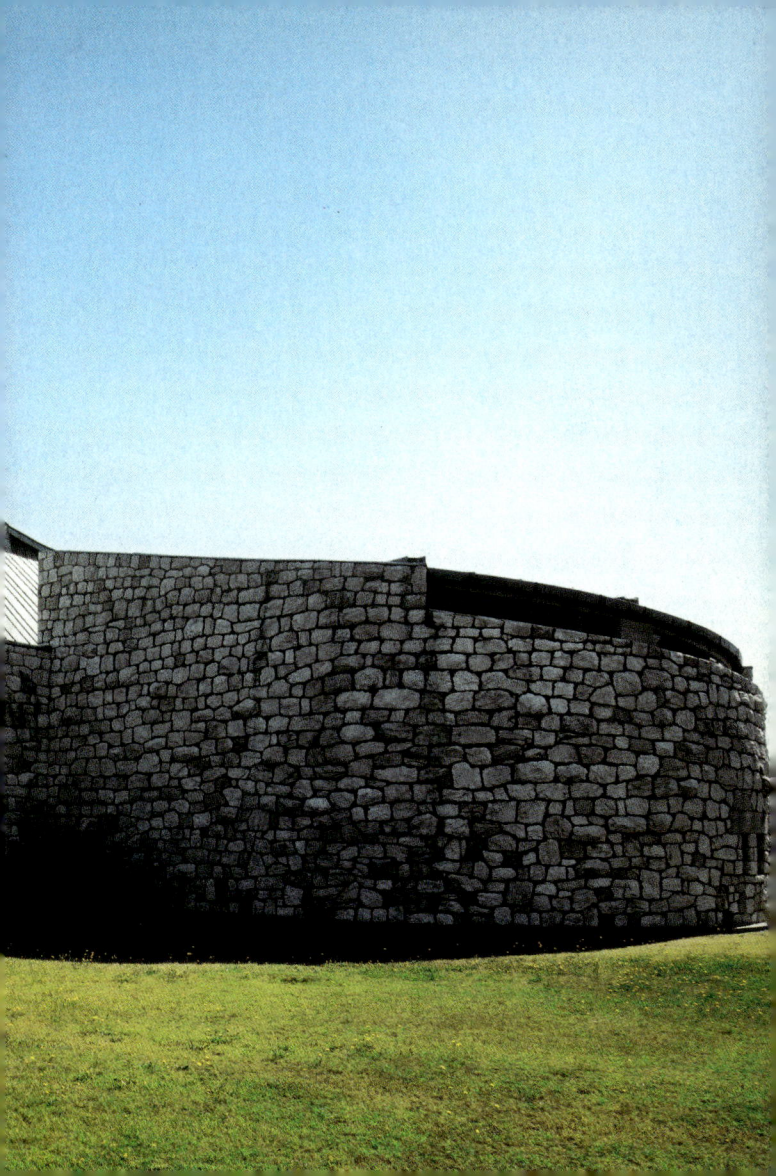

# Bibliography

ADRIANI, M., *Firenze sacra*, Florence 1990

BOCCHI, F., *Bellezze della città di Firenze*, Florence 1591; nuova edizione accresciuta da Giovanni Cinelli, Florence 1677

BUSIGNANI, A.-BENCINI, R., *Le chiese di Firenze*, 4 voll., Florence 1982-1993

COCCHI, A., *Le chiese di Firenze dal secolo IV al secolo XX*, Florence 1903

CALZOLAI, C.C. (ed. by), *La Chiesa fiorentina*, Florence 1970

CARDINI, D. (ed. by), *Il Bel San Giovanni e Santa Maria del Fiore*, Florence 1965

DAVIDSOHN, R., *Storia di Firenze*, Florence 1956

DEGLI INNOCENTI, P., *Le origini del Bel San Giovanni*, Florence 1994

DEL MIGLIORE, F.L., *Firenze città nobilissima illustrata*, Florence 1684

FANELLI, G., *Firenze. Architettura e città*, 2 voll., Florence 1973

GUALDO PRIORATO, G., *Relatione della città di Fiorenza e del Granducato di Toscana sotto il regnante Granduca Ferdinando II*, Cologne 1668; ristampa anastatica, Bologna 1971

HAINES, M.-RICCETTI, L., *Opera*, Florence 1996

HALL, M., *Renovation and Counter-Reformation. Vasari and Duke Cosimo in Santa Maria Novella and Santa Croce, 1565-1577*, Oxford 1979

HENDERSON, J., *Piety and Charity in Late Medieval Florence*, Oxford 1994

LANZONI, F., *Le Diocesi d'Italia dalle origini al principio del secolo VII*,

Faenza 1927

LOPES PEGNA, M., *Le più antiche chiese fiorentine*, Florence 1972

ID., *Firenze dalle origini al medioevo*, Florence 1962

MOROZZI, G., *Santa Reparata, l'antica Cattredale fiorentina*, Florence 1987

PAATZ, W., *Die Kirchen von Florenz*, Frankfurt am Main 1940

PAOLUCCI, A. (a cura di), *Il Battistero di San Giovanni a Firenze*, Modena 1994

QUILICI, B., *La chiesa di Firenze nell'alto medioevo*, Florence 1938

RICHA, G., *Notizie istoriche delle chiese fiorentine divise ne' suoi quartieri*, 10 voll., Florence 1757-1762; ristampa anastatica, Rome 1989

ROCCHI, G., *Santa Maria del Fiore*, Florence 1996

VASATURO, R.N., *Vallombrosa. L'Abbazia e la congregazione*, Vallombrosa 1994

VERDON, T. (ed. by) *La cupola di Santa Maria del Fiore*, Florence 1995

VERDON, T. (ed. by), *L'uomo in cielo. Il programma pittorico della cupola di Santa Maria del Fiore*, Bologna 1996

WOOD BROWN, J., *The Dominican Church of Santa Maria Novella at Florence*, Edinburgh 1902